D1329747

AMBITION AND POLITICS

AMERICAN POLITICS RESEARCH SERIES

AMBITION AND POLITICS

Political Careers in the United States

JOSEPH A. SCHLESINGER

MICHIGAN STATE UNIVERSITY

RAND McNALLY & COMPANY
Chicago, Illinois

AMERICAN POLITICS RESEARCH SERIES

Aaron Wildavsky, Series Editor

BARBER, *Power in Committees: An Experiment in the Governmental Process*

DYE, *Politics, Economics, and the Public: Policy Outcomes in the American States*

SCHLESINGER, *Ambition and Politics: Political Careers in the United States*

STEINER, *Social Insecurity: The Politics of Welfare*

Printed in U.S.A. by Rand McNally & Company
Library of Congress Catalog Card Number 66:19454

For

My Father and Mother

MONROE J. AND MILLIE SCHLESINGER

PREFACE

THIS STUDY REPRESENTS my long-standing conviction that we can learn more from the careers of political leaders than who they were and where they came from. Man's rise to political power is, after all, one description of the political system; the classical definitions of government, of monarchy, oligarchy, and democracy, hinge upon the manner in which the political leaders are chosen. In the United States the profusion of literature on the careers of politicians from state legislator to President testifies to the general belief that knowledge of these careers is important to our understanding of American politics.

In this study, therefore, I have sought a broad perspective on American political careers. Although much of the study concerns two offices, the offices of governor and senator, I have tried to place these offices within a general scheme of political advancement in the United States. Since the two-party system provides two important avenues of advancement, I have considered the careers of the major parties' nominees, their defeated as well as their successful candidates for office.

Within the American federal system the state is the primary political unit; the state, therefore, has been my principal unit of analysis. I have compiled data on the careers of officials in all the 48 states which formed the Union in the years 1914–1958. A longer time span, quite apart from the difficulties of gathering the data, would have encompassed a different political era. In 1914 the Seventeenth Amendment, which provided for the popular election of senators, took effect. But this was also the period in which other changes of significance for political advancement were adopted—the direct primary and women's suffrage. A shorter time period would have reduced the number of cases and made meaningless a discussion of order in careers. Some may question my bringing together data for this length of time without analyzing the changes which took place within the period. I can only say that when the data is analyzed by decades there is remarkable stability in the patterns of office movement.

The use which one makes of career data, however inclusive, depends, of course, on one's view of politics. Throughout this study the guiding notion has been that ambition for office moves politicians and that political careers are most revealing in what they tell us of these ambitions. Thus, while the data which I have used will be quite familiar to political scientists schooled in sociology and interested in political recruitment and socialization, my analysis will be more familiar to those who, under the influence of economics, see politics as a series of rational marginal choices made by men competing for power within a given set of political rules.

In preparing this study I received generous support from the Social Science Research Council and from Michigan State University, through both its All-University Research Committee and the Department of Political Science. Most of this work has, I hope, benefited from the critical reactions of colleagues and students. I want especially to thank Victor Jones, Robert Scigliano, Aaron Wildavsky, and James Wilson, all of whom read the manuscript and made perceptive comments. I should also like to thank Samuel Krislov for his helpful and stimulating suggestions. I, of course, take full responsibility for the final work.

Joseph A. Schlesinger

East Lansing, Michigan
December, 1965

TABLE OF CONTENTS

List of Tables

List of Figures

CHAPTER I

Introduction: Ambition and Opportunity

AMBITION LIES AT THE HEART of politics.[1] Politics thrive on the hope of preferment and the drive for office. The relation between personal ambitions and politics provides the rationale for this study of American political leaders. In most modern studies of political leaders the significance of office ambitions is obscure. A generation which is the intellectual heir of Marx and Freud favors a combination of social and psychological factors as the forces best able to explain the behavior of politicians. For the Marxist or the Freudian, the ambitious politician is an oversimplification. Human motives are complex, and, if they are not, they are modified by complex social and economic forces. The social scientist's rejection of the "self-interest" motive is reinforced by and, in turn, reinforces the widely held ethical position that politics ought not to revolve around personal ambitions. The intellectual's preference for political leaders motivated by ideology or principles is but a variant of the popular distrust of politicians because they are self-interested.

But the popular distrust is rooted in experience which the social scientist is unwise to ignore. In politics the relation between motive and action is more obvious than in any other social endeavor. The paradox is that it is the simplicity of this relationship which is so often slighted in political analyses. Of all those who perform for their fellow men, the politician leaves the clearest tracks between his purpose and his behavior. Personal ambition sparks all men's efforts to do more than subsist. But the place of personal ambition in the actions of the artist and of the saint presents us with the most complex of problems. The artist's

[1] In earlier usage the word "ambition" was more explicitly political; it comes from the Latin *ambitio,* meaning canvassing, or personal solicitation of honours (*Oxford English Dictionary*).

desire for immortality on earth and the saint's for immortality in heaven makes analysis of their motives difficult and, indeed, makes it unseemly for us to limit our discussion to the drive for immediate personal success. In politics, on the other hand, immediate personal success is so obviously the goal that the social scientist does well to give it primary consideration and surely errs to shun it. This is true even when principle or doctrine are the declared motive of the politician, as the career of Lenin so well demonstrates. Lenin was no more willing to delay his accession to power for the perfect Marxian revolution than is the American politician who polls the voters for policies to insure his election. This elementary relation between personal ambition and political action even in the most doctrinaire political activists is too often clouded by subtle explanations of political behavior.

In our concern with the complexity of human behavior, we should not forget that political institutions, and others as well, work because they simplify motives, because they make the behavior of politicians understandable and predictable. A political system becomes stable when it is able to control men's political ambitions. However complex the constitutional statement of governmental powers, its effectiveness depends upon the definition of how men are to gain and hold office. In stating the rules of officeholding, a constitution states the outlets for political ambitions and how they are to be achieved; if the explicit rules do not reflect the distribution of political influence within the society they are twisted until they do. Certainly no amendment or judicial decision has altered the American Constitution as much as the political parties have in redefining the role of the Electoral College in the selection of the President.

To slight the role of ambition in politics, then, or to treat it as a human failing to be suppressed, is to miss the central function of ambition in political systems. A political system unable to kindle ambitions for office is as much in danger of breaking down as one unable to restrain ambitions. Representative government, above all, depends on a supply of men so driven; the desire for election and, more important, for reelection becomes the electorate's restraint upon its public officials. No more irresponsible government is imaginable than one of high-minded men unconcerned for their political futures.

There is, of course, the delicate problem of balance. Men's ambitions must not so outrun the possibilities for their fulfillment that they refuse to play the game. Students from Aristotle to Brinton[2] have noted

[2] Aristotle, *Politics,* ed. by Ernest Barker (New York: Oxford University Press, 1946), pp. 202–54; see also F. Kort, "The Quantification of Aristotle's Theory of Revolution," *American Political Science Review,* XLVI (1952), 486–93; and Crane Brinton, *The Anatomy of Revolution* (New York: Norton, 1938).

that the gap between expectations and achievement is the essential factor in revolutions. Nevertheless, political ambition does not run wild in all men. Men must have their political ambitions excited as well as restrained. The political system must provide the refinements of power and status which attract as well as direct men's aspirations.

Only recently have we begun to realize how vital to the operation of the democratic system is the existence of men in key positions who are dominated by the office drive. James Wilson,[3] in his study of the club movement within the Democratic party, distinguishes between *amateurs* or those whose involvement in politics is based on policy goals and *professionals* who use policy issues as the means to gain office. Wilson argues that when political activists become predominantly amateur the leadership loses its flexibility and is pushed to extremes. It would appear that the validity of Wilson's proposition is borne out by the Goldwater movement in the Republican party. The Republican disaster of 1964 occurred not because the majority of Republican leaders held a conservative and demonstrably unpopular ideology. Delegates to earlier Republican conventions held ideological positions at variance with those of their own voters.[4] The significance of the 1964 Republican convention was that its delegates could not be swayed by the evidence that its choice would bring serious electoral defeat to the party.[5]

In this context we can see how democratic political parties perform a major service in transforming private goals into public morality. Political parties tie men's ambitions together, linking their fates over time. What may be the moral thing to do privately, then, such as to pursue personal principles at all costs, becomes immoral when it is followed publicly and others are injured. A party leader who advocates policies which, however principled, cost him election is to be praised if he alone suffers. But if he also brings down to defeat hundreds of his party colleagues he can be attacked on equally valid moral grounds.[6]

TOWARD AN AMBITION THEORY OF POLITICS

In calling attention to the importance of ambition for political analysis, I do not mean to imply that ambition as the motive for indi-

[3] James Wilson, *The Amateur Democrat* (Chicago: University of Chicago Press, 1962).
[4] H. McClosky, P. J. Hoffmann, and R. O'Hara, "Issue Conflict and Consensus among Party Leaders and Followers," *American Political Science Review,* LIV (1960), 406–27.
[5] Aaron Wildavsky, "The Goldwater Phenomenon, Purists, Politicians, and the Two-Party System," *Review of Politics,* XXVII (1965), 386–413.
[6] The distinction between private and public morality or the "fiduciary relation" is discussed by William H. Riker in *The Theory of Political Coalitions* (New Haven: Yale University Press, 1962), pp. 24–27.

vidual political action has been entirely neglected. There has been considerable concern for understanding why men have political ambitions. This theme runs through the work of Lasswell[7] and is the dominant question posed by the Georges in their psychoanalytic biography of Woodrow Wilson.[8] But the answer to the question of why men have ambitions does not move us far toward understanding the consequences. No man is likely to obtain a major political office unless he wants it. His motives in wanting the job may run the gamut of human desires. But I would argue that no political system functions well if it relies upon chance to assure that individual motives will work for the public good. What is needed, therefore, is a theory of politics which explicitly accepts the assumption that politicians respond primarily to their office goals, in effect an ambition theory of politics, rather than a theory which explains personal ambitions.

An ambition theory of politics follows from the propitious development of *party theory* which has taken place in the last 20 years. Schattschneider adumbrated the outlines of a party theory; the economist Schumpeter made the theory more explicit; and Anthony Downs has elaborated it.[9] In one sense the party theory of these men is ambition theory: its basic assumption is that the party is ambitious to govern and that it adopts policies which permit it to govern under the rules of political competition. Ambition in party theory, however, is that of the team rather than of individual politicians. As such, party theory is a gross simplification of the democratic process, whose most interesting and important problems concern why politicians do or do not act as teams. Even in Great Britain, where the party system comes closest to representing the two-party model in the real world, one of the most important forces affecting policy is the factional conflict related to

[7] The problem of why men want power is a theme which runs throughout Harold Lasswell's work, but it is most completely stated in his *Power and Personality* (New York: Norton, 1948).

[8] Alexander L. George and Juliette C. George, *Woodrow Wilson and Colonel House; a Personality Study* (New York: Day, 1956).

[9] The development of theory for an explicitly two-party system is in E. E. Schattschneider, *Party Government* (New York: Holt, 1942); Joseph A. Schumpeter, *Capitalism, Socialism, and Democracy*, 3rd ed. (New York: Harper, 1950); and Anthony Downs, *An Economic Theory of Democracy* (New York: Harper, 1957). Related theoretical works whose attention remains focused on the immediate control of governmental decisions are Robert A. Dahl, *A Preface to Democratic Theory* (Chicago: University of Chicago Press, 1956); Duncan Black, *The Theory of Committees and Elections* (Cambridge, England: Cambridge University Press, 1958); Riker, *The Theory of Political Coalitions;* and James M. Buchanan and Gordon Tullock, *The Calculus of Consent* (Ann Arbor: University of Michigan Press, 1962).

opposing ambitions within the major parties. In the United States, even if the parties were cohesive teams, which they are not, there would still be differences within a party deriving from its varying relations to government. Governmental control means different things to a presidential candidate, a congressional committee chairman, a state governor, and a state legislator. Therefore, while party theory is extremely important to the development of ambition theory, the latter starts from a more valid premise. Party theory, by assuming cohesive behavior, is, in effect, a special case of ambition theory—one of whose principal problems is that of explaining when politicians will act cohesively.

Here it should be said that the primary purpose of this study is not to relate personal ambitions to politics in an elaborate theoretical scheme. I shall attempt (in Chapter VII) to relate ambition and party theory in a formal way and to examine the usefulness of both concepts for understanding material such as the data on American political careers gathered for this study. At the same time, I expect such data to inform us only by inference about the relation of personal ambitions to politics. Nevertheless, it should be understood that it is the central role of ambition in politics which has determined the present gathering of data and its presentation in this study. Conversely, I would assert that a comprehensive theory of politics based on personal ambitions must rest upon findings such as those presented here about political opportunities.

It is appropriate, therefore, that I at least suggest the outlines of a comprehensive theory and the problems which its elaboration presents. Ambition theory focuses on the ways in which men cooperate—form organizations, coalitions, or factions—to serve their political ends. Shifting party alignments, party factions, relations among officeholders at various levels of government are related to strategic differences in ambitions and in the electoral conditions which satisfy them. At the same time ambition theory can be brought to bear on specific overt acts such as the votes of a legislator or the policy proposals of a governor. In this instance ambition theory does not pose a criterion different from the widely held and occasionally tested hypothesis[10] that a legislator responds to his constituency; it differs in that it asserts that the constituency to which the legislator is responding is not always the one from which he has been elected, and that it is more important to know what he wants to be than how he got to be where he now is.

[10] Duncan MacRae, Jr., "The Relation between Roll Call Votes and Constituencies in the Massachusetts House of Representatives," *American Political Science Review,* XLVI (1952), 1046–55; Lewis A. Froman, Jr., *Congressmen and Their Constituencies* (Chicago: Rand McNally, 1963); Frank Sorauf, *Party and Representation* (New York: Atherton Press, 1963).

The central assumption of ambition theory is that a politician's behavior is a response to his office goals.[11] Or, to put it another way, the politician as officeseeker engages in political acts and makes decisions appropriate to gaining office. His problem consists, first, in defining his office goal or goals and, secondly, in relating his current activity to them. To do the latter is obviously not a simple task, involving as it does a host of uncertainties; at the same time the means of advancing in politics is not a mystery.

A theory of politics based on ambitions, therefore, has to consider carefully alternative strategies of advancement. With respect to elective offices, our ambitious politician must act today in terms of the electorate of the office which he hopes to win tomorrow. For, while political advancement is certainly not solely a matter of satisfying electorates, winning votes is the focal problem of all democratic officeseekers. Fortunately we know enough about electoral behavior to base the discussion of this variable of ambition theory upon solid findings. On the other hand, we know little in a systematic manner about the second major variable, the office goals of politicians. The present study is concerned primarily with that question.

THE PROBLEM OF ISOLATING POLITICAL AMBITIONS

We must note first that the ambitious politician is an abstraction and that a theory based on such a partial view of what moves the politician cannot explain all of his behavior, even the specifically political. Politicians are no more driven by the single motive of office than businessmen are guided solely by the desire for profit or doctors by the urge to heal. Each has a life beyond his occupation which impinges on the way he performs. But the abstraction of the businessman or doctor guided by his occupational aims has been useful, if only to discover when, in fact, other values do intrude on his behavior. Even the abstraction of the

[11] While the proposition that men's ambitions guide their behavior is imbedded in most political analysis, only rarely has it been given systematic examination. Some studies which have shown a positive relationship between expectations or ambitions and political behavior are Samuel Krislov, "Constituency versus Constitutionalism: the Desegregation Issue and Tensions and Aspirations of Southern Attorneys General," *Midwest Journal of Political Science,* III (1959), 75–92; Duncan MacRae, Jr., *Dimensions of Congressional Voting* (Berkeley: University of California Press, 1958); and Donald R. Matthews, *U.S. Senators and Their World* (New York: Vintage, 1960), pp 109–10. The best use of political ambition as the focus for historical analysis is in Lewis Namier's studies of the development of parties in the British Parliament: *Personalities and Powers* (New York: Harper, 1965), pp. 13–38; and *The Structure of Politics at the Accession of George III,* 2nd ed. (London: Macmillan, 1965).

doctor or businessman does not always present simple answers to the problems of assigning motives. Thus we can ask if the psychiatrist charges high fees because it is essential to his therapy or because he wants money? Since the politician is also always a citizen, it is never possible to abstract him as pure officeseeker, in the same degree to which we can isolate the businessman or the doctor. The politician's other interests are always involved in his decisions as politician. Thus the ambitious politician, well-imbued with a professional attitude toward issues, would, we hope, restrain his use of an issue which might gain him votes but would also erode the system.

The problem of isolating political ambitions in the real world is compounded by the partial nature of officeholding in politicians' careers. Frequently a public official maintains a private occupation. Sometimes this provides supplementary income for a public position which does provide basic support, as when a congressman retains a law practice or engages in public relations or pursues private investments. For a large share of American elective offices such an outside occupation is essential, since the public position pays nothing or gives only partial support. When an individual obtains all of his income from his occupation it is easier to perceive him as motivated by abstract occupational objectives. But does the legislative lawyer represent his clients or his constituents? What ambitions guide the part-time mayor who owns a real estate agency or a mortuary?

Furthermore, a political career is not only partial in the sense that a man can hold other jobs concurrently; it is also sporadic in that there is always the prospect of long periods out of office. A man's current behavior in office, then, may have no relevance at all to future political office but much to future employment with corporations or other interest groups. In other words, more than most occupations, officeholding is intertwined with other occupations in the economic system; most officeholders and candidates must have another occupational base with related ambitions. Office, therefore, is at best only a part of the career ambitions of politicians.[12]

The difficulties of isolating office ambitions from other motives

[12] For a general summary of literature on the occupational backgrounds of politicians there is Donald R. Matthews, *The Social Background of Political Decision Makers* (New York: Doubleday, 1954); W. Bell, R. J. Hill, and C. R. Wright, *Public Leadership* (San Francisco: Chandler, 1961). On specific occupations there is Heinz Eulau and John D. Sprague, *Lawyers in Politics* (Indianapolis: Bobbs-Merrill, 1964); R. S. Wells, "The Legal Profession and Politics," *Midwest Journal of Political Science,* VIII (1964), 166–90; Joseph A. Schlesinger, "Lawyers and American Politics: A Clarified View." *Midwest Journal of Political Science,* I (1957), 26–39; William A. Glaser, "Doctors and Politics," *American Journal of Sociology,* LXVI (1960), 230–45.

warn us of pitfalls in a political theory based on such ambitions; but they should not close our minds to the utility of such a theory. Of all the motives which may drive a politician, his office drives are the ones the external observer can discern with some assurance. Whatever the informal rules may say about the propriety of reluctance, and however much the American political style requires that ambition be played down, there comes a time when a man must make overt his intentions to seek a public office. He must enter his name in the primary, permit himself to go before a convention, or do whatever is required to place himself before the electors. Public offices are not prizes handed out by committees which the receivers can graciously appear not to have sought. True, those who make the open efforts at office do not exhaust the ranks of the ambitious. Nor can the observer say much about the intensity of one man's ambitions compared with those of another. Surely men sometimes make overt efforts to get an office which they do not expect to win and perhaps really do not want to win. Yet it is not difficult for the observer to make some assessment of a man's chances and to make some place in the theory for mock candidates. The attainment of office remains the one observable goal that we have in politics, a fact on which the political system itself rests, and which, for that reason, can provide a theoretical base for the understanding of politics.

THE ASSIGNMENT OF AMBITIONS

Since it is impossible to assign specific ambitions to individual politicians except at the time when a man openly seeks an office, we can develop a theory of ambitions only if we adopt reasonable assumptions about when such ambitions occur. The most reasonable assumption is that ambition for office, like most other ambitions, develops with a specific situation, that it is a response to the possibilities which lie before the politician. A man in an office which may lead somewhere is more likely to have office ambitions than a man in an office which leads nowhere. This assumption has virtue because it is part of the relevant situation: it is one commonly made by most observers; therefore the assumption creates the opinion to reinforce itself. The small band of governors in sizeable and competitive states and the conspicuous members of the Senate who together compose the presidential "hopefuls" are hopeful as much because of the expectations of others as because of their own.[13] Each lesser office has its own band of hopefuls which

[13] Henry Taylor, *The Statesman* (orig. ed., 1838; New York: Mentor Books, 1958), p. 92.

exists in the minds of the observant public; and public opinion affects the politician because it defines his success or failure. A New York governor who does not make the Presidency has failed in a sense in which his counterpart in Mississippi or South Dakota cannot fail. Politics is, after all, a game of advancement, and a man succeeds only if he advances as far as his situation will permit.

The relation between a man's ambitions and his current situation is further reinforced by the circularity of human behavior. If lieutenant governors have become governor in the past, then men who want to become governor will first seek to become lieutenant governor. This circularity, which has been used to attack the significance of patterns of political advancement, is, in fact, essential to the realistic assignment of ambitions. It makes little difference to the theory of ambitions whether men adopt the ambitions suitable to the office or attain the office because of their ambitions. It is sufficient to conclude that governors of New York will behave as though they were presidential candidates while governors of Mississippi or South Dakota will not.

An ambition theory need not assume that office goals are constant in their intensity and direction for the same individual or for different individuals. As a man does or does not progress in his career the possibilities change, and, if he is reasonable, so will his ambitions. The hopes which lie in the hearts of young men running for their first offices are secret. Some are undoubtedly already forming their first presidential inaugural address, while others have no thought of the future. But, as a career develops, success spurs ambition and failure dampens it. What is reasonable for a 30-year-old state legislator is ridiculous in his colleague of 60. Each politician faces the problem of keeping his ambitions and his possibilities constantly aligned. The independent influence of ambition upon opportunity occurs early in a man's career; as he moves on, both in office and in age, the possibilities modify his ambitions.

My basic inference, then, should be clear: the ambitions of any politician flow from the expectations which are reasonable for a man in his position. Obviously the inference will not hold true in all cases, but I assume that it holds true in enough cases to permit generalizations about the impact of personal ambitions upon the political system.

THE DIRECTION OF AMBITION

One of the most important ways in which office ambitions vary is in their direction. The office structure of the United States, for example, provides a variety of outlets for office goals, including the opportunity to leave public office. Each direction has its own constituency, and it is, therefore, essential to define the ambition before inferring its impact. Failure to consider more than one direction for ambition is the major weakness of party theory, which assumes a horizontal direction—to govern.

I would suggest that there are three directions which office ambitions may take. Ambitions may be *discrete:* The politician wants the particular office for its specified term and then chooses to withdraw from public office. If he is a candidate, the political tensions he experiences are simply those caused by the immediate objective. If he is an officeholder, he has no political tensions, (i.e., office ambitions). This type of ambition is certainly not uncommon for many lesser local offices, for the state legislature, and for higher offices as well. Indeed, the Twenty-Second Amendment prescribes this ambition for American Presidents once they have been reelected.

Ambitions may also be *static:* The politician seeks to make a long-run career out of a particular office. In this case the tensions he experiences derive primarily from his constituency. How widespread such ambitions are we cannot tell, for the possibilities of making a career of one office are varied. Nevertheless, it is certainly a marked goal of many American congressmen and senators.

Finally, ambitions may be *progressive:* The politician aspires to attain an office more important than the one he now seeks or is holding. Here, at the least, he is under tension not only from his current constituency but also from that of the office to which he aspires. A likely assumption is that progressive ambitions dominate and are suppressed only when they appear unreasonable in terms of the chances.

We can also assume that one type of ambition is unlikely to remain constant for any one politician over his lifetime. A city councillor may start with discrete ambitions but find politics so exciting that he develops static or progressive goals. Later failure may temper his expectations. Many a congressman retires voluntarily after a lengthy term of office. In his last term his ambitions have shifted from static to discrete. A theory of ambitions, however, is not so much concerned with predicting what a man's ambitions will be over his entire career, but rather with taking a man's current ambitions and predicting from them his political behavior. A legislator's votes and a governor's policies are therefore a consequence of current rather than possible future ambitions. This does not mean that a politician's ambitions may not combine both short- and long-run goals. It is a matter of assigning relative weights to each type of ambition.

THE STRUCTURE OF POLITICAL OPPORTUNITIES

In developing an ambition theory of politics we can bring order to the office ambitions of politicians only if we can find order in their chances or opportunities for office. It is therefore necessary to discover, if possible, the structure of political opportunities. The structure may be clearly defined, as in a hereditary monarchy which limits chances and ambitions to the family tree. Or it may be difficult to discern structure: potential candidates may emerge everywhere. In a democracy such as the United States, where there are a great many independent elective offices with great disparities in status, there are also likely to be great differences in the numbers of people able to gain office. The structure of political opportunities in the United States must therefore be constructed from numerous and varied chances at offices ranging from drain surveyor or fence viewer to President.

If politicians' ambitions are to be ordered, there must be some stability of opportunities. The direction of the ambitions fostered by an office depends upon the way in which officeholders and the electorate typically treat the office, as well as upon the route it provides for political advancement. The office of governor enjoys prestige in itself and has also been a good steppingstone to federal office. But it is also, as we shall demonstrate, an office which few men can hope to hold for very long. Viewed with all other offices, the governorship is likely to produce progressive ambitions, although the object of these ambitions must depend upon the state, for all governorships are not equal. The congressman, on the other hand, is in a position which combines intrinsic satisfactions with the possibilites of long tenure; we would expect such a position to foster static ambitions. We would expect to find discrete ambitions where offices are intrinsically undesirable or lacking in satisfactions, as in the case of the lowly-paid state legislatures, and where there is little hope of advancement.

It should be clear that I do not include in the structure of political opportunity all of the opportunities that lie before a politician. It is especially important to distinguish between social and political opportunities. There is abundant evidence that all men do not have an equal chance at public office in the United States.[14] Everywhere political advantage reflects social and economic advantages; officeholders are a very unrepresentative sample of the population at large. But a structure of political opportunities independent of the social system does exist,

[14] Matthews, *Social Background,* provides data on the non-representativeness of American public officials.

and it may vary from state to state. Thus, for example, senators may come predominantly from the upper social strata, but the chances that a Virginia gentleman may become a senator are considerably less than those of a Kentucky gentleman because of the differences in office tenure between the two states. It may be, as some have said, that today only millionaires can become President; but only those millionaires in strategic political posts can hope to turn the trick. In the game of politics the political as well as the social system determines the players.

CAREER DATA AND AMBITION THEORY

The structure of political opportunities is a matter of empirical observation; it is with such observation that the main body of this study is concerned. The data from which I shall construct the opportunity structure in the United States are the office careers of major political figures. Since the compilation of such data has long been attractive to social scientists, it is important to note how ambition theory leads me to use the data differently.

A wealth of accumulated data exists about the backgrounds of Presidents,[15] Cabinet members,[16] Supreme Court judges,[17] senators,[18] congressmen,[19] governors,[20] and state legislators.[21] Yet, despite the

[15] Presidential backgrounds are covered most thoroughly in P. T. David, R. M. Goldman, and R. C. Bain, *The Politics of National Party Conventions* (Washington: Brookings, 1960).

[16] On the Cabinet, see Richard F. Fenno, Jr., *The President's Cabinet* (New York: Vintage, 1959). C. Wright Mills, *The Power Elite* (New York: Galaxy, 1959), presents varied data on the backgrounds of American political leaders, including the Cabinet members, especially in pp. 400–403.

[17] Cortez A. M. Ewing, *The Judges of the Supreme Court, 1789–1937* (Minneapolis: University of Minnesota Press, 1938); John R. Schmidhauser, "The Justices of the Supreme Court: A Collective Portrait," *Midwest Journal of Political Science,* III (1959), 1–57; Sidney S. Ulmer, "Public Office in the Social Background of Supreme Court Justices," *American Journal of Economics and Sociology,* XXI (1962), 57–68.

[18] An early study of senatorial careers is George H. Haynes, *The Election of Senators* (New York: Holt, 1906). The recent period is covered by Matthews, *U.S. Senators and Their World.* See also Andrew Hacker, "The Elected and the Anointed, Two American Elites, Senators and Corporation Presidents," *American Political Science Review,* LV (1961), 539–49.

[19] The membership of the United States House of Representatives has not been systematically examined in any published work, although there are frequent tabulations of the characteristics of members for particular Congresses, such as those published by *Congressional Quarterly* at the beginning of each session. See also David Truman, ed., *The Congress and America's Future* (Englewood Cliffs, N.J.: Prentice-Hall, 1965), especially the articles by S. P. Huntington and H. D. Price.

[20] Joseph A. Schlesinger, *How They Became Governor* (East Lansing: Governmental Research Bureau, Michigan State University, 1957).

[21] State legislators' backgrounds were examined by Charles Hyneman in "Who

industry which has gone into the accumulation of these data, they have been notably fruitless in producing predictive propositions, in relating data to behavior. And this failure has been due primarily to the lack of a useful political theory. Theory there is, but it is generally social or psychological. One may find, therefore, in the literature on political careers, answers to questions about the social system or evidence of social stratification. There are interesting cases of psychopathology. But inference from a politician's origins or his personailty to his political behavior does not work.[22] The social or occupational composition of Congress is no guide to its voting behavior. A classification of leaders according to personality types holds little promise of predicting matters of political consequence: for example, that an agitator such as Eugene Talmadge would develop the theme of racial intolerance while a Huey Long would excoriate the exploiting capitalists.[23]

Certainly a man's background is important to his endeavors as a politician. Matthews has shown, for example, that former congressmen adjust to the norms and folkways of the Senate more rapidly than do former governors.[24] But there is little evidence that former governors vote differently from former congressmen, or even that they are barred from eventual leadership of the Senate or inner circle.[25] Before we can

Makes Our Laws?" *Political Science Quarterly,* LV (1940), 556–81, reprinted in J. C. Wahlke and Heinz Eulau, eds., *Legislative Behavior* (Glencoe, Ill.: Free Press, 1959). J. C. Wahlke, Heinz Eulau, W. Buchanan, and L. Ferguson, *The Legislative System* (New York: Wiley, 1962), contains information on New Jersey, Ohio, Tennessee, and California. For the Wisconsin legislature, see Leon Epstein, *Politics in Wisconsin* (Madison: University of Wisconsin Press, 1958); on Pennsylvania, see Sorauf, *Party and Representation;* and on Oregon, see Lester Seligman, "Political Recruitment and Party Structure: A Case Study," *American Political Science Review,* LV (1961), 77–86.

[22] James D. Barber, in *The Lawmakers* (New Haven: Yale University Press, 1965), has shown a relationship between personality variables for legislators and a measure of their total activity in the legislature. From this he draws some imaginative inferences about the different roles they might play in politics.

[23] For an interesting attempt to develop a conceptual model of leadership behavior which does take into account the complexity of motives which I explicitly exclude, see Lewis Edinger, "Political Science and Political Biography," *The Journal of Politics,* XXVI (1964), 423–39, 648–76. I would argue that we are not likely to get very far in understanding the impact of personality differences until we have developed empirically testable theories which hold the personality variable constant.

[24] Matthews, *U.S. Senators and Their World,* Ch. V.

[25] Morton Grodzins, in his article, "American Political Parties and the American System," *Western Political Quarterly,* XIII (1960), 974–98, points out that, in the voting on the National Airport Act of 1946, a disproportionate number of ex-governors in the Senate were responsible for the provisions that required state involvement in the administration of the grant program to cities for airports. Findings of this type inevitably raise questions of interpretation. The background perspective implies that these senators voted as they did because they were ex-

determine the political consequences of the background differences among senators, we must find the relationship between the group life of the Senate and political decisions. In other words, Matthews' finding, at least in the form in which I have stated it, is interesting in relation to the Senate as a social not as a political system.

The difficulty is that background data have tended to draw political scientists away from their political perspective. Since the data are about politicians' pasts we are drawn to the assumption that they are creatures of their past. Surely there is truth in that assumption. It would be absurd to deny that the social composition of Congress affects its behavior in some way, or that politicians' personalities determine their reactions to political events, or that their previous office experience affects the way they go about their business. But to seek answers to political behavior in this manner is to see politics as the product of the social system or of individual psychology. Investigations of this type, therefore, test social and psychological rather than political theories. But they will be able to explain political events, the way a congressman votes, for example, only if social and psychological theories develop to the point where they can explain or predict behavior within a limited institutional framework.

If, on the other hand, we accept the central place of ambition in politics, we gain a political perspective on background data. A politician's biography is, after all, the story of one man's political ambitions. It may not tell us all of his aspirations, when they emerged or when they changed. But it does tell us what overt moves he has made toward gaining public office. We can say with certainty that, whatever other ambitions he had, these office ambitions he did have. Thus, when a congressman becomes a senator, the interesting questions do not revolve entirely around the impact of his congressional experience upon his senatorial behavior; there is also the effect of his ambition to become a senator upon his behavior in the lower house. Looking back on a man's career, we can see where he was going and attempt to determine what relationship existed between his future and his behavior at any previous stage. True, we cannot tell all of his ambitions from his career; but we can tell some, and particularly those which mattered.

When we collect the political biographies of many politicians we can observe whatever order there is in political careers. But what we make of that order is very much a matter of theoretical perspective. When that perspective, for example, focuses upon the recruitment of

governors. Ambition theory, however, leads us to note that a disproportionate number of ex-governors in the Senate come from states with one party dominant and that their constituencies appear to be particularly responsive to efforts at preserving state powers.

political leaders, the primary concern is the type of man, classified according to social or personality traits, who wins public office; little is made of the data on office experience as such. From the perspective of ambition theory, however, such mundane data as the tenure and turnover of officeholders, office succession, and the ages of elective officials take on major significance. The order which emerges from these data on political careers becomes "the structure of political opportunities"; we assume that opportunities arouse expectations and, in turn, give direction to personal ambitions.

This is not to say that an interest in political recruitment precludes the use of aggregate data on the office careers of elective leaders. But when the concern is primarily with recruitment, the tendency is to ask how men become President, senator, or governor. Within the framework of ambition theory, the aggregate data indicate rather which men are in the best position to become governor, senator, or President and, therefore, which men are likely to have such ambitions. In ambition theory the emphasis in analyzing such data is not on *how* one advances in politics but on *who* will want to advance.

As an example of the utility of ambition theory in interpreting career data, consider the standard question: Is the elected executive with legislative experience advantaged in his relations with the legislature? In answering this question, preoccupation with the process of political recruitment as the major influence upon political behavior leads to the assumption, which has wide acceptance, that the President who emerges from the Senate, or the governor from the state legislature, will get along better with the legislature because he knows its personnel and its customs. Legislative-executive relations become mostly a social affair, and the executive's effectiveness largely a matter of personal contacts and sensitivity to the legislators' various roles.

Lyndon Johnson to the contrary, the evidence to support the above assumption is not overwhelming. Ambition theory allows us to take the same data on the office experience of executives and arrive at a different view of executive-legislative relations. From this perspective, legislative experience in the background of Presidents and governors indicates that movement between the two types of office is possible and, therefore, that there will be some legislators with executive ambitions. There is revealed a link between the executive and the legislature which cannot exist in a situation where there is no reasonable expectation that a legislator can be elected to executive office. But note that from the perspective of ambition theory, even where the legislative-executive links exists, the precise way in which legislators improve their chances to advance can vary. Whereas in one instance cooperation with the executive may be the course, in another open conflict may well be the choice. Whereas, then, concern with political recruitment prompts us to ask how legislative experience affects the ability of the executive to deal with the legislature, ambition theory leads us to ask what the legislative experience of executives in a given political setting tells us about legislative behavior. When we know which legislators are in a good position to advance to executive office, we will be better able to consider the effect of legislators' strategies for advancement upon legislative action, a consideration which the concern for the recruitment of political leaders or their past tends to slight.

Regretfully, in this study I shall not do much with the strategies of advancement. Thus, in the present example I shall not ask what a legislator should do to maximize his changes of becoming governor or President. Nevertheless, it is through the interaction of opportunities and strategies that ambition theory can hope to explain the specifics of legislative or other political behavior. In my preoccupation with the discovery of the structure of opportunities I may appear to neglect ambitions. Yet I hope that I have made it clear that the entire enterprise stems from a concern with the impact of ambitions on politics and that I am mapping out one of the principal variables of a theory based on that motive.

SOME GENERAL CHARACTERISTICS OF THE STRUCTURE OF POLITICAL OPPORTUNITIES IN THE UNITED STATES

I should now make some general observations about the way political opportunities are structured in the United States. The most salient characteristic of the system is the proliferation of outlets for political ambition. Besides the thousands of local offices, the federal system provides, at the national and state levels, bicameral legislatures and independently elected executives. All of these offices have fixed terms which run for four years or less with few exceptions. Thus there are numerous more or less conspicuous and presumably desirable positions. Furthermore, almost all of these offices are elected independently; that is, there are few tie-in elections like that for the Presidency and Vice Presidency.

Not only are the outlets for political ambition multiple; they are also open in the sense that the lines of advancement are not prescribed by the legal system. Most of the nominations for office are made independently of others; that is, different combinations of people make the nominations for each office. With the exception of age and residency, there are few prerequisites for office, particularly any which require prior office experience. In fact, constitutional restraints often take the opposite course; they bar reelection, as in the case of second-term Presidents or many governors; occasionally they even bar election to another office, as is the case for executive officers in New Mexico who cannot run for any other executive office in the state.

Open access broadens the chances to obtain an office and loosens or blurs the opportunity structure. One consequence is that American politics may be entered at any level and at any stage in a man's career. One does not have to decide early in life that politics is to be one's life work and then advance up the ladder of office. Many men do, but there are enough examples of those who have reached the highest rungs without touching those below to increase the uncertainties of the system. For the politician calculating his chances, this means that he can never know with certainty who are to be his competitors or all of the sources from which they may come. It also means a constant renewal of personalities, a system in which new faces are always becoming prominent, one in which political generations are very short.

The open character of political opportunity in the United States forces the politician to treat public office as an avocation. The books on career counseling ignore politics as a profession, and the many "how to go into politics" books consist, by and large, of explanations of legal requirements. The politician needs another means of support, preferably one compatible with officeholding. For a large proportion of politicians, the law has served this function. In the words of Woodrow Wilson, "The profession I chose was politics; the profession I entered was the law. I entered one because I thought it would lead to the other."[26]

Nevertheless, there is structure to the opportunities for political office in the United States. Any elective system of opportunities is full of risks for the politician. But if we look at the American system from the standpoint of ambitions we can see that the risks tend to foster some ambitions and reduce others. The risks for those with progressive ambitions are not equally distributed among officeholders. Career risks are maximized in a situation in which, in order to seek a higher office, a man must give up his current office. The congressman who reaches for the Senate and fails loses everything, as did Alvin Bentley of Michigan in 1960. We would expect, therefore, that those congressmen who did seek to become governor or senator would be men who either came from

[26] Quoted in Eulau and Sprague, *Lawyers in Politics.* While there has been much speculation about the impact on American politics of the high proportion of lawyers among legislators, there is little evidence that they act cohesively; see David Derge, "The Lawyer as Decision-Maker in the American State Legislature," *Journal of Politics,* XXI (1959), 408–33.

unsafe seats or were sure of advancement. This does not mean that ambitious men will not take the risk. Congressman Bentley may have failed in 1960, but Congressman Kennedy of Massachusetts succeeded in 1952. Both were wealthy men for whom the risks were entirely of a political nature. Nevertheless, the opportunity structure tends to reduce, if not eliminate, the likelihood that congressmen will develop progressive ambitions.

There are other officials for whom the risks of seeking advancement are either negligible or for whom there are no risks at all. It is among these men that we expect to find progressive ambitions. Governors with restricted terms of office are free to seek advancement. Men whose terms of office overlap that of the office they seek are in a no-risk situation. Thomas Dewey could without risk run twice for the Presidency while he was governor of New York because his term as governor overlapped that of the Presidency.[27] The trend of recent constitutional changes in Connecticut, Michigan, New York, and Ohio to give up the two-year term for governor for a four-year term, elected at the presidential midterm, is explainable only partially as an attempt to separate state politics from national trends. It also eases the burden of governors who want to be President.

Senators, because of the six-year terms, are also in good position to seek the Presidency. Only in alternate elections must they seek reelection during a presidential year. If we look at the 14 senators who were nominated for the Presidency or Vice Presidency from 1900 through 1964, we find that 11 were in the happy state of facing no risk of losing office. One of the three whose senatorial election did coincide with that of the Vice Presidency was Lyndon Johnson in 1960; the Texas legislature resolved his problem by permitting him to run for both offices at the same time. Another senator to take the chance was Warren Harding in 1920, and it was not much of a chance. The only senator to lose his position because he sought the Presidency was Barry Goldwater in 1964—another facet to the *amateur* character of his nomination. Probably most senators would be happy to get a presidential nomination, regardless of its timing with respect to their own terms. But the relation between terms does lead some to be more interested at one time than at another. It was probably not accidental that Estes Kefauver made his major bids for the Democratic nomination in 1952 and 1956 and had to face senatorial elections in 1954 and 1960.

Another factor which gives structure to American political opportunities is, of course, the two-party system. In effect, it means that for

[27] On the other hand, Adlai Stevenson reluctantly had to give up the chance for reelection as governor of Illinois in order to run for the Presidency in 1952.

almost any office of consequence a man must be nominated either as a Democrat or a Republican. Without saying anything more about the content of the nomination, whether it requires acceptance by a strong organization or means simply that the label is attached, the two-party system does force the ambitious politician to take into account the competitive chances of each party for the office to which he aspires. Indeed, each party has its own opportunity structure, and the individual politician by opting for one party must calculate his chances within that structure. But, as I have pointed out above, while party theory is an ambition theory, they are not to be equated. By the same token, the party system is related to the overall structure of political opportunities, but in what way is a matter for empirical analysis.

Together the two-party system and the differential risk factor provide stability for the American opportunity structure, which in turn contributes to the stability of the American political system. Few politicians can have any direct or purposeful impact on the range of opportunities available to them. Each politician must work within an opportunity structure that he cannot alter. This is not to say that he cannot improve his own chances, but rather that the conditions he must cope with are not his to create. A politician continually makes decisions which affect his own ability to advance. He must choose his party, time his entry into politics, select his constituency, decide which offices to run for. The sum of these decisions by politicians everywhere certainly affects the general character of the system, but the individual politician, like the individual producer under conditions of perfect competition who cannot affect the prices of his products, is unable to affect the general structure of opportunities.

The structure of opportunities is certainly not fixed. Wars and changing economic bases have their observable impacts on political chances. To the extent that the party system is related to political opportunity, the shifting tides of party strength both nationally and within the states have their effect. The decade of the thirties saw Republican chances shrivel while those of the Democrats blossomed. There is a secular trend eroding sectional party strength and producing a more even two-party system. Increased chances for Republicans in the south and for Democrats in the midwest certainly alter the opportunity structure.

Most of the changes in the structure, however, are slow and predictable. For example, the distribution of population among the states, together with the Electoral College, provide the ground rules for the achievement of the Presidency. We can predict that if the present population trend continues the western states will become more important at the expense of the eastern and midwestern states. Yet politically it is a glacial change. Another change may be a decline in the chances of governors and a rise in the prospects of senators to become President. Certainly the 1960 and 1964 presidential elections did give senators an unprecedented prominence. But the change, if it be one, is far from revolutionary, for senators have always been important and governors certainly cannot yet be counted out. One might argue that the structure of political opportunities is one of the aspects of American life most resistant to change. The long history of legislative resistance to reapportionment and legislators' capacity to preserve as much of the status quo as possible in the face of the need to redistrict is testimony to the politicians' determination to keep their opportunities structured and predictable.

THE MEASUREMENT OF THE STRUCTURE OF POLITICAL OPPORTUNITIES

The stability of the American opportunity structure is essential to the measurement of its size and shape. Stability enables us to consider statistically the careers of many politicians over a number of years. We are not led astray in bringing together data from long periods of time, although we must be careful to note changes over time.

By the size of the structure I mean the total number of opportunities or chances, good or bad, for getting ahead in politics. In other words, the size of the structure consists of the number of offices available and the frequency with which new men attain them. The shape of the structure derives from the ways in which men typically advance in politics. If everyone has an equal chance at every office there is no form. Differential chances give shape to the structure of opportunities.

Since I intend to measure the place of the the states in the structure, I should point out that their structures may have the same shape but different sizes, or the reverse. Thus, two states may have the same rigid pattern of advancement from the legislature to the office of governor, but in one state a more rapid rate of turnover in the latter office will increase the size.

This study does not claim to measure the complete network of political opportunities in the United States. It does take some soundings and attempts to get at the outline of the real opportunity structure in order to see what generalizations might be made. The study proceeds as follows: (1) First we seek the outlines of the national structure of opportunities, with particular reference to the position of the states within the national system. Since the states are building blocks in the political career system, which includes the major federal offices, some assessment of the progressive ambitions of state leaders for national office is essential to defining the national structure as well as the states' internal structures of opportunities. (2) In Chapter III we measure the size of the opportunity structures in the several states, concentrating upon the major elective offices in terms of numbers and real turnover of personnel. (3) In Chapter IV we assess the party systems of the states to determine their relation to the size of the opportunity structure. (4) In Chapters V and VI we measure the shape of the opportunity structures within the states, with particular reference to the offices of governor and senator. (5) Having presented the empirical evidence, we are in a position in Chapter VII to return to the theoretical problem of relating ambition theory to party theory through our knowledge of the opportunity structure. We can also elaborate the implications of these findings for party organization in the United States. (6) In Chapter VIII the internal differences and similarities between the parties within a state are examined, so that it is possible to explore further the impact of party systems on political opportunities. (7) In Chapter IX we turn to a consideration of the timetable of individual careers within the structure of opportunities, an analysis essential to the further empirical development of an ambition theory of politics. (8) Finally, in Chapter X we examine the findings of this study for general implications about the American political system.

CHAPTER II

Political Opportunity in the United States: The National Structure

CONCERN FOR THE IMPORTANCE of office ambitions in politics leads me to analyze the opportunities for elective office in the American states. Although most of this study deals with the states, the perspective of ambition requires us to note that the states do not set the bounds for American political opportunities and ambitions. The American political system is national in scope. One of the major reasons that state politics are not independent of national politics is that national opportunities arouse in state politicians national ambitions.

But if there is a national structure of opportunities, the states do not share equally in these opportunities. This fact is critical to a comparative description of the states' opportunity structures; it determines the extent to which the offices in the states' control comprise the opportunities available to their politicians. Our major concern in this chapter, therefore, is the standing of the states in the national opportunity structure.

Ambition theory, however, raises two additional questions which should be asked first in the national context. Ambition theory, as distinct from party theory, leads us to ask if, and to what extent, the structure of opportunities is independent of the party system. Then too, since ambition theory implies that opportunities control ambitions and direct men's expectations, we should ask how orderly is the advancement to office in the United States.

THE PLACE OF THE STATES IN THE NATIONAL STRUCTURE OF OPPORTUNITIES

The national opportunity structure has two foci, the Presidency and the Congress. The Presidency includes not only the offices of President and Vice President but the many officials in the executive and the judiciary whom the President appoints. The Congress has its own career opportunities. Since, however, they are largely dependent upon offices in the control of the states, I shall examine the opportunities for national congressional office as part of the states' opportunity structures. In the following discussion of the national opportunity structure I shall deal only with the opportunities associated with the Presidency. While there is only one critical elective office in the presidential office complex, there are many significant offices which Presidents influence or appoint and for which other men strive. The Vice Presidency, the Supreme Court, and the Cabinet all draw men from major offices in the Congress and in the states. The coalitions created to capture the Presidency also have as their major target, and are indeed cemented by, the desire to control these offices as well. The Vice Presidential nominee has usually been selected to balance the presidential ticket for both geographical and factional reasons.[1] A President's Cabinet and Supreme Court appointments are properly seen not merely as a reflection of his desire to get the most able men for the job, but also as his payment for political debts and as a device for forging his policies. We shall consider, then, the people who hold the posts surrounding the Presidency as having reached the peak of the national opportunity structure and as forming the national political elite.

In the period 1900–1958 there are some 238 individuals who are either presidential or vice presidential nominees, Cabinet appointees, or Supreme Court members. Their careers in the aggregate provide us with our data for the analysis of the national opportunity structure. The contributions of the states to the complex of offices surrounding the Presidency are determined simply enough by calculating the proportion of the 238 national officials who came from each state.[2]

In Table II-1 we see the 48 states ranked according to an "index

[1] The most thorough historic survey of the factors involved in the selection of both presidential and vice presidential candidates is Paul T. David, Ralph M. Goldman, and Richard C. Bain, *The Politics of National Party Conventions* (Washington: Brookings, 1960). See also Irving G. Williams, *The Rise of the Vice Presidency* (Washington: Public Affairs Press, 1956).

[2] The state attributed to a particular individual is that of his official residence at the time of his nomination for national office.

TABLE II-1
The Positions of the States in the National Leadership Group

		Percentage of the Electoral College (A)	*Percentage of the National Leadership Group (B)*	*Index of Advantage (B/A)*
Mass. N. Y.	Mo. Iowa	15.81%	38.23%	Heavily Advantaged (2.23–2.51)[a]
Ohio N. M. Utah Neb. Tenn.	Ind. Colo. W. Va. Kan.	16.07	23.10	Moderately Advantaged (1.07–1.78)
Ill. Va. Pa. Ky. N. J. S. C. Mich. Md. Vt.	Wyo. Ore. Tex. Calif. Minn. Conn. R. I. Wash.	44.05	34.88	Moderately Disadvantaged (0.50–0.99)
Ala. Wis. N. C.	Ark. Okla. Ga.	12.25	3.79	Heavily Disadvantaged (0.19–0.41)
Ariz. Del. Fla. Idaho La. Me.	Miss. Mont. Nev. N. H. N. D. S. D.	11.83	0.00	Completely Disadvantaged (0.00)

[a] The range of indices of advantage for states in the category.

of advantage," the measure of the extent to which a state has received its share of representation in the presidential complex.[3] From Table II-1 we note that 13 states have enjoyed an advantage in the presidential complex. The advantaged states represent 32 per cent of the total Electoral College strength, while they provide 62 per cent of the national leadership group, or slightly less than twice as much as their Electoral

[3] The Electoral College allotment following the 1950 census has been used as the standard. Since the distribution of Electoral College votes has been constantly shifting, no single year is completely representative of the six decades covered, although the variations in results would not be very great. The 1950 figure tends to overestimate the advantage given to states suffering from a continual decline in Electoral College strength. An index of advantage of 1.00 means that a state's proportion of national leaders is just what one might have expected according to its Electoral College strength. Indices over 1.00 are measures of disproportionate representation and below 1.00 of underrepresentation.

College strength warrants. At the other end of the scale, there are 12 states with a total electoral college strength of 11.83 per cent which have provided the national leadership group with no members at all. The most heavily advantaged state is Massachusetts, with more than two and one-half times the number of national leaders which its Electoral College strength warrants. New York is close behind.

Much of the distribution of the states' positions in the presidential office complex is not surprising. Size and competitiveness advantage a state, and the practice of giving all of a state's Electoral College votes to the presidential candidate with a plurality maximizes the importance of both these qualities. Thus we find the large and competitive states of New York and Ohio advantaged, the small and strongly committed states of Mississippi and South Dakota completely disadvantaged.

TABLE II-2

State Position in the National Leadership Group Related to Position in the Senate

Position in the Senate[a]		*Relative Advantage in the National Leadership Group*				
		No. of States				
		Advantaged		*Disadvantaged*		
		Heavily	*Moderately*	*Moderately*	*Heavily*	*Completely*
No. of States						
Advantaged	Very Heavily	0	2	3	2	10
	Heavily	0	2	2	1	1
	Moderately	1	3	5	2	1
Disadvantaged	Moderately	2	1	3	1	0
	Heavily	1	1	4	0	0

[a] Based on Robert A. Dahl, *A Preface to Democratic Theory*, pp. 114–15. Copyright © 1956 by The University of Chicago Press, publishers, and reproduced by permission.

But the distribution of the states also indicates that more than size and competitiveness are involved in a state's standing. If, for example, size were the major factor, my index of advantage would be the exact inverse of a similar index calculated by Robert Dahl for the United States Senate. Table II-2 indicates that there is some validity to this proposition, but it is important to note that it is only in *some* degree valid. The cluster of states in the upper right-hand cells, 27 small states which have been relatively advantaged in the Senate, are at a disadvantage in the presidential complex. Five states in the lower left-hand corner of the table are disadvantaged in the Senate and advantaged in the presidential complex. But there still remain 16 states which are either advantaged or disadvantaged in both the Senate and the presidential complex. Such large states as Illinois, Pennsylvania, New Jersey, Michigan, Texas, California, Minnesota, and Wisconsin find no advantage in either office system. Smaller states such as Iowa, New Mexico, Utah, Nebraska, Tennessee, Colorado, West Virginia, and Kansas find favor in both systems. Thus, while none of the very large states are severely deprived in the presidential system and none of the smallest states are highly advantaged, we must also conclude that size is only a partial explanation of the states' positions.

Even when we consider party competition along with size we do not get a complete explanation of the presidential structure of opportunities. The eight states which we have noted as being disadvantaged in both the Senate and the presidential complex are not noticeably less competitive for the office of President than those large states which are advantaged. In the period 1900–1956, Illinois, Pennsylvania, New Jersey, and Minnesota changed parties in presidential elections four times, Texas three times, California five times, Michigan six times, and Wisconsin seven. While size and competition, then, are relevant to our problem, additional factors are needed to explain the position of the states within the national opportunity structure.

Part of the answer to the exceptional importance of some states in the structure is their representation of regional interests. For example, the border states of Missouri, Tennessee, and West Virginia gain in importance from their marginal position which enables the parties to make concessions to the one-party south without actually favoring its states. In other words, the weakness of some states due to lack of competition strengthens others which are marginally competitive. Apart from the border states, the other states advantaged in the presidential complex represent a bloc ranging from Iowa westward and south to include Kansas and Nebraska and the three southern mountain states, Utah, New Mexico, and Colorado. Part of the importance of these states comes from our definition of major office; we have included the posts of the secretaries of agriculture and the interior, which often fall to members of these states. But, on closer examination, it is evident that non-regional offices such as supreme court justice, the secretaries of war, the treasury, and commerce, and even presidential and vice presidential nominations also fall to men from these states: Alfred Landon and Henry Wallace are conspicuous examples. We can say that the need for the presidential party to take into consideration regional interests explains some of this overadvantage. But the interesting fact is not that men advance to the presidential complex from the underpopulated western states, but that they advance consistently from the same few. As a result, other western states are underrepresented or have no representation at all, as in the case of the Dakotas, Nevada, Montana, and Idaho.[4]

[4] It should be clear that for the smallest states our figures are also very small. States such as Vermont, Delaware, or Nevada which have a minimal Electoral

THE NATIONAL STRUCTURE OF OPPORTUNITIES AND THE PARTY SYSTEM

Do the states' standings in the national opportunity structure simply reflect their standings within the two major parties? If so, our concern for the national opportunity structure should be subordinated to an understanding of the party system. The evidence, however, points to the existence of a national structure which may be affected by the party system but which transcends the parties.

In recalculating the states' indices of advantage in the presidential office complex according to the party of the appointing President, I have found 27 states advantaged in one or the other party and 7 states which are advantaged in both parties. These 7 states shape much of the national structure of opportunities; together they provide 45 per cent of all the national leaders. Included in this group are the conspicuous states of New York and Ohio; but the remainder of the states are far less conspicuous—Iowa, Missouri, Tennessee, Utah, and New Mexico.

TABLE II-3
Party Similarity and Difference in State Sources of National Leadership

Advantaged in Both Parties	*Advantaged in Republican Party Only*	*Advantaged in Democratic Party Only*	*Disadvantaged in Both Parties*	
N.Y.	Mass.	Neb.	N.J.	Fla.
Mo.	Kan.	Ky.	Md.	Idaho
Iowa	Ore.	S.C.	Wash.	La.
Ohio	Vt.	W. Va.	Ala.	Me.
Utah	Wyo.	Colo.	Wis.	Miss.
N.M.	Ill.	Va.	N.C.	Mont.
Tenn.	Calif.	Ind.	Ark.	Nev.
	Minn.	R.I.	Okla.	N.H.
	Mich.	Tex.	Ga.	N.D.
		Conn.	Ariz.	S.D.
		Penn.	Del.	
Percentage of Total Leadership Group				
44.53%	24.36%	22.69%	8.42%	

College strength are adequately represented in the leadership group if they have one or two members. The distribution, therefore, among these states may well be a matter of chance. Such significance as can be attributed to these figures rests, therefore, upon their regional quality as well as upon the tendency for both parties to use the same states. The cutoff date of 1958, for example, has led us to exclude two representatives from Arizona, Secretary of the Interior Udall and presidential candidate Goldwater. From a condition of complete non-representation up to 1958, Arizona would have to be considered now as adequately represented. Of course Arizona is also one of the nine states which gained Electoral College strength in 1960.

The advantaged states in each party have to some degree been rewarded for their party loyalty but not entirely. Among the states favored by the Republican party are states which at one time or another have been strongholds of Republicanism: Massachusetts and Vermont, Michigan, Illinois, and Minnesota in the midwest, California and Oregon in the far west. Democratic favorites are found among the border states, in the south, and in southern New England where Connecticut and Rhode Island have been favored. But the parties have also favored states conspicuous for their lack of partisan support. The Republican party has given preferential treatment to Missouri and Tennessee and has even used men from Texas, Virginia, and Georgia, while it has neglected such strongholds of Republicanism as New Hampshire, Maine, and South Dakota. The Democratic party has been quite generous to Iowa, Nebraska, and Pennsylvania, despite the lukewarm attachments of these states for most of the period under consideration to the Democratic cause. Seemingly the two parties are concerned to boost the morale of their adherents in areas where they are weak. As a result, the opportunities for advancement in national politics are often better for men in the minority party of such swing states as Missouri and Pennsylvania than for men of the majority party in one-party states.

The explanation of the advantage enjoyed by some of the smaller states within the two parties may lie in part with organization. Certainly Missouri's great importance emerges not solely from its position at the confluence of all of the major political streams in America, but also from the strong organizations which have been able to exploit this position.[5] Well-organized parties in regions where others are not well organized are in a particularly good position to claim all of the influence which a national party is willing to allot to the region. For example, in the west there is evidence that New Mexicans have developed effective organizations, based on ethnic divisions, in a region not otherwise noted for its cohesive parties.[6] In contrast to New Mexico, North Dakota has long been disfavored in the presidential complex, a situation which the state's maverick senator, William Langer, fought constantly and in vain to remedy. Langer's failure was undoubtedly related to his state's disorganized politics which allowed a maverick to monopolize for a very long time one of its senate seats.[7]

[5] On Missouri party organization, see John Fenton, *Politics in the Border States* (New Orleans: Hauser, 1957); and Maurice M. Milligan, *Missouri Waltz* (New York: Scribner's, 1948).

[6] On New Mexico parties, see Charles Judah, *The Republican Party in New Mexico* (Albuquerque: Division of Research, Department of Government, University of New Mexico, 1949); T. C. Donnelly, ed., *Rocky Mountain Politics* (Albuquerque: University of New Mexico Press, 1940).

[7] As chairman of the Senate Judiciary Committee in 1953 and 1954, Republican

THE RELEVANCE OF STATE OFFICE TO NATIONAL OFFICE

In analyzing the national structure of opportunities I have assigned major importance to the states' political systems. It is possible, however, that our figures tell us nothing about the states as political units but merely reflect the distribution of influence within a nation state. In other words, if such writers as Floyd Hunter and C. Wright Mills are correct in their concept of a national elite, then the geographical sources of the members of that elite are less an index of the strength of the local political unit than an index of the strength of important commercial and industrial centers.[8] Thus, New York and Massachusetts are the home states of many national leaders, not because of their politics but because New York City and Boston are two of the principal financial and intellectual communities of the nation.

While our figures do not allow us to test directly the power center hypothesis, we can isolate the relevance in any overt sense of state politics in the careers of national leaders. A man who reaches the top ranks of national politics either has or has not held some kind of state office. If he has, we can assume that state politics has probably been more relevant to his advancement than if he has not. Thus, while Dwight Eisenhower advanced directly to the Presidency from New York, his advancement was less a tribute to New York politics than was the presidential nomination of Thomas Dewey. When Charles Wilson and Robert McNamara became Cabinet members, it was less a sign of the importance of Michigan in national politics than it was of the strength of the automobile industry.

Of the 238 national leaders we have been considering, 81 or one-third did not hold prior public office in their home states. For this purpose I have considered congressional offices as part of the state office complex. These 81 men support the proposition that there is a national elite independent of the localities. Their concentration (Table II-4) in the states with large metropolitan centers—over one-half of them come from New York, Illinois, Ohio, and Pennsylvania—strengthens the notion that their advance is not due to local political strength. The remaining two-thirds of the presidential complex, however, stand as testimony to the fact that the state political systems are the places

William Langer was an incessant source of trouble to the Eisenhower administration. He was particularly troublesome over judicial appointments and openly delayed confirmation because no major appointments had gone to the State of North Dakota. See *The New York Times,* December 17, 1954.

[8] Floyd Hunter, *Top Leadership, U.S.A.* (Chapel Hill: University of North Carolina Press, 1959); C. Wright Mills, *The Power Elite* (New York: Oxford University Press, 1956).

TABLE II-4
National Leaders Who Had Never Held Public Office in the Control of the States

States from Which Leaders Came	*Number of Leaders*	*Percentage of Total*
New York	21	25.93%
Illinois	8	9.88
Ohio	6	
Missouri	6	22.23
Pennsylvania	6	
Iowa	5	6.17
Massachusetts	4	4.94
California	3	
Michigan	3	
Maryland	3	18.50
Colorado	3	
Virginia	3	
Texas	2	2.47
Kansas	1	
Minnesota	1	
New Jersey	1	
New Mexico	1	
Utah	1	9.88
North Carolina	1	
Tennessee	1	
Connecticut	1	
	81	100.00

where most national leaders get their start. An understanding of the structure of opportunities within the states, therefore, is critical to our analysis of the national structure.

If we recalculate the states' indices of advantage in the presidential office complex, leaving out the 81 officials who have not held local office, there is a general improvement in standings. Six additional states are advantaged—Kentucky, South Carolina, Wyoming, Vermont, Oregon, and New Jersey; while only one, Colorado, loses its advantaged position. Since Massachusetts, which ranked first before, is even more advantaged, we are lead to infer that its standing derives more from the quality of its politics than from its position as a power center. New York loses in importance, but only slightly; it must still be characterized as heavily advantaged. The importance of the border states is enhanced, as well as that of the western-southwestern bloc which we noted earlier. These alterations, then, do not require us to revise our earlier conclusions.

How much the relative standings of the states with respect to the major presidential offices are also reflected in the rest of the federal hierarchy is a matter for investigation. Other studies have shown that state office experience is a significant route to the federal administra-

TABLE II-5

Relationship between State Advantage in Top National Group and in Secondary Positions

Secondary Position		*Top Leadership Group (1900–1958)*	
		Total Number of States Which Are	
		Advantaged N = 13	*Disadvantaged N = 35*
Federal Regulatory Commissioners[a]	Advantaged	61%	37%
	Disadvantaged	39	63
		100	100
Higher Civil Servants (1940 Sample)[b]	Advantaged	69	26
	Disadvantaged	31	74
		100	100

[a] Based on figures in Pendleton Herring, *Federal Regulatory Commissioners* (Cambridge: Harvard University Press, 1936). Herring's total was 143. The state index of advantage was calculated as above by relating the state's proportion in the Electoral College in 1950 to its proportion of such commissioners.
[b] Based on figures in Reinhard Bendix, *Higher Civil Servants in American Society* (Boulder: University of Colorado Studies, 1949). Bendix's sample consisted of 234 bureau heads and other major non-political officers. These figures were recalculated into the index of advantage.

tion. A sampling of political executives in the Truman, Eisenhower, and Kennedy administrations shows that 40 per cent have had state or local experience.[9] Earlier studies which categorized the state origins of top administrators reveal results similar to those I have found. Those states advantaged in providing the top leaders are similarly advantaged in providing federal regulatory commissioners[10] and the bureau heads.[11] For example, Massachusetts, which, as we noted, has an exceptional position in providing top leaders, also ranks second only to New York in providing regulatory commissioners and bureau heads. Similarly, western states such as Kansas, Iowa, and Colorado retain their advantage in the lower reaches of the federal hierarchy. Such evidence as exists,

[9] Dean E. Mann, "The Selection of Federal Political Executives," *American Political Science Review,* LVIII (1964), 97.
[10] Pendleton Herring, *Federal Regulatory Commissioners* (Cambridge: Harvard University Press, 1936), p. 108.
[11] Reinhard Bendix, *Higher Civil Servants in American Society* (Boulder: University of Colorado Studies, 1949), p. 24.

then, leads us to infer that these figures are fair estimates of what has been the relative positions of the states as sources for federal office.

I am, in fact, satisfied that the relative standings of the states in the presidential office complex can serve as a measure of the interdependence of state and national office. We can, I think, consider the 12 states with no representation in the presidential complex to have truncated structures of opportunity. The leaders of these states have had to satisfy their ambitions either within the states themselves or in Congress. Free, to all intents and purposes, of the tensions of national ambitions, the leaders of these states have in turn undoubtedly fostered the independence of their states' political systems to a degree which would not be the case if they had national ambitions and therefore national perspectives. In this instance the opportunity structure operates much like the electoral system which allows one-party states, insulated from national electoral tides, to develop a high degree of independence from national politics.[12]

On the other hand, the more numerous the outlets for national office which a state's leaders enjoy, the more closely related is its political life to the national scene. Politicians in Ohio, Massachusetts, or New York cannot ignore national politics; even if they have no national ambitions themselves, they can be sure there are others around them who do. Every aspect of state politics can be affected by the degree to which the leaders of that state can expect to advance in national politics. A governor who has good prospects of advancement has a powerful instrument to affect other politicians—their own hope for advancement. If men do act out of gratitude for past favors, ambition theory points to the importance of future hopes in controlling behavior. Regardless of whether or not a governor is strong or weak in a formal institutional sense, a governor with strong prospects for advancement can influence legislators and administrators in a way in which one without prospects cannot hope to do.

At the same time, and for the same reasons, national leaders are closely involved with the states advantaged in the presidential complex. They cannot afford to treat the politics of these states as a matter of purely local concern. Both as candidate and as President, John Kennedy had to deal continuously with the competing factions of the New York Democratic party. His brother's ability to obtain that party's nomination for United States senator in 1964 was but a mark of the relation between national and New York state politics which has existed for a long

[12] Electoral independence is discussed by V. O. Key, Jr., *American State Politics* (New York: Knopf, 1956), pp. 18–51.

time in both parties. The reverse of the Kennedy transfer was effected in 1900 by Boss Thomas Platt who rid himself of troublesome Theodore Roosevelt by advancing him from the New York governorship to the Vice Presidency.[13]

Indeed, when a state is an important feeder into the national hierarchy, national leaders cannot ignore what is happening even in the state's opposite party. One of the major exceptions to the rule that national leaders do not get involved in the nominations for lesser office occurs when the opposite party is grooming a potentially effective national candidate. There is probably very little of such long-range planning in American politics, but it is most likely to occur in the states most advantaged in the presidential complex. Thus, in 1907 Congressman Theodore Burton of Ohio was persuaded by Theodore Roosevelt to risk all of his accumulated power in Congress to run for mayor of Cleveland against Tom Johnson, a man who looked as though he might rise to more than local prominence.[14] In 1964 it was not difficult to conclude that astronaut-hero John Glenn had national party blessing when he announced his candidacy for the Ohio Senate seat of fellow-Democrat Stephen Young. The object of national Democratic concern was surely not Mr. Young who had been a loyal Democrat, nor was it simply fear that the Democrats might lose some of their lopsided Senate majority. Certainly a major factor in the national party's interest was the probable Republican senatorial candidate, Robert Taft, Jr., who was also a potentially attractive presidential candidate for his party.

THE SHAPE OF THE NATIONAL STRUCTURE OF OPPORTUNITIES

The third question posed by ambition theory is whether national political opportunities have sufficient focus to provide politicians interested in advancement with reasonable expectations. If we break down the presidential office complex into the Presidency, the Cabinet, and the Supreme Court, we find three distinctive careers leading to each office. The career leading to the Presidency is overwhelmingly political; over two-thirds of the nominees for President and Vice President between 1900 and 1958 have come from a major elective office. In contrast, the typical career leading to the Cabinet is non-political; that is, its members come mostly from administrative non-elective positions; close to one-

[13] Theodore Roosevelt, *Autobiography* (New York: Scribner's, 1920), p. 308.
[14] Forrest Crissey, *Theodore E. Burton, American Statesman* (New York: World, 1956), pp. 146–54.

TABLE II-6
Last Previous Office of Members of the National Leadership Group (1900–1958)

Last Office	Presidential and Vice Presidential Candidates		Cabinet Members		Supreme Court Justices	
	Rep.	*Dem.*	*Rep.*	*Dem.*	*Rep.*	*Dem.*
Major Elective						
President or Vice President	9.1%	4.5%	—%	1.45%	5.0%	—%
U. S. Senator	22.7	27.2	2.2	4.35	—	20.0
U. S. Representative	4.5	4.5	3.3	8.70	—	—
Governor or other state office	31.8	31.8	4.4	4.35	10.0	—
Defeated candidate for President or Vice President	—	4.5	1.1	2.90	—	—
	68.1	72.5	11.0	21.75	15.0	20.0
Administrative						
Federal Cabinet	9.1	4.5	8.9	4.35	10.0	33.3
Federal sub-Cabinet	—	—	11.1	20.30	—	—
Federal administration	4.5	13.6	25.6	21.70	—	6.7
State administration	—	—	—	2.90	—	—
	13.6	18.1	45.6	49.25	10.0	40.0
Court System						
Federal judge	4.5	—	—	2.90	35.0	20.0
State judge	—	4.5	1.1	1.45	25.0	—
Federal lawyer	—	—	2.2	5.80	15.0	6.7
	4.5	4.5	3.3	10.15	75.0	26.7
Others						
Major party administration	—	—	7.8	11.60	—	—
Defeated governor or senator	—	4.5	3.3	—	—	—
Local elective officer	—	—	1.1	1.45	—	—
No recent public office or nomination	13.6	—	27.8	5.80	—	13.3
	13.6	4.5	40.0	18.85	0.0	13.3
Total	99.3	99.6	99.9	100.0	100.0	100.0)
N	(22)	(22)	(90)	(69)	(20)	(15

half of the Cabinet members advanced from lesser posts within the federal bureaucracy. The Supreme Court has drawn its membership almost entirely from men in lesser legal posts. In effect, chances at all of these positions can hardly be described as randomly distributed.

It is true that there is no evidence of certain ascent from post to post; nor are the three avenues to high national office entirely distinct. Secretary of Commerce Hoover went on to the Presidency; William Jennings Bryan, his party's presidential candidate, was willing to accept Cabinet office; Charles Evans Hughes and Earl Warren sought the Presidency and went on to the Supreme Court; William Howard Taft won the Presidency and then became a Supreme Court justice; Wendell

Willkie and Dwight Eisenhower sought the Presidency without benefit of public office. But the evidence shows that these men were aberrations. There is sufficient clarity in the routes to top national office for politicians at the lower level to place their expectations in a reasonable perspective.

We should also ask if party distinctions are relevant to the ordering of national opportunities. Here the evidence supports our earlier contention about the relative independence of the national opportunity structure from the party system. Within both parties men advance to high national office mostly from similar positions.

Nevertheless, we should note that, on balance, the Democratic career is typically more "political" than the Republican career. The Republican party has given its presidential nomination to men without public office, Willkie and Eisenhower. A much higher proportion of Cabinet members named by Republican Presidents have never held public office. If we examine the types of offices from which nominees come, we find that the Democrats consistently follow the more political course, choosing a higher proportion of presidential candidates, Cabinet members, and Supreme Court justices from elective positions. The greatest discrepancy is in the parties' attitudes toward the court; some 75 per cent of the Republican nominees come from the court system, while only 27 per cent of the Democratic nominees come through this "normal" channel. In effect, the Republican party has set the career patterns for the non-elective positions in the national structure, while the Democrats have set the pattern for the elective or more purely political offices.

The reasons for the differences between the two parties probably lie in each party's peculiar function in American politics. The Republicans as the more conservative party have had closer ties to the business community and have been more willing and able to draw leadership from the business elite. At the same time, as the party with the narrower social base, the Republicans, in making nominations for the top elective or political offices, have had a greater need for figures who can transcend party. Since the 1930's the majority of voters have turned to the Democrats, and the Democrats have had little need for a Willkie or an Eisenhower. Their advantage has come from playing up party affiliation and record. The Republicans have accepted the more regular, the legal, route in making nominations to the Supreme Court. The Democrats with a more political view of the proper functions of the court have gone to the Senate (Hugo Black and James Byrnes), to the office of attorney general (Frank Murphy, Robert Jackson, and Tom Clark) or completely outside the ranks of officeholders (Louis Brandeis and Felix Frankfurter).

CONCLUSIONS

Our analysis of the national structure of opportunities has been preliminary to the examination of the states' structures which follows. Guided by our concern for the impact of personal ambitions upon the political system, we have sought to answer three questions. First we have defined the relative contributions of the states to the presidential office complex. In so doing, we have found marked differences in the opportunities afforded politicians by the individual states, although two-thirds of our national leaders have come from some type of state office. We also find order in the careers of high national officials and we conclude that reasonable expectations for national advancement are not scattered at random among the states' politicians. While there are differences between Republican and Democratic officeholders with respect to their geographic origin and office experience, the structure of opportunities in both parties is very similar. This finding justifies the discussion of a structure of opportunities independent of the party system.

CHAPTER III

The American States and the Number of Political Opportunities

IN THE LAST CHAPTER I discussed the national structure of political opportunities in the United States in broad and rather imprecise terms. The discussion was, however, a necessary introduction to the question of the states' structures of opportunities which concern me here and which I hope to describe with greater precision. In this chapter I shall attempt to measure what I have called earlier the size of the structure of opportunities, or the frequency with which new men can hope to attain office. Such opportunities can be measured for particular offices, or they may be considered in the aggregate for all the offices in a state. Again it is our concern for the impact of ambitions which directs our task. The general level of opportunities in a state has, I assume, much to do with the excitation of ambitions among politicians. And differences among offices have much to do with the ways in which both those who hold an office and those who want one treat them.

Of course our figures will be, at best, statements of probabilities. The chances of any one politician are much a matter of being in the right place at the right time. Before his defeat for the Presidency Richard Nixon was reportedly prone to philosophising about politics in this vein.[1] Certainly his own career, at least up to that point, had been a prime example of good fortune. In 1946, when he won election to Congress as part of an overwhelming Republican landslide, there was no way to predict that 14 years later he would be running for President.

[1] Stewart Alsop, *Nixon and Rockefeller* (Garden City, N.Y.: Doubleday, 1960), pp. 184–201.

Even within the target area of a particular office it is difficult for a politician to assess his chances accurately. As astute a politician as Franklin Roosevelt was unhappy about having to run for governor of New York in 1928 because he did not predict a good Democratic presidential year until 1936.[2] The politician must bring into focus simultaneously his own availability for an office and the chances of his party.

At the same time the politician's sense of the probable outlets for his ambitions must be aroused by external events; it must come from the accumulated experience of men in positions similar to his own. Thus, since the turnover in United States senators in Kentucky is about four times that in Virginia, politicians eyeing the senatorship in Kentucky ought to feel about four times as sanguine as their counterparts in Virginia. And, indeed, the scrambling among Kentucky politicians is certainly both a cause and an effect of their chances. On the other hand, the slowness of turnover in Virginia enhances the value of timing. As governor of Virginia in 1933, Harry Byrd could accept appointment to the Senate and begin a career which lasted over 30 years because newly elected Franklin Roosevelt appointed Virginia's Senator Swanson to his cabinet. A slight difference in timing might have led Byrd to political oblivion, as it has, undoubtedly, many another Virginia politician. Precision in timing would appear to be less important in Kentucky, where men such as Alben Barkley, John Sherman Cooper, and A. B. Chandler could all aspire to the Senate within a relatively brief period of time. The opportunities to become senator in these two states are characteristically different.

We should, therefore, be able to measure opportunities for office by the rate of change of personnel in that office. But it is important that we distinguish between the real turnover, or actual changes in personnel, and the legal rate which is defined by electoral frequency. In trying to measure the *real* turnover we run into a time problem. When the politician contemplates his chances of becoming governor, President, or senator he thinks of such possibilities within a specific time period, the span of his own political life. But *political* time runs by two calendars: the normal chronology of months and years, and the electoral calendar which measures time in two-, four-, and six-year office terms. Is political time the same in a state where the terms of office are four years as it is where the terms are only two years? To the extent that the sense of the passage of time is derived from the regular occurrence of events, time passes twice as quickly in the states with biennial elections. Terms of office are an important political measure; the expressions

[2] Alfred B. Rollins, *Roosevelt and Howe* (New York: Knopf, 1962), p. 234.

"third-term governor" and "freshman senator" have meaning apart from the number of years involved. The sense of longevity in office is related as much to the number of times a man has been reelected as it is to the number of years he has been in office. A governor who has run successfully for six two-year terms is marked by three times as much campaigning as a senator who has won two six-year terms, although their time in office is the same. Both the sense of longevity and the sense of opportunity emerge from some combination of chronological and electoral time.

Real turnover in office, therefore, is related both to time perceptions as well as to the generally prevalent attitudes about the proper tenure for a particular office. We shall note shortly that the office of governor is one of very high turnover. Since the term of office for governors has been increasing over the years, there is a resultant increase in their tenure, but the actual number of years they spend in office has not increased at the same rate as the length of terms. For example, in Massachusetts governors had a one-year term until 1920 and the typical governor could expect to be elected to three terms. After that, as in most states with two-year terms, the typical governor could expect at most one reelection. And, if we compare them with states with four-year terms for governors (excluding those which permit no reelection), we find that gubernatorial tenure in the latter exceeds that in the former, but not by twice as much.

To measure political opportunities, then, we must take into account both electoral and chronological time. We can measure electoral time in terms of the frequency with which new men are elected to an office or the frequency of personnel change according to the electoral timetable. I call this measure the *personnel turnover rate*. When offices have the same terms of office the rates are comparable. But where the terms of office differ we must find a common denominator. We must translate the personnel turnover rate into chronological time. By multiplying the personnel turnover rate by the number of elections in a given time period we obtain a figure which states the normal *rate of opportunities,* or the frequency with which a new man has gained the office in that particular time period. Twelve years is the most convenient time period since it is the lowest common multiple of two, four, and six, the standard office terms in the United States. Twelve years is also a sufficiently long period, given the rapid turnover of political leadership in the United States, to warrant being called a political generation. While the figures I shall use to determine the size of the states' opportunity structures do not refer to any particular twelve-year period, they are distilled from the data which I gathered for the period 1914–1958.[3] That is to say, the personnel turnover rate for each of the offices is calculated on the basis of the election series in each state from 1914 through 1958. Those rates are then translated into the twelve-year generation or political opportunity rate by multiplying them by six, three, or two (depending upon whether the office carries a term of two, four, or six years), i.e., by the number of elections for a particular office in a twelve-year period.[4]

TABLE III-1

The Opportunities to Become Senator, Governor, and Congressman in the United States

Office	No. of Offices	A No. of Elections (1914–1958) (A)	B No. of Personnel Changes (1914–1958) (B)	C Personnel Turnover Rate (B/A)	D No. of Elections in 12 years	E Opportunity Rate (C × D)
Governor	48	822	548	.667	204	136.07
Senator	96	819	399[b]	.487	192	93.50
U. S. Representative	435	9,509[a]	2,228	.234	2,610	610.74

[a] The reapportionment of congressional seats every 10 years—ignored in 1920—makes impossible the tracing of turnover continuously for all congressional seats. Where it was possible a seat was traced on through a reapportionment, but where the district lines were seriously reordered, the count of electoral turnover started over with the new apportionment. Therefore the figure stated above does not include all congressional elections between 1914 and 1958.

[b] Personnel changes among senators were determined according to each senatorial seat in a state.

We are now equipped to measure the size of the opportunity structures of the states. But we can get a better idea of the meaning of the

[3] The election year 1914 was chosen as the starting point for the analysis because it was the first in which United States senators were popularly elected. Also, by that time the direct primary method of nomination had spread widely among the states. The cutoff date of 1958 coincides with the period for which career data on candidates was gathered.

[4] In a few instances the states have made changes during the period 1914–1958 in the terms of office of the governor. In 1939 New York changed from two- to four-year terms, and in 1947 Idaho increased its terms to four years. New Jersey in 1950 went from a three- to a four-year term. In these cases the personnel turnover rate was calculated, as it has to be, without regard to terms. The opportunity rate, however, was calculated using the new and longer term only. As a result, the opportunity rate probably overestimates tenure in office and therefore underestimates real opportunities, because the turnover rate would normally be lower during the shorter office period. That, of course, is due to the mixing of time senses noted above. Ohio changed to a four-year term for governor in 1958, and a number of other states have extended their terms since then. In these cases the calculations have been made with the old, or two-year, term.

measurements by answering the question, What are the relative chances in national terms of becoming governor, senator, or congressman? We must also recognize, however, that the answer, stated in national terms, will tell us little directly about office careers since all of these offices must be obtained within states and districts. (Table III-1 gives the method of making the calculations.)[5] The personnel turnover rates (Column C) show that the turnover rate for governors is about three times that of congressmen, or that two-thirds of the elections for governor produce a new man in office while that is true for less than one-quarter of the congressional elections. Senators range somewhere in between, gaining, on the average, a little better (.487) than two terms. When we translate these figures based on the total experience of 1914–1958 (Column C) into chances per 12-year generations by multiplying them by the number of elections (Column D), we obtain the opportunity rate. We see, then, that in 12 years there are 610 chances to become one of 435 congressmen and 93 chances to become one of 96 senators; and we note that, despite the fact that there are twice as many senators as governors, the real chances of becoming a governor are greater, 136.07 in 12 years.

CONSTITUTIONAL PRESCRIPTIONS AND THE SIZE OF THE STATES' STRUCTURES OF OPPORTUNITIES

While we wish to assess as accurately as possible the size of the states' opportunity structures, we must recognize that constitutional prescriptions set the bounds. Political opportunity arises within an institutional framework, clearly marked and not easily changed by the ambitious politician. The number of elective offices and the terms prescribed by the Constitution establish the maximum number of opportunities. On the other hand, constitutional restraints which prevent men from succeeding themselves in office establish the minimum number of opportunities for achieving office. According to our measure of opportunities, the maximum number is equivalent to a personnel turnover rate of 1.00.

[5] The formula for calculating the political opportunity rate is as follows: For any office

political opportunity rate = (personnel turnover rate) × (potential turnover in 12 years)

or

$$\frac{\text{no. of elections with change in personnel, 1914–1958}}{\text{no. of elections, 1914–1958}} \times \text{(no. of elections in 12 years)}$$

or

(the average real turnover in personnel) × (constitutional maximum turnover)

In measuring the opportunity structures of the states I focus upon nine offices,[6] although not all nine are elective in every state. Presumably, the fewer the elective offices provided for in the Constitution, the smaller the size of the political opportunity structure. In only twenty-six states are all six of the state executive posts which I deal with elective.[7] Four states, Maine, New Hampshire, New Jersey, and Tennessee, have only one elective executive officer, the governor. Table III-2 indicates the elective posts in each state. The number of congressmen, of course, varies with the state's population.[8]

As far as terms of office are concerned, the federal Constitution prescribes uniform terms for the offices of senator and representative. But the length of terms for state offices varies among the states from two to four years. Most states have the same terms for all of their state executive offices but there are exceptions. In Delaware the governor, the lieutenant governor, and the attorney general have four-year terms, the auditor and treasurer two-year terms. The reverse is true in Minnesota and Ohio, where all officials have two-year terms except the auditor whose term is four years.[9]

Constitutional restraints upon succession also vary among the states. Most commonly they apply to the governor. Some fifteen states permit only one four-year term for governor: Pennsylvania, West Virginia, Virginia, Kentucky, North Carolina, South Carolina, Georgia, Florida, Alabama, Mississippi, Louisiana, Indiana, Missouri, Oklahoma, and Idaho. Delaware, New Jersey, Maryland, and Oregon permit two consecutive four-year terms. In New Mexico only two consecutive two-year terms are permitted; in Tennessee, three consecutive two-year

[6] Besides United States senator, governor, and United States representative, the offices are the minor statewide elective positions most common in the states: lieutenant governor, attorney general, auditor, treasurer, and secretary of state. In addition I have considered the lower house of the state legislature.

[7] Since 1938 the lieutenant governor of New York, although still elected, is chosen on a joint ticket with the governor. As a result the office has lost much of its independent political strength and cannot be considered part of the elective hierarchy of the state, as it was, for example, when Herbert Lehman moved from lieutenant governor to governor. Therefore I have not included it within the elective opportunity structure of New York. Michigan adopted a similar arrangement beginning with the election of 1964. For a brief discussion of the minor state elective offices, see Byron Abernethy, *Some Persisting Questions Concerning the Constitutional State Executive* (Lawrence: Governmental Research Center, University of Kansas, 1960).

[8] The figures for the legislative offices for the United States Senate and House and the state legislatures are composites for each state. There are, of course, great differences among the districts of some states in the number of opportunities they provide to new men. Thus, the figures presented here define the general character of tenure in such offices and the general differences among the states, while obscuring significant variations within a state.

[9] In 1958 Ohio shifted to a four-year term for all state offices.

terms.[10] The constitutional restraints upon governors do not, for the most part, apply to lesser state officials. But Alabama and Kentucky impose the same one-term limitation on all elective state officers; in New Mexico all state officers, including the governor, may have only two terms and may not succeed to any other state office. Restricted terms for the fiscal offices of auditor and treasurer are common, and, in a few states such as Colorado and Utah, they have restricted terms when the governor does not. In Mississippi the state's auditor and treasurer cannot succeed themselves or each other.[11]

TABLE III-2

Opportunity Rates for Selected Offices—By States

The rate is the number of times, on the average, the office becomes available to a new man during a 12-year period. (The average is calculated from the experience, during the period 1914–1958, except for the state legislatures.) For those offices which consist of more than one seat, the figures are an average. To determine the actual opportunities to hold any one of these offices, the figure given for the office should be multiplied by the number of seats in the state, e.g., senator by 2 and the others by the size of their delegations.

SYMBOLS: ( ) A career office, one held typically for 12 or more years consecutively (a rate of 1.00 or less).
____ A transitory office, one held typically for 4 years or less (a rate of 3.00 or more).
* The office does not exist, as an elective post, in the state.

	Senator	*U. S. Cong.*	*Gov.*	*Lt. Gov.*	*Att'y Gen'l*	*Sec. of State*	*Treas.*	*Auditor*	*Lower House State Legis.*
A. States with generally high rates of opportunities—no career offices of significance.									
Colo.	1.06	1.24	3.66	4.43	3.13	2.60	6.00	6.00	4.37
Del.	1.47	4.44	2.18	3.00	3.00	*	5.70	5.40	5.01
Ind.	1.06	1.52	3.00	3.00	2.70	3.90	3.39	4.43	4.47
S. D.	1.07	1.24	3.39	3.91	3.13	3.39	3.39	2.87	3.39
Mich.	1.20	1.31	3.13	4.44	4.44	3.13	2.35	2.09	2.88
Ohio	1.16	1.66	3.33	4.20	3.65	3.13	2.61	1.09	3.54
Ky.	1.50	1.30	3.00	3.00	3.00	3.00	3.00	3.00	4.13
Ill.	1.30	1.62	1.91	2.18	1.64	1.36	6.00	1.91	2.35
Iowa	1.29	1.14	3.13	3.39	2.61	2.08	1.81	1.57	3.19
Pa.	1.22	1.81	3.00	3.00	*	1.25	3.00	3.00	2.92
Mo.	1.06	1.85	3.00	2.18	1.91	1.36	3.00	1.36	3.64
Idaho	1.30	1.57	2.10	2.25	2.70	2.60	1.20	1.20	3.74
Conn.	1.30	2.72	2.62	2.29	1.43	2.15	2.00	*	3.93
Minn.	1.06	1.39	3.13	3.13	1.56	(0.79)	1.82	1.63	2.44
Wyo.	1.20	2.05	2.57	*	*	2.25	3.00	1.50	2.42
W. Va.	1.41	2.39	3.00	*	2.18	1.34	1.09	(0.82)	n.a.

[10] Joseph K. Kallenbach, "Constitutional Limitations on Reeligibility of National and State Chief Executives," *American Political Science Review,* XLVI (1952), 438–54.

[11] Restraints on specific offices are based on *Index Digest of State Constitutions* (Dobbs Ferry, N.Y.: Oceana, 1964).

TABLE III-2

Opportunity Rates—*Continued*

	Senator	*U. S. Cong.*	*Gov.*	*Lt. Gov.*	*Att'y Gen'l*	*Sec. of State*	*Treas.*	*Auditor*	*Lower House State Legis.*
B. States where the opportunites to become U.S. senator or congressman are low, but where they are high for state offices.									
N. M.	(0.84)	2.71	4.36	4.09	4.36	3.00	3.82	3.55	4.40
Ala.	(0.48)	(0.96)	3.00	3.00	3.00	3.00	3.00	3.00	2.30
Neb.	(0.94)	1.96	3.13	3.13	3.13	1.57	3.65	1.57	3.31
Ariz.	(0.66)	1.36	3.13	*	2.61	2.61	6.00	1.56	3.84
N. D.	(0.72)	1.58	2.87	3.90	3.12	(0.88)	3.66	(0.88)	3.13
Okla.	(0.94)	1.74	3.00	1.36	1.36	3.00	3.00	3.00	4.21
Kan.	(0.75)	1.19	3.66	3.39	2.87	1.82	2.09	1.30	4.00
Mass.	1.06	(0.87)	3.11	3.46	2.77	(0.69)	3.23	1.39	2.94
Ark.	(0.82)	(0.90)	3.42	2.62	3.00	1.36	1.91	2.18	3.98
Vt.	(0.95)	1.36	4.18	4.70	2.09	1.57	1.04	(0.52)	4.27
Miss.	(0.62)	(0.78)	3.00	3.00	1.36	(0.55)	3.00	3.00	1.26
Wis.	(0.94)	1.55	3.65	2.87	2.99	1.30	1.81	*	3.07
R. I.	(1.00)	1.32	2.87	3.65	2.08	1.57	2.35	*	2.30
La.	(0.94)	1.14	3.00	3.00	2.18	1.09	1.64	1.09	1.18
N. C.	(0.94)	(0.96)	3.00	3.00	1.36	1.09	(0.55)	(0.82)	3.94
Tex.	(0.76)	(0.90)	3.42	2.96	3.14	*	1.43	*	3.76
C. States with generally low opportunities, except for governor and legislature.									
Mont.	(0.50)	2.09	1.64	2.45	2.45	1.06	3.00	(0.55)	3.61
Utah	(0.75)	1.82	1.81	*	1.91	1.64	3.00	3.00	4.17
Wash.	(0.88)	1.21	1.91	1.64	1.64	1.36	3.00	(0.27)	3.47
Nev.	(0.63)	2.87	2.00	1.75	2.00	(0.75)	(0.75)	*	3.75
Calif.	1.06	1.20	2.25	2.50	1.25	(0.25)	(1.00)	*	2.66
Ore.	(0.88)	1.17	2.36	*	(1.00)	1.50	1.50	*	3.70
S. C.	(0.70)	1.08	2.40	1.93	(0.64)	(0.64)	(0.64)	*	3.22
N. J.	1.56	1.47	2.57	*	*	*	*	*	2.01
Md.	1.13	1.61	1.75	*	2.00	*	*	*	2.19
N. Y.	1.06	1.43	1.67	*	1.33	*	*	*	1.37
N. H.	(0.83)	1.69	4.18	*	*	*	*	*	3.74
Me.	(0.94)	1.28	3.40	*	*	*	*	*	4.19
Tenn.	(1.00)	1.08	3.42	*	*	*	*	*	4.52
Fla.	(0.58)	1.14	3.00	*	1.25	(0.25)	(0.50)	*	3.59
Va.	(0.38)	1.08	3.00	2.10	1.20	*	*	*	2.97
Ga.	(0.70)	(0.96)	2.10	*	1.50	(0.75)	(0.38)	*	4.16
Number of states where offices fit each career category.									
(Careers)	27	7	0	0	2	9	6	6	0
Transitory	0	1	30	21	12	8	20	10	32
Intermediate	21	40	18	14	28	22	15	15	15
	48	48	48	35	42	39	41	31	47

The effect of constitutional restraints upon the number of opportunities in each state may be seen in Table III-2. The rate of opportunity for any one office, as defined earlier, will lie somewhere between the minimum and maximum set by constitutional prescription. Of course, where succession in office is prohibited, the minimum, the maximum, and the rate of opportunities will all coincide. Thus, in Colorado, where the treasurer and auditor may serve but a single two-year term, we find an opportunity rate of 6.00, indicating that in twelve years there will be a different person in each office six times. Where the term of office is four years without possiblity of reelection, the opportunity rate is 3.00, as it is for all of the statewide elective positions in Kentucky. Having called attention to the constitutional prescription, I shall focus upon the rates of opportunity as the most precise measure of the size of the opportunity structures of the states.

THE RATES OF OPPORTUNITY FOR SELECTED OFFICES WITHIN THE STATES

The nine offices from which I have chosen to construct the opportunity structures of the states are of general but varied importance. Seven have statewide electorates: United States senator, governor, and the lesser state executive offices of lieutenant governor, attorney general, secretary of state, state treasurer, and state auditor. I have also included the seats in the lower house of the federal Congress and the lower house of the state legislature[12] whose electorates fall within districts of the state. While these offices do not comprise all of the elective office opportunities within the states, they do represent the principal outlets for political ambitions.

[12] The opportunity rate for the state legislatures is a projection from the experience of but a single legislature, that one sitting during 1950, and for that reason the figure is less reliable than the others presented. State legislative turnover rates are calculated from the information on the number of terms of office of the members of the 1950 legislature as presented in Belle Zeller, *American State Legislatures* (New York: Crowell, 1954). That information has been translated into the present measure by devising the turnover rate and then adjusting it to the term of office. The reliability or typicality of these figures has been tested by comparing them with those presented by Charles Hyneman in his article, "Tenure and Turnover of Legislative Personnel," *Annals of the American Academy of Political and Social Science,* CXCV (1938), 23. Hyneman's figures cover ten legislatures for the period 1925–1935. In every one of the ten states his figures show a lower turnover rate than Zeller's figures, but the relative positions of the states remain the same; states with high turnovers are high on both calculations for two different periods. Therefore, I conclude that the experience of the single legislature chosen here probably overestimates turnover, yet the relative positions of the states are probably accurately stated.

The opportunity rates make it possible for us to characterize offices according to the role each can play in a man's political career. It also identifies the types of ambition a particular office is likely to foster. Only offices for which the opportunity rate is low can realistically produce static ambitions. Particularly at the extremes, the opportunity rate is useful in designating office types. Thus I shall call high turnover posts, or offices with a rate of 3.00 and more, *transitory* offices. These offices, in other words, are held typically for four years or less. I shall call *career* offices, those offices with a rate below 1.00 or offices held typically for twelve or more successive years by the same man. For offices which fall between the rates of 1.00 and 3.00, I use the designation *intermediate,* to signify their unclear role in political careers.

Classified according to office types, the states fall into three broad groups. First there are those states with no career offices of major significance, states where many posts are actually transitory (group A). The second group (B) also has generally high rates of opportunity for state offices, but one or both of the congressional offices are career posts. Finally, there are 16 states (group C) which have generally low opportunity rates, with some exceptions for the office of governor and the state legislature. Some states fall in this group because they have so few elective offices, e.g., Maine, New Hampshire, and Tennessee.

Of all the offices considered, the office of United States senator emerges most clearly as a career office. Of course, its term is also the longest. But in some states tenure is exceptionally long, as in Virginia, where an opportunity rate of 0.38 indicates an average tenure of just under 32 years. In Montana the average term is 24 years, and in Alabama just under 24 years. The shortest average senatorial tenure is found in Kentucky, eight years, and New Jersey, just under eight years. In general the United States House of Representatives also allows long tenure; the office of representative is transitory only in Delaware, although the average tenure in most states falls below 12 years. But there are 7 states, Massachusetts and 6 from the solid south, where the average congressman lasts 12 or more consecutive years. In Mississippi the average is over 15 years. While long tenure in the federal offices is especially noticeable in the south where the one-party system is the base, the two federal posts are generally the offices with the lowest turnover. In no state do the chances to gain a single Senate seat equal that for governor; only in Delaware, Kentucky, Illinois, New Jersey, Maryland, New York, and Idaho do the chances to gain both Senate seats combined equal or surpass the chances to gain the single office of governor.[13]

[13] The relatively low turnover indicated here for the office of governor in New York, Idaho, and New Jersey may be an underestimation due to the change in term of office in all three states. See above, footnote 4.

Among the states the transitory offices are the three state executive offices which are most political: the offices of governor, lieutenant governor, and attorney general. In no state is the office of governor or lieutenant governor a career post; the office of attorney general qualifies as a career office only in Oregon and South Carolina. High turnover in these posts is characteristic of most states whether there is a legal requirement for high turnover or not. The three minor elective offices, essentially administrative, give mixed results. In many states these offices have very high opportunity rates, particularly for the offices of treasurer and auditor. But most of these cases reflect the legal inability of incumbents to succeed themselves. Where there are no legal restraints, these offices show a clear tendency to become career offices. For example, in Florida and California for the period from 1914 through 1958 there has been only one change in the office of secretary of state.

In fact, legal restraints with respect to the minor administrative offices are not infrequently circumvented. In some states, notably Colorado and Oklahoma, the practice of rotation of offices negates the constitutional objective. In Colorado from 1914 to 1958 there were six men who played this game of musical chairs, moving in and out of the offices of auditor and treasurer. The most successful was Homer Bedford who, after 1932, held these two offices alternately thirteen times. Only one break occurred in his career in the two offices. While during the period there were 46 elections for the two offices in which no incumbent was or could be reelected, only 17 individuals served as either treasurer or auditor. Similar instances exist in Oklahoma; A. S. J. Shaw had the longest round—six terms alternating as treasurer and auditor. Other states with instances of office rotation are Alabama, Illinois, and Louisiana. Two states, as we noted earlier, Mississippi and New Mexico, have specific consititutional provisions to prevent this practice.

It is interesting to note that such artifices as rotation for circumventing constitutional prescriptions have never been successfully used by governors, lieutenant governors, or attorneys general. It is possible that politicians are not particularly fond of these jobs, but there is no apparent reason to suppose that the office of state treasurer has any greater long-range appeal than that of attorney general or governor.[14] Governor Earl Long of Louisiana reportedly proposed to defy the constitutional prohibition on succession by running for lieutenant governor and then having

[14] The inherent weaknesses of the office of lieutenant governor make it unlikely that any but those using it to further their ambitions would want it. A lieutenant governor of Nebraska, Robert Crosby, expressed his reactions in "Why I Want to Get Rid of My Job," *State Government,* XX (1947), 139–94, 204.

the newly elected governor resign in his favor, but he never had a chance to test the scheme.[15] It is clear, however, that where the electorate is willing, constitutions can be circumvented.

In effect, the distinction between career and transitory offices seems to be ingrained in the American political system. The voters are willing to allow congressmen to hold their jobs for life; and the minor state officials whose jobs have no conspicuous political content may also hold on for decades. But the same attitude which fostered the two-term tradition for President and then sanctified it with the Twenty-Second Amendment is reflected in the high turnover for all of the conspicuously political executive posts at the state level.[16] We need not dwell here on the causes of this attitude, but it is important to our analysis because of its consequences for the structure of political opportunities. Driven by the desire for both security and advancement, the politician must assign different values to each office in accordance with the part it can play in his career. The more transitory the office, the more its holders must handle it primarily in terms of where it can lead. The more careerlike an office, the more likely it will be sought by men for itself and the more likely they will behave in that office according to some internal rules. Thus, the proverbial clublike atmosphere of the Senate emerges because, for most of its members, being a senator is the final political goal and they can, therefore, concentrate upon their current activities without a constant eye to future office. Similarly, state treasurers and secretaries of state may, even though elected, behave independently of other state leaders such as the governor because they can develop different career expectations.

Indeed, our classification of offices according to their rates of opportunity helps reveal the basis for many of the weaknesses in state government in the United States. The most transitory positions in the elective hierarchy are precisely those which can best provide the leadership to resolve state problems, the governor, attorney general, and lieutenant governor. It is not that the offices do not attract capable men, but that the nature of these offices forces capable men to look outside the range of the states to satisfy their political ambitions. They must

[15] A. J. Liebling, *The Earl of Louisiana* (New York: Simon and Schuster, 1961). Although Long sought the Democratic nomination for lieutenant governor on a ticket with James Noe who was seeking the governorship, both denied that Noe planned to resign in favor of Long should they be elected. See *The New York Times,* November 30, 1959.

[16] Roberta S. Sigel and David J. Butler, "The Public and the No Third Term Tradition: An Inquiry into Attitudes towards Power," *Midwest Journal of Politics,* VIII (1964), 39–54, indicates that within a sample of Detroit voters there was considerable support for the restraint on presidential tenure.

move on, and the only way is up and out of the state to federal office, preferably to the Senate where a man can settle down. Only political leaders who see their future tied to the state can be expected to take strong stands on such ubiquitous state problems as the tax structure and legislative apportionment. Why jeopardize a future in politics for a present which can, at best, last two or three more years? Thus, while the office of governor has been a means of advancing in American politics, its incumbents have not been noted for their great contributions to their states. During the Progressive era, it is true, there were a number of strong governors who did have an impact. Governors such as Hiram Johnson in California, Albert Cummins in Iowa, and Robert LaFollette in Wisconsin fostered many state reforms. But it is worth noting that one of their more lasting reforms was the structure of political opportunities. The twin products of the era, the direct primary and the popular election of United States senators, changed the ground rules and reflected in each case the difficulties these ambitious men had with the old political order. Their goal accomplished, each moved on to the Senate to complete his public career, far from the problems of state government.

OPPORTUNITY RATES AND THE SIZE OF THE STRUCTURE OF OPPORTUNITIES WITHIN THE STATES

While the differences among the opportunity rates for a specific office play an important role in shaping the political careers of individuals who seek the office and in defining their behavior in office, we can determine whether political opportunity as such is high or low only by combining the opportunity rates for particular offices. To the extent that political ambitions are generalized, frustration in one direction leads to the transfer of energies to other more accessible outlets. If such outlets or offices do not exist or if they also have low opportunity rates, then ambitions are frustrated; in that case, ambition must be curbed or it will produce conflict within the leadership group. The size of an opportunity structure is difficult to measure with complete accuracy, especially when the selection of offices has been arbitrary and disparate. It is feasible only if we assume that the direction of individual ambition is not fixed but is conditioned by the availability of outlets. While it is true that many men who would run for governor or senator would never run for state auditor, the reverse is much less likely. The direction of ambition is upward, and the various offices we have measured are not of equivalent political status. But if we think of the size of the opportunity structure as

TABLE III-3
General Opportunity Levels, by States

	Number of Chances to Achieve Major Office during a 12-Year Political Generation		
	Constitutional		*Real (Based on Personnel Turnover)*
	Minimum	*Maximum*	
Pennsylvania	12	199	69.05
New York	—	268	66.89
Ohio	—	175	58.42
Illinois	6	172	58.10
Michigan	—	148	45.42
California	—	199	44.35
Indiana	15	97	39.30
Missouri	6	88	35.32
Colorado	12	64	32.90
Texas	—	160	32.17
Kentucky	18	70	31.61
New Mexico	18	52	30.28
Wisconsin	—	94	29.98
Connecticut	—	52	29.41
Massachusetts	2	124	28.95
Alabama	18	76	27.60
Oklahoma	12	58	27.04
Minnesota	—	91	26.71
Delaware	3	34	26.66
Iowa	—	88	26.30
New Jersey	1.5	91	26.27
Nebraska	3	64	25.91
West Virginia	3	55	25.61
South Dakota	3	52	24.69
Kansas	—	76	23.79
North Carolina	6	94	23.22
Louisiana	6	70	23.00
Arkansas	—	70	21.53
Arizona	6	46	19.99
North Dakota	3	52	19.89
Mississippi	12	58	19.83
Virginia	3	74	17.86
Idaho	6	35	17.79
Vermont	—	46	17.36
Maryland	1.5	52	17.29
Rhode Island	—	46	17.16
Utah	6	31	16.51
Montana	3	34	16.33
Washington	—	64	16.15
Georgia	3	76	15.73
Florida	3	64	15.28
Tennessee	3	64	15.14
South Carolina	3	55	14.13
Wyoming	3	25	13.75
Oregon	3.5	40	12.80
Nevada	—	25	11.48
New Hampshire	—	22	9.21
Maine	—	28	9.11

TABLE III-4
General Opportunity Levels,[a] by States
(Adjusted to Population, 1950)

	Maximum Chances	*Real Chances*
Delaware	10.69	8.38
Nevada	15.62	7.17
Wyoming	8.61	4.73
Vermont	12.18	4.60
New Mexico	7.63	4.45
South Dakota	7.97	3.78
North Dakota	8.39	3.21
Idaho	5.95	3.02
Montana	5.75	2.76
Arizona	6.14	2.67
Colorado	4.83	2.48
Utah	4.50	2.40
Rhode Island	5.81	2.17
Nebraska	4.83	1.95
New Hampshire	4.13	1.73
Connecticut	2.59	1.47
West Virginia	2.74	1.27
Kansas	3.99	1.25
Oklahoma	2.60	1.21
Arkansas	3.67	1.13
Kentucky	2.38	1.07
Iowa	3.36	1.00
Maine	3.06	1.00
Indiana	2.47	1.00
Mississippi	2.66	0.91
Minnesota	3.05	0.90
Alabama	2.48	0.90
Missouri	2.23	0.89
Wisconsin	2.74	0.87
Louisiana	2.61	0.86
Oregon	2.63	0.84
Maryland	2.22	0.74
Ohio	2.20	0.74
Michigan	2.32	0.71
Washington	2.69	0.68
South Carolina	2.60	0.67
Illinois	1.97	0.67
Tennessee	1.94	0.66
Pennsylvania	1.90	0.66
Massachusetts	2.64	0.62
North Carolina	2.31	0.57
Florida	2.31	0.55
Virginia	2.23	0.54
New Jersey	1.88	0.54
Georgia	2.20	0.46
New York	1.81	0.45
Texas	2.07	0.42
California	1.88	0.42

[a] These are expressed by figures which represent the number of chances per 100,000 population to achieve a major political office during a single political generation (12 years).

something which looms before men in the lower reaches of politics—legislators, local officials, district attorneys, and party workers, an undifferentiated combination of outlets probably does reflect accurately what is available to them.

The combined totals for the opportunity rates of the individual offices measured earlier (except for the state legislature) are presented in Table III-3. Since these figures include both Senate seats and all of the congressional seats, the relative positions of the states tend to reflect population size, but not completely. Over an average 12-year period there were 1,273 chances for new men to achieve significant statewide office or to go on to the federal Congress, i.e., one-third the constitutional or maximum chances. The results are impressive. It is impossible to say how they compare with other political systems, but they reveal a vast number of political opportunities in the United States.

The chances, adjusted to population size (a consideration most relevant to the sense of opportunity), are presented in Table III-4. Here we see that the chances for office, per 100,000 population, range from a high of 8.38 in 12 years in Delaware to less than one-half (0.42) in Texas and California. The political hopeful in Delaware, then, has about 20 times as much chance to gain an important political office as the officeseeker in the larger states. Of course, this situation is not very different from the proverbial one of fishes and ponds, although some of the big fish in the little ponds can, in this case, get to be big fishes in the big pond of Congress.

AN EQUILIBRIUM OF CHANCES FOR POLITICAL OFFICE?

Our analysis of the opportunity structures of the states thus far reveals that, given the relatively fixed number of offices, the per capita chances of obtaining office rise very rapidly in the smaller states (see Table III-5). Yet once the population of a state rises above one million, there does not appear to be much variation in the chances for major

TABLE III-5
Per Capita Chances to Gain Major Political Office, Related to Population of State (1950)

Population	*Number of States*				
	Per Capita Chances in a 12-Year Period				
	0.42–0.49	*0.50–0.99*	*1.00–1.99*	*2.00–2.99*	*3.00+*
Under 1,000,000	0	0	2	4	8
1,000,000 to 2,999,999	0	8	8	1	0
3,000,000 to 4,999,999	1	8	1	0	0
5,000,000 and over	3	4	0	0	0

office. In states of 1.5 million and more, the variation in per capita chances does not exceed 1, although the variation in total population goes to almost 15. We have, of course, built into our calculations a population adjustment by including the office of federal representative, whose number varies according to population. Nevertheless, the range of differences among the states is sufficiently small to prompt the speculation that in many of the states there is an equilibrium of chances—that, within these states, if the chances for advancement in one office tend to be small, they will be greater for other offices. As in any pressure system, and certainly political ambitions are analagous to physical pressures, there must be outlets if the system is not to burst.

We can test the proposition that there is an equilibrium of chances for the three principal offices in the control of the states, the two United States Senate seats and the governorship. As we have seen, there is considerable variation in the opportunity rates for these offices among the states. While the two senate seats have fixed six-year terms, governors enjoy either two- or four-year terms with different types of restraints upon reelection. There is, therefore, considerable room for adjustment among the three offices. The opportunity rate, adjusted as it is to a standard twelve-year period, makes it possible to combine the chances for the three positions (Table III-6). On the average, for the 48 states there are 4.82 chances in 12 years to become either governor or senator. The distribution among the states is at the same time concentrated; the total chances in 36 of the states come to more than 4 and less than 6 in a 12-year period. Thus, a low rate of opportunity for the office of senator is compensated for by a high opportunity rate for the governorship.

TABLE III-6

Combined Opportunity Rate for Governor and U.S. Senator

Real Chances in 12 Years to Become Governor or Senator[a]	*Number of States*
6.00+	3
5.50–5.99	9
5.00–5.49	12
4.50–4.99	8
4.00–4.49	7
3.50–3.99	6
3.00–3.49	2
2.50–2.99	1
	48

[a] The maximum number of chances, i.e., where the incumbent is never reelected, would be 7.00 in states where the governor has a four-year term and 10.00 where the term is two years.

In considering the question of equilibrium it is also important to relate the size of the states' opportunity structures to the office outlets in the national presidential system which we discussed in the last chapter. Specifically, where the outlets in the presidential office complex are low, the internal outlets should be high if political opportunities are to be balanced; where outlets in the presidential complex are high, there is less pressure to maintain high rates of opportunity in the internal politics of the state. I have tested this proposition by correlating the rank order of the states according to (a) their per capita real chances—Table III-4, and (b) their index of advantage in the presidential office complex, calculated only for those national leaders who have held some state office.[17] We obtain the expected negative correlation (−0.79). Here, then, is more evidence to support the proposition that the variety of elective offices available in the United States do form a national system and that ambitions frustrated at one level of government or by one particular office may be satisfied elsewhere.

There are, of course, many reasons why the relationship between internal and external opportunities in the states are inverse. Some have only a peripheral bearing upon my proposition. Because the presidential electoral system favors the large states, the large states will obviously find favor in the presidential office complex. This, combined with the mathematical decline in per capita opportunities for the state's offices as the population increases, is enough to give us a negative correlation. There are, then, intervening factors which help balance political opportunities. Within the context of the theory of ambition, however, the mechanisms of control are less important than the fact that there is indeed control and balance.

The proposition that opportunities for political office reach some kind of balance in a political system has as its corollary the proposition that where balance is not achieved dissatisfaction and tensions among the politically ambitious will emerge. Severe factionalism within political parties may be one expression of such tensions. The internal and external measures of opportunity we have devised provide us with an index of those states where opportunities generally have been lowest and where, then, internal dissension should be highest. There are four states which have no outlets in the presidential system and which also have few (below the median of 1.00 per 100,000) internal outlets: Florida, Maryland, Louisiana, and Mississippi. While there is no precise measure of party factionalism which we can apply to the states, these four states are

[17] The index of advantage used here is the one based on those members of the national leadership group who have had some kind of previous state office experience. See Chapter II.

conspicuous examples of high factionalism. Key's study of the southern states rated Florida and Mississippi as states with very fluid factions, highly personal in character, the situation one might expect in a state where there is an undifferentiated sense of frustration among politicians. Louisiana is the best example of a one-party state with dual factionalism, a product of the Long regime and its opposition.[18] There one of the more flagrant examples of frustrated ambition in American politics has utilized class divisions to create a political organization for its power drives. As for Maryland, Fenton asserts that its Democratic party is clearly divided between Baltimore and Tidewater factions.[19] The kinds of internal dissension in these states ranges from the extreme personalism of Mississippi to the well-organized factions of Maryland; in both cases the lack of good career outlets beyond the state only exacerbates internal conflict.

A second group of states has below average rates of internal opportunities and, although they have some outlets at the national level, they are disadvantaged in terms of their population.[20] Large states such as Texas and California, which fit this category, certainly have had far more turbulent and factional internal political histories than a state such as New York. Because we have no comparative measure, it is risky to assert that some of the other states in this grouping have higher levels of internal dissension than those outside the group. All I propose is that, within the framework of ambition theory, these states should have high levels of dissension and factionalism.

CONCLUSIONS

In this chapter I have measured one dimension of the states' opportunity structures—their size. First I have assessed the chances for individual offices in the states. These findings are particularly important for the development of ambition theory because they define the role each office can play within political careers. Second I have measured the size of the structure of opportunities within a state; this measure provides the politically ambitious with some sense of the possibilities of gaining not a particular office but any positon of significance. While I have found marked variations at the extremes, in the more sizeable states there

[18] V. O. Key, Jr., *Southern Politics* (New York: Knopf, 1949).
[19] John Fenton, *Politics in the Border States* (New Orleans: Hauser, 1957), pp. 171–89.
[20] States with internal per capita chances of less than 1.00 and with indices of advantage of less than 1.00 in the national leadership group are California, Texas, Georgia, Virginia, North Carolina, Pennsylvania, Illinois, Washington, Michigan, Wisconsin, Alabama, and Minnesota.

appears to be an equilibrium of chances for political office. Finally I have sought to relate the states' internal structures of opportunity to their position in the national office hierarchy. Here I find limited evidence to indicate that the level of political opportunities is related to political stability or dissension.

This measurement of the opportunity structures of the states is far from complete. I have examined only a few of the offices in the states. I have studiously ignored party competition as an influence upon political opportunities. But, before I could talk meaningfully about the relevance of party for political opportunities, it was necessary to develop an independent measure of opportunity. Now that I have such a measure, it is possible to relate political opportunity to the party battle.

CHAPTER IV

Party Competition and the Opportunities for Political Office

THE TWO-PARTY SYSTEM has an obvious impact upon political opportunity in the United States. While the federal system and the independent election of officeholders help keep opportunities open, the two-party system or the requirement that candidates run as Democrats or Republicans restricts opportunity. Indeed, much of the scholarly neglect of the structure of opportunities is due to the equation of political opportunity with party competition. Within the framework of party theory, political opportunities are considered to be high or low in relation to the degree of party competition. But the problem is not as simple as that. In the last chapter we saw that the rate of opportunity varies greatly with the office; it is by no means obvious that these variations reflect simply differences in party competition. In this chapter, therefore, we are interested in examining the relation between the opportunities for new individuals to achieve office and the parties' opportunities and in discovering whether these opportunities are identical or whether there are indeed differences.

Before we consider the pattern of party competition in the states, it is important to note the incomplete or non-independent character of the states' party systems. While scholars may dispute the reasons for the maintenance of a national two-party system, its existence has forced the states to fit their political conflicts into the Republican-Democratic mold. The states are tied to the national duopoly by the ambition of their leaders to advance nationally. Although voters respond primarily to the national party labels, they have shown time and again over the past century that they can support parties and leaders outside the two-party mold. There has, after all, been a long line of semisuccessful new party movements in recent American history. The Greenbackers, Farmer's Alliance, Prohibitionists, 1912 Progressives, Non-Partisan Leaguers, Wisconsin Progressives, and even the Dixiecrats all achieved notable successes at the state levels, capturing major offices and legislatures. Their universal decline came about not because of rejection at the polls—a party which cannot endure defeat is not much of a party; they failed because they were cut off from the national opportunity system. Their senators and congressmen were lonely men deprived of the perquisites of seniority and party position in Congress; many other outlets for ambition too—the expectations on which party organization thrives, the federal judgeships and important federal appointments—all were closed to a state party outside the Republican-Democratic framework. There is no better proof that frustrated ambition rather than electoral decline has killed off third parties than their desertion, in almost every instance, by their leaders, who moved off into one of the other major parties. While the 1912 Progressives died as a party, many of their major leaders, men such as Gifford Pinchot and Harold Ickes, continued their careers in the Republican and Democratic parties, and a minor figure such as Alfred Landon could emerge later in a major position. Men such as Henry Shipstead of Minnesota, William Langer of North Dakota, and Strom Thurmond of South Carolina also continued in two-party politics after their third-party movements had disappeared.

THE STRUCTURE OF POLITICAL OPPORTUNITY AND THE RANGE OF PARTY COMPETITION

Our principal problem is defining the extent to which the size of a state's structure of opportunity depends upon competition between the two parties. We have seen in Chapter III that opportunities vary greatly among the states. We also know that there are great differences in the attachments of the states to one or the other party. Furthermore, even within a state, competition is not evenly dsitributed among all the offices. In an earlier study I attempted to measure, or at least to define, with some precision the meaning of party competition, which is as elusive a concept as opportunity.[1] In that study I examined the degree of party competition for those offices we have considered here as forming the states' opportunity structures (excluding the state legislature). For only a few states, and these were primarily the ones dominated by a single

[1] Joseph A. Schlesinger, "The Structure of Competition for Office in the American States," *Behavioral Science,* V (1960), 197–210.

party, could it be said that the same degree of competitiveness faced the candidates for each of these major offices. There were some extreme instances: Ohio, for example, where the Democrats generally controlled the governorship and the Republicans the minor offices of attorney general and treasurer; or Wyoming where the Democrats dominated the Senate and the Republicans the lower federal house seats. In effect, for most states there was a sufficiently great range of competitiveness among the offices that the conditions surrounding one office were not indicative of those surrounding others. The description of a state's politics in terms of a simple, two-party, government-and-opposition model is bound to be inaccurate.

Given the range of party competition within and among the states, should we not question the meaning of party as such in the deliberations of the voters? It is true that we can arrive at explanations of the variations in competition for office which do not exclude the voter's awareness of party. Electoral timing, for example, may help account for the variations. All of the officers whom I consider are not selected at the same time; senators run on a different timetable from governors and other state officials. When voters make different partisan decisions in different years, it cannot be assumed that they are ignoring considerations of party. Similarly there is the question of different jurisdictions. When voters choose men of one party for federal office and those of the other party for state office there is not necessarily a contradiction in party terms. Yet such explanations do not account for all of the variety which I have found in the conditions of competition between the two parties. The fact remains that electorates do select officials at the same times and for the same jurisdictions from different parties.

Of course we already know from survey analyses that partisan considerations do not explain all the votes cast in elections. Partisan sentiments may or may not coincide with the voter's attitude toward the personalities of the candidates and with his perception of the issues. We also know that the degree of party influence varies from election to election; it appears to be higher in midterm than in presidential elections. And, at the same time, presidential elections do not always generate the same degree of partisan reaction. The presidential election of 1948 was largely decided by partisan identification; but a few years later the impact of party attachment was markedly reduced.[2]

My findings provide further evidence of the extrapartisan dimension in elections. The great variations in the degree of party competition

[2] A. Campbell, P. Converse, W. Miller, and D. Stokes, *The American Voter* (New York: Wiley, 1960), pp. 523–38; A. Campbell, "Surge and Decline: A Study of Electoral Change," *Public Opinion Quarterly*, XXIV (1960), 397–418.

among the states suggest that in those states where the range of competition from office to office is greatest, party labels are least important in affecting the vote. But we must also consider the implication of the variations, from office to office within a state, in partisan choice. To preserve a purely party explanation of this electoral phenomenon, we should have to assert that each office generates its own party system. In other words, in the state of California the office of attorney general has generated a competitive party system while the office of secretary of state has generated a one-party system controlled by the Republicans; i.e., within a single state, there exist party systems as different as the competitive party system of Massachusetts and the one-party system of Mississippi. Is it not more sensible to seek an explanation over and above party for the behavior of voters in states such as California?

I would propose that, over and above the party system, the opportunity structure intrudes, and that is the hypothesis I shall now test. In the last chapter I have pointed out that we can measure the frequency with which new men are elected to an office or the frequency of political personnel change according to the electoral timetable—the personnel turnover rate. In my earlier study of party competition I used another measure of electoral turnover, the party changes in office control. If we apply both measures to the eight basic offices in the opportunity structures of the states[3] for the time period 1914–1958 and confront the measures, I believe we can begin to decide to what extent opportunities for office reflect the competitive two-party system and to what extent they form their own structure independent of the party system.

There is, of course, a simple, direct relation between party competition and turnover in office personnel. With only the rarest exceptions, a change in party means a change in the officeholder. To that extent, party competition regulates the flow of political opportunities, and, to the extent that the two parties contest on equal terms and frequently alternate control, the turnover in office personnel must be high. But in my study of party competition I discovered that even for the most competitive offices the rate of change in party control was relatively low. Indeed, for most of the offices in the states' opportunity structures it was possible for changes in personnel to take place independent of the party system. The separation, therefore, of competitive party influences from influences other than party competition upon personnel turnover is fundamental to an understanding of the opportunities for political careers.

In Table IV-1, I have compared the differences in the personnel turnover rate and the rate of party change for the eight offices in the

[3] The state legislatures have not been included in this analysis.

TABLE IV-1

The Relationship between Party and Personnel Turnover (1914–1958)

Office	*No. of States*[a]	*No. of Elections*	*No. of Party Changes*	*No. of Personnel Changes*	*Percentage of Party Change*	*Percentage of Personnel Change*	*Percentage of Personnel Changes over and above Party Changes*
Governor	32	611	187	361	30.60%	59.08%	28.48%
Senator	48	819	198	396	24.17	48.35	24.18
Lieutenant Governor	27	505	107	320	21.18	63.36	42.18
State Treasurer	29	549	89	238	16.21	43.35	27.14
State Attorney General	40	680	104	355	15.29	52.20	36.91
State Auditor	24	428	65	156	15.18	36.44	21.26
Secretary of State	36	634	90	237	14.19	37.38	23.19
U. S. Representative	48	9,509	1,098	2,228	11.54	23.43	11.89

[a] The states which do not permit reelection to the office are excluded.

states' opportunity structures for the period 1914–1958. The table reveals that party competition is highest for the governorship; in 30.6 per cent of the gubernatorial elections considered there is a change in party control. For the offices of senator and lieutenant governor the rate of party change is moderate; 24 and 21 per cent respectively of the elections for these offices mean a change in party as well as in personnel. For the remaining offices the rate of party change is low; for congressmen a change in party control takes place in only 11.5 per cent of the elections.

In each instance the changes in personnel are higher than the changes in party. Changes in personnel are highest for the office of lieutenant governor; in 63.4 per cent of the elections considered a personnel change takes place. Changes in personnel are lowest for the office of congressman; in only 23.4 per cent of the congressional elections does a change in personnel take place. Certainly there is a positive relation between personnel and party change; the rank order correlation between the two is +0.81. But the relation is not stable. The last column of Table IV-1 notes the differences between the two variables. These figures give us the personnel changes in elections over and above the changes due to party competition; in other words, they measure the minimum effect upon changes in office personnel of factors other than party competition. These factors play the largest part in the personnel changes for the offices of lieutenant governor and attorney general; the differences between the two variables are 42 and 37 per cent. Such factors are of moderate importance in the personnel turnover among governors, senators, treasurers, auditors, and secretaries of state; the range of difference goes from 21 to 28 per cent. Factors other than party competition are least important in the personnel changes among congressmen, where the difference between party and personnel changes is only 12 per cent. At the very least we must conclude that the relative effect of party competition and of factors other than party competition upon opportunities for office differ markedly with the office.

We can, however, refine our measure of the effect of factors other than party competition upon political opportunities. It does not yet give us all the changes in personnel which would have occurred with or without a change of party. Specifically it does not take into account the problem of incumbency. If the party in control of an office does not renominate the incumbent, the party's defeat does not really account for the change in personnel. In Table IV-2 I have corrected the measure of such factors to account for incumbency in the offices of governor and senator. (Not included are the southern one-party states and the northern states which do not permit reelection for governor.) Note that for

TABLE IV-2

The Impact of Party Competition on Personnel Changes in the Offices of Governor and Senator (1914–1958)

	Governor	*Senator*
Number of states[a]	29	36
Number of elections	542	616
Percentage of elections with change of party (X)	33.2	32.0
Percentage of elections in which incumbent was defeated (Y)	17.4	19.5
Percentage of elections with personnel changes (Z)	60.0	52.6
Percentage of elections with a change in personnel over and above party changes (Z − X)	26.8	20.6
Percentage of elections in which there was a party change, but which would have produced a personnel change anyway (X − Y)	15.8	12.5
Percentage of elections in which personnel changes occurred over and above party influence (Z − X) + (X − Y) = (Z − Y)	42.6	33.1

[a] Southern states and, for governor, those states which do not permit succession in the office have been excluded.

both offices the maximum impact of party competition is about the same; a change in party control has taken place in about one-third of the elections considered. Changes in personnel are somewhat higher for the governorship, running to 60 per cent of the elections, as compared to 52.6 per cent of the elections for senator. When we break down these figures to isolate incumbency, we find that in a little under half the instances of party change, a personnel change would have taken place in any event because the incumbent was not running. When we combine these instances with the personnel changes over and above party changes, we find the impact of these other factors upon opportunities in 42.6 per cent of the gubernatorial elections and in 33.1 per cent of the senatorial elections under consideration. In other words, a good share of the opportunities for both offices arise not from party competition but from factors outside the two-party system.

Certainly relevant questions arise which my measure of these other factors in personnel changes does not help us answer: it cannot indicate those instances where party defeat might have been averted had the incumbent senator or governor been the candidate. In other words, it is possible and even likely that the opportunity structures of the states have their impact upon the states' party systems, but, given the limitations of the data, I cannot assign with certainty a role to each system. But the data do allow me to assert the existence of an opportunity system independent of the party system. Moreover, the hypothesis on incumbency, which the earlier measure could not reach, I have tested for the two most competitive offices in the states' opportunity structures in the most competitive states, the offices for which the party system should be most important in defining opportunities. For most of the other offices party changes occurred less than half as often as for the office of governor, making the impact of party competition[4] upon opportunity appear slight indeed. At the very least, then, these data allow us to deny the party system a dominant role in determining political opportunity in the United States.

TABLE IV-3
Correlations between Percentage of Personnel Change and Percentage of Party Turnover (Elections 1914–1958)

	Number of States[a]	*Correlation*
U. S. Representative	48	0.86
Auditor	24	0.81
U. S. Senator	48	0.76
Secretary of State	36	0.73
Governor	32	0.69
Lieutenant Governor	27	0.60
Attorney General	40	0.38
Treasurer	29	0.36

[a] For each office the number of states includes only those which permit some succession in the office.

My conclusions about the relation of the two-party system to political opportunity are strengthened when we move from the gross impact of party competition to its relative impact from state to state. Table IV-3 measures the relation between the states' differences in personnel change and their rates of party competition and presents the correlation coefficients for the two variables. This analysis reveals the special relation of party competition to turnover in political office. The table shows that the office which is generally least competitive, the office of United States representative, is the office for which there is

[4] In this discussion my standard of competitiveness is the frequency of change of party in control of an office. While undoubtedly much of the sense of competitiveness comes from the closeness of the vote, the differences in volatility of constituencies makes the likelihood of actual shift in control an equally valid measure. See Joseph A. Schlesinger, "Stability in the Vote for Governor," *Public Opinion Quarterly,* XXIV (1960), 85–91.

the closest relationship between party competition and personnel change. In other words, although throughout the states the office is one in which changes in both personnel and party are infrequent, the variations in change which do occur are most directly related to conditions of party competition. On the other hand, there is no general relation between relatively non-competitive offices and the differences in opportunities for those offices among the states. The opportunities for the offices of attorney general and state treasurer, which generate much less party competition than the offices of senator, governor, and lieutenant governor, are relatively unaffected by differences in party competition. Here again is evidence of an opportunity system which is independent of the party system. Within the opportunity system, some offices are typically held by the same person for a long period of time, while others are offices with a high turnover. For both types of offices party competition varies from state to state in no clear pattern, giving the mixed relationship between personnel turnover in political office and the level of party competition which I have just described.

The dual measure of turnover in political office, the measure of party competition and of factors other than party competition, now allows me to elaborate my statement of the roles played by various offices in political careers and the types of ambitions they are most likely to foster. The offices of governor and lieutenant governor for which the chances are always high regardless of party competition are offices which can only foster what I described earlier as discrete or progressive ambitions. My analysis of the impact of competitive factors upon these two offices sustains the impression conveyed by their opportunity rates in the preceding chapter: providing little expectation of longevity to their holders no matter what the conditions of party competition, these are transitory offices in men's political careers. Much the same can be said of the offices of attorney general and state treasurer, despite the fact that these offices generate much less party competition. (For the special circumstances surrounding the office of state treasurer see Chapter III.) In contrast, the offices of United States senator and representative lend themselves to what I have called static ambitions. My conclusions about the effect of party competition, its direct relevance to the chances for both offices (although the office of senator is by far the more competitive), do not alter my earlier description of these offices as career offices for politicians. The minor state offices of secretary of state and state auditor, offices with low turnover in personnel and relatively unaffected by conditions of party competition, are certainly posts likely to nurture static ambitions. The two-party system within the states, then, does not require me to alter my scheme of either office roles or ambitions.

FACTORS OTHER THAN PARTY COMPETITION AFFECTING POLITICAL OPPORTUNITIES

In my discussion thus far of political opportunities I have emphasized the significance of factors beyond the two-party system, but I have not identified them. Undoubtedly they are many and difficult to isolate, but it is appropriate to speculate upon a few. The offices which comprise the states' opportunity structures vary greatly in importance and demand varying skills in the legislative and executive branches of government. Personnel turnover in some of these offices, then, may be due largely to the attitudes of the holders; they may find a particular office without inherent satisfactions or they may consider it a likely steppingstone to a more desirable place. But personnel turnover is also likely to be affected by the attitudes toward the personnel needs of a particular office of those influential in the process of selection, the attitudes of the writers of constitutions, of party leaders, and of voters. Finally, built into the process of selecting public officials are factors affecting personnel turnover which are not the product of conscious decision.

An example of the last factor is the age at which men typically reach a particular office. Human mortality assures some turnover in political office. But the state, unlike most organizations, does not assure turnover by establishing retirement ages for elective officials. In contrast to the state, large corporations are able to guarantee a system of open careers by keeping men out of the top posts until they are near the age of retirement. The typical president of the large corporation holds his position a much shorter time than the typical United States senator.[5] Nevertheless, although there is little conscious use of age in politics, the complexities of reaching the very highest office allow age to affect the opportunities for such office. Undoubtedly much of the resentment of John Kennedy's drive for the Presidency came from the feeling that in his early forties it was out of turn. Harry Truman, whose arrival at the Presidency had been at the more typical and appropriate age, expressed this feeling openly and bluntly before the 1960 Democratic convention.[6] For the Presidency has been an office not normally attained until the late fifties, thereby assuring for that reason alone turnover in office. In this century, two Presidents, Harding and Franklin Roosevelt, died in office of natural causes, and two others, Wilson and Eisenhower, were disabled

[5] Andrew Hacker, "The Elected and the Anointed, Two American Elites, Senators and Corporation Presidents," *American Political Science Review,* LV (1961), 539–49.

[6] *The New York Times,* July 3, 1960.

during their terms by ailments associated with aging. For the offices in the states' opportunity structures which are our primary concern, however, the age pattern does not noticeably affect opportunity.

Of much greater significance for the size of the states' opportunity structures is the value which a particular office has taken on for those who aspire to political careers. The value of a particular office involves not only its contribution to the size of a state's opportunity structure but also its contribution to the form or shape which I defined in the introductory chapter as the pattern of movement from office to office. I shall devote the next two chapters to the shape of the states' structures of opportunity. But it is relevant to the number of opportunities for office that there are certain offices, notably the lesser state executive offices of lieutenant governor and attorney general, which are conspicuously regarded as steppingstones. Of course, as is true for much of my analysis, it is difficult to assert whether the treatment of these offices as steppingstones is due to their inherent qualities or to the accumulated attitudes of politicians. But the contrast in the inherent importance of the two offices leads us to give more weight to the politicians' attitudes. In state government the office of lieutenant governor has probably the least inherent importance apart from its stand-in potential. It is, therefore, hardly an office that ambitious politicians would wish to hold for very long. On the other hand, in most states the attorney general is the most important official next to the governor in terms of the scope and content of his activities; his office may very well provide inherent satisfactions. Nevertheless, both these offices are passed on rapidly. The similar behavior in dissimilar offices suggests that, if we must choose between the inherent qualities of a particular office and the type of individual it attracts as causes for a turnover in personnel, it is the latter factor which is more decisive.

Of course it is always difficult to distinguish with certainty the willingness of an officeholder to pass on a particular office from the demands of others that he do so. The constitutional prescriptions which forbid the reelection of governors in many states provide the most obvious evidence of the influence of desires other than the officeholder's upon turnover. Similarly, when an incumbent faces strong competition either in primaries or in conventions, we can note the impingement of ambitions other than the officeholder's upon the opportunities for the office he holds. Of those officeholders who retire before the observable evidence of conflict, we cannot assess with any precision those who do so voluntarily or because of external pressures.

But the attitudes of other politicians and of party organizations toward incumbents will differ according to the office and to conditions of party competition. As we have seen, the office of governor is one of high turnover. Nevertheless there is evidence that, where parties face increasing competition, they value incumbents more highly for their proven vote-getting abilities. Both the legal and customary limitations on the governor's tenure have emerged in states dominated by one party. In a competitive situation, what might be considered the instinctive demand of other politicians for rapid turnover in high office is counteracted by the need for partisan politicians to subdue their personal office ambitions in order to reap the benefits accruing to their party from continued control of the state's principal office.

The attitudes of other politicians toward the incumbent, then, depend upon the worth of his office for their ambitions. Consistently my data has shown a much higher turnover in executive offices, notably the offices of governor and President, than in legislative offices, particularly congressional office. At the same time, for the two types of office there is an inverse relationship between a man's ability to satisfy other men's ambitions and his longevity in office. In legislative office longevity increases a man's usefulness to others; the longer an executive is in office, the less effective he is in these terms. In congress, though not in all state legislatures, the rules of seniority place a formal value upon longevity. But, over and above the formal advantages, the legislator can use time to develop skills and contacts which make him more useful than a beginner in affecting appointments and otherwise serving the ambitious. However much other men may want to be congressman or senator, the longer the incumbents in these offices remain, the more capable they become of satisfying the needs and desires of fellow politicians. For the executive the opposite is true. His capacity to satisfy the ambitions of others is highest at the beginning of his term, and it is higher in his first term of office than in his second. No appointments a President or governor makes receive as much attention as his initial appointments; these appointments represent best the forces which coalesced to make him governor or President and the support which he considers essential to his initial undertakings. As a presidential regime wears on, Cabinet appointments tend to become primarily internal promotions. The executive, of course, does not lose his appointive powers; throughout his term he retains more power to satisfy the ambitions of those who seek public posts than any single legislator. But only the new executive can bring the shake-up in government which is most satisfying to the ambitious. When party competition is stable, therefore, the pressure within parties is undoubtedly greater for turnover in the executive office than among legislators.

But longevity in office is affected not only by the politician's attitude but also by the voters' attitudes toward incumbency. Unfortunately, survey analyses have yet to deal with voter attitudes toward different offices. But there is no particular reason to assume that the differences in party competition among offices indicate the electorate's preference for one party in the governor's mansion and the opposite party in the state senate as well as in the lesser executive office of secretary of state. For minor executive offices with no marked controversial or partisan functions, the electorate may simply prefer to ignore party and retain an officeholder whose name is known and whom it has no cause to reject. The differences in the electorate's approach to legislative as opposed to executive office may indicate more complex attitudes toward government. Some of the differences stem from the differences in electorates. Legislative electorates are normally more homogeneous and less competitive than the electorates of governors and the President. But our evidence indicates that there is also a greater willingness to accept long tenure for legislators than for chief executives and their closest formal associates, lieutenant governors, probably because it is much easier for the voter to associate governmental responsibility with the executive than with the legislator. Even if the legislature has been obstructionist and "do-nothing," the group aspect of legislative office helps protect the individual legislator from voter reaction in a way in which the governor or President, alone and conspicuous, can never be protected. The governor and the President are most vulnerable to the accumulated grievances of voters which produce the rejection of incumbents. This is not to say that legislators are immune to changes in voter attitudes; American political history easily demonstrates the contrary. But American politics also demonstrates that revulsion against the legislator must penetrate the electorate more deeply, that there is a time lag which means that the voters will grant to the legislator the long term which they will not permit the executive.

CONCLUSIONS

The primary objective of this chapter has been to demonstrate that, within the states, political opportunity has its own structure independent of the states' party systems. An analysis of political opportunity, therefore, which restricts its attention to party chances at governing gives an incomplete picture of men's chances for public office. I by no means wish to imply that the states' party systems are irrelevant to American political behavior; I do mean to say that their relevance for political opportunity is best understood within the total structure of opportunities. In the next two chapters I shall complete my analysis of the states' opportunity structures by adding shape to their size. I shall then be able to return to the relationship of party to opportunity.

CHAPTER V

The American States and Patterns of Opportunity: The Base Office

THUS FAR I have been most concerned with measuring the size of the states' opportunity structures or the number of real chances new men have for attaining political offices of significance. But the number of opportunities tells us little about the patterns of opportunity or the typical lines of advancement in political office. In other words, while we can now estimate the chances of advancing to elective offices in the states, we do not know whether the chances are random or whether they take on form. If the turnover among officeholders is high in Delaware and low in California, the question still remains for both political systems, Are the chances high and low for everyone? High turnover may be accompanied by a system of succession so rigidly defined that we can accurately predict the next governor, senator, or congressman, or there may be no regularity in succession to office at all. But whether there is regularity or not is of central importance to a theory of politics which posits ambition as its dynamic. Ambition can serve as a control in politics only if the expectations of advancement are in some sense clear. In this chapter and in the next, therefore, I am concerned with the lines of advancement within the states leading to the two top political offices, the offices of governor and United States senator.

In this chapter I am interested in the early office experiences of the states' top political leaders. I am interested in whether or not there are common experiences, in whether or not there are special modes of entry to major political careers in the states. Such modes of entry I shall call base offices. In the next chapter I shall consider whether or not there are series of offices which lead to the states' top political posts.

The concept of a base office or a common set of experiences for political leaders is helpful in defining institutional relationships. We should not expect a legislative body whose members have few expectations of advancement to behave in the same way as one which holds out bright prospects. One of the most powerful controls which the British executive has over Parliament is the fact that membership in Parliament is the base office for a Cabinet career. A foreign observer, impressed by the British Cabinet but ignorant of Parliament, would be forced to examine the entire parliamentary system if he set about studying the office careers of Cabinet members. Were he to do so for a long period of time, he would discover that, while Parliament has remained the principal base office for a Cabinet career, the House of Lords has declined in relation to the House of Commons as the source for Cabinet ministers. Thus, he could infer not only that the Cabinet has a means of controlling members of Parliament through their ambitions, but also that the upper house had declined in importance in relation to the lower house. Similarly, if the United States Senate becomes widely acknowledged as the principal avenue to the White House, the power of the Senate in the structure of government will undoubtedly be affected, as well as the distribution of influence within the Senate itself.

The concept of common or basic office experience is also helpful for our understanding of the democratic political elite. Several studies have demonstrated that there are important differences in the attitudes of American political leaders and their followers. The leaders are more ideological in their response to issues and parties.[1] At the same time they appear better able to understand and accept democratic procedures.[2] Their followers accept democracy as an abstraction, but they are more likely to reject such democratic procedures as free discussion. Here is a paradox: the most ideological segment of the population is also the most prepared to accept the give-and-take of democracy. The paradox is explained by the leaders' ambitions for office, either for themselves or for their party, by their experience that within the democratic framework ambition is best satisfied by adhering to democratic rules. As V. O. Key has suggested, "A major function of the guarantees of civil

[1] A. Campbell, P. Converse, W. Miller, and D. Stokes, *The American Voter* (New York: Wiley, 1960), pp. 188–265; V. O. Key, Jr., *Public Opinion and American Democracy* (New York: Knopf, 1961); H. McClosky, P. J. Hoffman, and R. O'Hara, "Issue Conflict and Consensus among Party Leaders and Followers," *American Political Science Review*, LIV (1960), 406–27.

[2] Samuel Stouffer, *Communism, Conformity and Civil Liberties* (New York: Doubleday, 1955); Key, *Public Opinion*, Ch. 2; H. McClosky, "Consensus and Ideology in American Politics," *American Political Science Review*, LVIII (1964), 361–82.

liberties is to keep competing political elites from putting each other into jail; they need to be more alert about such matters."[3]

Critical to the formation of the democratic office elite in the states, to the development of its motives and attitudes, is induction into political office. Is there a common experience which most leaders have shared? Is there a base office which has instructed them in and reconciled them to the ways of the political system? My data on political careers in the states consist solely of the external indices of office experience. Such indices can tell us nothing directly about the influence of office experience upon leaders' attitudes. But, as I shall demonstrate, the data do allow us to justify the use of the concept of base office with respect to American political careers.

I would suggest two types of elective office for the base offices of the states' opportunity structures. The first is state legislative office. In every state the legislature brings together for a period of between one and seven months a sizeable number of politically-minded men from all parts of the state. It is, therefore, a natural breeding ground for political ambition and a logical base office. Another likely base office is the complex of offices elected at the local level and concerned with the making of policy—the offices of city councillor, alderman, county supervisor, and mayor, all of which abound in profusion throughout the nation. The number and accessibility of *state legislative* and *local elective* offices make it likely that many careerists in politics will at some point have held such office. They are, therefore, good places to look for the apprenticeship or sifting of political leaders. Nor need we consider these two types of base office mutually exclusive; they can be stages within a distinctive career pattern.

But there are other possible base offices or political filters. The appointive political offices in the states are one possibility. These I have grouped together and called the *administrative* office. As a category, administrative office is probably too heterogeneous, but there is a common factor: in some way the holders of these offices have been co-opted into the office system. The category expresses a similarity in the relation between the public office and the politician who holds it; the administrative politician has had close enough contacts with men in public office and enough of a desire for office to accept appointment.

The final type of base office I shall suggest are the offices associated with the court system, the law enforcement offices. The position of the judge and of the court has always been of special importance in American politics. Some of these offices are elective, others appointive. Public attorneys, sheriffs, and judges have had many opportunities to

[3] Key, *Public Opinion,* p. 138.

advance to other public offices. But the reverse has also been true. Important positions on the bench have been major goals of politicians in other branches of government. In any event, the obvious movement in the states from positions of law enforcement to higher office justifies considering law enforcement offices as the fourth type of base office.[4]

Let us now consider the extent to which each of the base offices I have described is used by the states or the extent to which there is some formal mode of entry to political opportunity in the states. For this purpose, I shall determine the distribution of base office experiences among a state's elective leaders.[5] By leaders I mean here, and for the remainder of my analysis of political careers, the candidates of the two major parties for the offices of governor and senator. The nominees for the office of governor are from the period 1900–1958, the nominees for the office of senator, from the period 1914–1958. In my analysis of base office experience, no candidate has been counted twice; that is to say, a man renominated for governor or senator does not reappear in the totals, nor do the many senators who have served first as governors. The sample groups together the nominees of both major parties.[6] At least for the moment, the assumption is that with respect to a politician's basic office experience, party makes little difference.

TABLE V-1
The Distribution of Base Offices among the States

Percentage of Major Leaders to Have Held Base Office	*Number of States in Which Base Offices Are Held*			
	State Legislative	*Law Enforcement*	*Adminis-trative*	*Local Elective*
60% and over	7	2	0	0
50–59	9	6	4	0
40–49	13	12	5	1
30–39	10	15	15	10
20–29	6	9	18	7
Under 20	3	4	6	30
	48	48	48	48

[4] Joseph A. Schlesinger, "Lawyers and American Politics, A Clarified View," *Midwest Journal of Political Science,* I (1957), 26–39.
[5] Note that by *base* office I do not mean *first* office. The base office is defined as a common form of experience, regardless of whether or not it is the first public office in a politician's career. There is certainly much overlap between the two categories. The first-office category will be used in later chapters and will always be referred to as such.
[6] The sample does not include the occasional Republican nominees in the southern states. The total number of politicians on which the present discussion is based is 1879. For a state breakdown of the leadership group, see Appendix A.

An overall view of the states' use of base offices reveals that experience in the state legislature is by far the commonest office experience of the states' political leaders. In 16 states, over half of the leaders have been in the state legislature (see Table V-1). The range in legislative experience, however, is great, going from a high of 78 per cent in Vermont to a low of 11.4 per cent in Michigan. Law enforcement experience is the second most important type of base office; law enforcement experience ranges from a high of 68.8 per cent in Kentucky to a low of 14.3 per cent in Massachusetts. Although administrative experience is also common, in fewer states is it a conspicuous mode of entry; administrative experience is highest among state leaders in Michigan, 56.8 per cent; lowest among the leaders of North Dakota, 9.1 per cent. Of the four base offices, local elective experience is least significant, reaching 40 per cent in only one state (Maine, 43.2 per cent); in one state, Nevada, no leader has had local office experience. The failure of local elective office to emerge as a significant base office does not mean that local office as such is insignificant; a great proportion of the law enforcement offices and many of the administrative offices are local in character. It means rather that the traditional local policy positions which make up the category of local elective office are not, in most states, on the main path to high office.

It is important to note that, if the states are classified by the degree to which their leaders use the four base offices, they tend to group themselves in regional patterns. The regional pattern is strongest for the two most important base offices and suggest an inverse relationship (Figures V-1, V-2). Legislative experience is most important for the leaders of states along the east coast, and in the north, to the west of the Great Lakes. Law enforcement experience is strong in the backgrounds of state leaders in the south, and most important for the leaders of the border states and other areas of the midwest and southwest. The two types of office experience are by no means mutually exclusive, but in no state does a majority of leaders have both types of experience. The regional distribution of the minor base offices is less distinctive. Local elective experience, however, is heaviest in the New England states, while administrative experience is most common in various northern states to the exclusion of most of the south and southwest.

My overall view of basic office experience among the states' leaders appears to justify my use of the concept of base office as one means of defining the shape of the states' structures of political opportunity. Of the four base offices I have suggested, two are common enough in the experience of the states' leaders to merit the designation of base office.

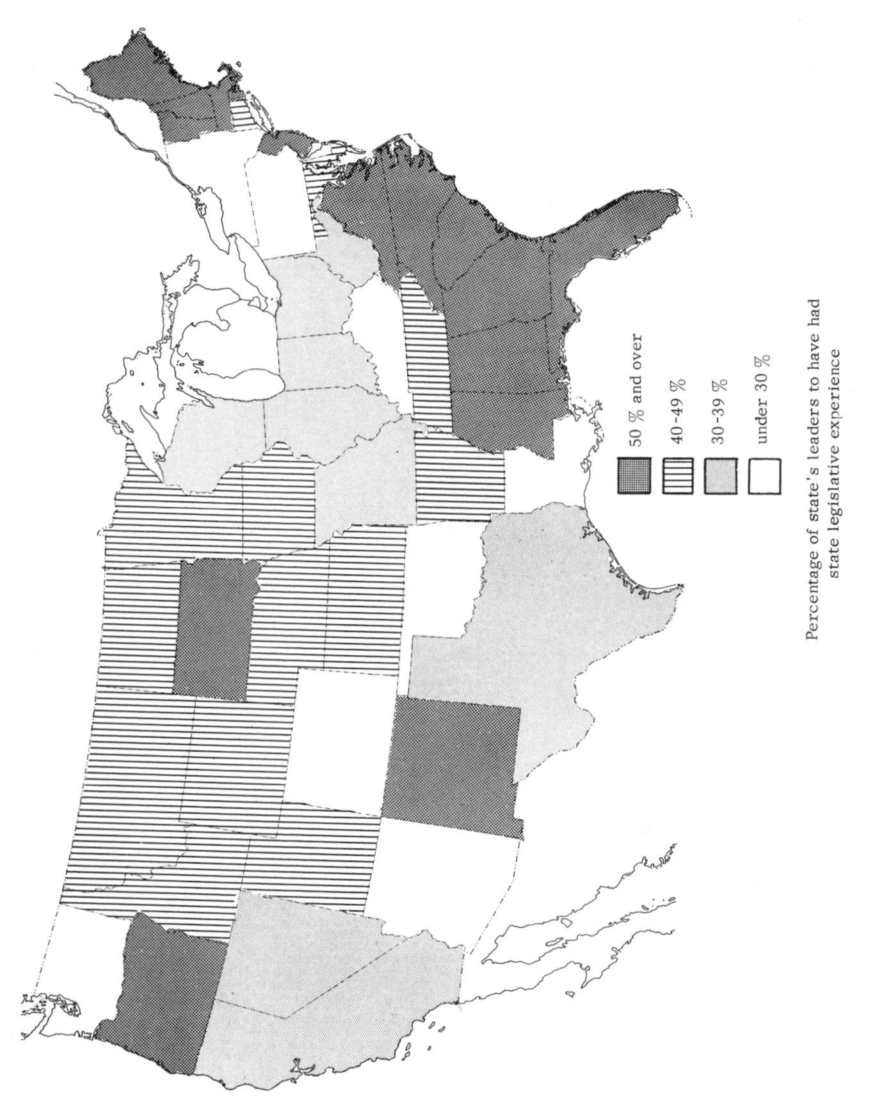

FIGURE V-1
The State Legislature as Base Office

Moreover, their use is neither entirely uniform nor scattered among the states. The states' use of these base offices varies from almost mandatory to negligible; and, equally significant for the concept of shape, the variations are regional. It is, therefore, worthwhile to examine the use of base offices in the states more closely, to seek explanations of their use, and

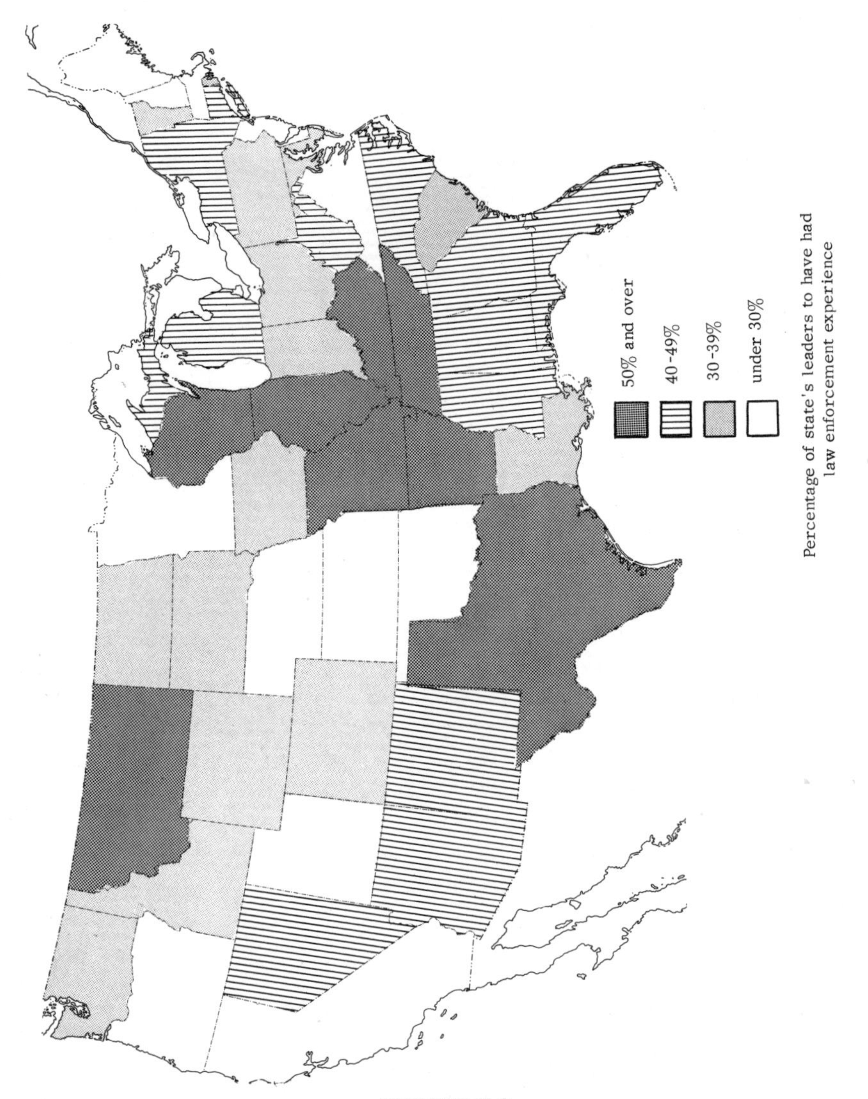

FIGURE V-2
Law Enforcement Positions as a Base Office

then to consider the place of the base office in a state's total structure of opportunities.

The relationships among the four base offices are especially revealing. Table V-2 gives the rank order correlations for the four base offices. The calculations have been made by region, for the nation at large, and

TABLE V-2

Rank Order Relationships between Base Offices

Regions	*Legislature and Law Enforcement*	*Legislature and Local*	*Legislature and Administration*	*Law Enforcement and Local*	*Law Enforcement and Administration*	*Local and Administration*
New England (6 states)	−.31	+.71	+.03	−.83	+.54	−.37
Midwest (11 states)	−.35	−.44	−.40	+.10	+.36	+.29
Far West (11 states)	−.35	+.21	+.33	−.55	+.18	−.25
Border (4 states)	−1.00	+.40	+.40	−.40	−.40	−.40
Mid-Atlantic (4 states)	−.20	+.80	+1.00	−.40	−.20	+.80
Total, Non-southern (36 states)	−.41	+.38	−.01	−.38	+.15	+.07
South (12 states)	+.08	+.51	+.06	−.25	−.20	−.18
Total (48 states)	−.26	+.18	−.14	−.41	−.10	+.20

for the nation excluding the south.[7] Thus it is possible to discern both the general relationship among the offices and regional peculiarities. The table reveals that experience in the state legislature is associated primarily with experience in local elective office and that both these types of experience are generally incompatible with law enforcement experience. The negative correlation between legislative and law enforcement experience, although small for all 48 states (—.26), is consistently negative for all regions except the south where there is no relation at all (+.08). We might note also the consistently negative correlation between law enforcement and local elective office, except in the midwest (+.10). In contrast, the correlation between legislative and local elective office is positive from region to region, except in the midwest (—.44). We can conclude, therefore, that these are compatible offices within a state's opportunity structure.

A consistent relationship between administrative office and the other base offices is less apparent. There is a positive relation between administrative and law enforcement offices, but not in the areas where law enforcement experience is most important—the mid-Atlantic, the border, and the southern states. Nor is the relation of administrative experience to the state legislative-local office complex consistent. Undoubtedly the heterogeneous character of the administrative office category makes it more difficult to isolate its part in the states' opportunity structures. Nevertheless, as a departure from promotion within the elective system, the frequent use of men with administrative experience as a source for political leaders probably indicates a merging of administrative and electoral politics, and its supplemental use, a compensation for a deficiency in the use of one of the other base offices. If we examine the states where administrative experience is common to many of the state's leaders, we find, in most instances, very infrequent use of one of the other base offices. Michigan, which ranks highest in its use of administrative office as a base office, makes the least use of the legislature. In Nevada and Kentucky, administrative experience is common to 44 per cent and 47 per cent of the states' leaders, but there is a marked deficiency in local elective office experience among the leaders of both states

[7] Regions—*New England:* Maine, Vermont, New Hampshire, Massachusetts, Rhode Island, Connecticut; *Midwest:* Ohio, Indiana, Illinois, Michigan, Wisconsin, Minnesota, Iowa, North Dakota, South Dakota, Nebraska, Kansas; *Far West:* Montana, Idaho, Wyoming, Colorado, Utah, Nevada, Arizona, New Mexico, Washington, Oregon, California; *Border:* Maryland, West Virginia, Kentucky, Missouri; *Mid-Atlantic:* New York, New Jersey, Pennsylvania, Delaware; *South:* Virginia, North Carolina, South Carolina, Georgia, Florida, Alabama, Mississippi, Louisiana, Arkansas, Texas, Tennessee, Oklahoma. The correlation is Spearman's Rank Correlation Coefficient, from M. J. Moroney, *Facts From Figures* (Pelican A236; Baltimore: Penguin, 1956), p. 335.

(0 per cent and 7 per cent). Vermont alone uses administrative office (54.3 per cent) along with another base office, the legislature (78.0 per cent), to a high degree. The varying rank order correlations for administrative office confirm its supplemental character as well as its reflection of the deficiency of other base offices in a state's opportunity structure.

The use of different base offices by the states is highly suggestive of differences in the states' political systems. Two base offices are in common use: the state legislative office and the law enforcement office. But these offices are used generally not only by different states but by different regions, and they are, undoubtedly, different responses to different political conditions. Three possible explanations of the use of different base offices by the states are worth exploring: (1) The states' use of different base offices reflects institutional differences which make it more or less likely that a particular office will serve as the base office in a particular state's opportunity structure. (2) The different base offices are indicative of the more than 100-year span in which the states' constitutions were written, and of the fact that American attitudes toward offices has not remained constant throughout that period. (3) Differences in base offices among the states reflect differences in political styles, in ways of organizing for political action, and in the political issues of major concern. These explanations are by no means contradictory; indeed the regional character of the use of base office suggests that they are closely related.

The simplest institutional explanation for the use of different base offices by the states is that varying political structures provide different formal chances for a particular office. This explanation is easily tested for the office of state legislator. State legislatures vary in size from a total of 424 members in both houses of the New Hampshire legislature down to a mere 81 in both houses in New Jersey. Population also varies, so that, presumably, the more per capita chances to become a legislator

TABLE V-3
Relationship between Legal Opportunities to Be a State Legislator and the Legislative Base

Maximum Per Capita Legal Opportunities to Be a State Legislator Expressed As One Chance per	*Number of States in Which the Percentage of Leaders with Legislative Experience Is*	
	High (42.4%–78.0%)	*Low (11.4%–42.2%)*
High (629–9,065 thousand)	15	9
Low (9,750–52,931 thousand)	9	15

in a particular state, the more likely that the office will be a base office for the state's political leaders.[8] In Table V-3 I have related the per capita chances to be a legislator with the distribution of the base office and find some support for the proposition that the office is used more as a base office in states where the formal chances are the greatest.

But the regional distribution in the use of the office of state legislator as a base office weakens the proposition that the number of formal chances to become a legislator is the critical factor. Of the nine states listed in Table V-3 whose leaders have more legislative experience than the per capita chances to become legislator warrant, six are in the south, a region marked by its use of the office of legislator as a base office. Of the nine states whose leaders have less legislative experience than the per capita chances warrant, four are mountain states and three are border states. Here again is evidence of regional factors intruding upon the institutional provisions for the use of the office of state legislator as a base office.

It is more difficult to test the importance of formal chances in the use of law enforcement office as a base office. There is no simple measure of the availability of legal office in the states. We can, however, try for a measure which approximates the measure of per capita chances to obtain legislative office. The states do differ greatly in the size of the legal staffs attached to the offices of the attorney general. These differences reflect a variety of administrative arrangements, but they probably indicate also variations in the amount of the states' legal work. We can, therefore, assume that the size of the attorney general's staff is an approximation of the number of formal chances for gaining legal office within a state; by dividing the state's population by the size of the staff we arrive at the approximate per capita chances to become a law enforcement officer.[9] Table V-4 gives us the results, which are negative: there is no apparent relation between the per capita chances and the use of the law enforcement office as a base office. Indeed, both the legislative and law enforcement offices are sufficiently numerous for one or the other to be the base office in the opportunity structures of all the states. Since, then, there is no deficiency in the formal chances for either office, and since the evidence of a positive relation between

[8] In this instance the chances to become a legislator have been defined in maximum terms, i.e., the frequency of election. A four-year period is used to take into account two- and four-year terms. Both houses of the state legislatures are used. The population figures are those of 1950.

[9] The size of the law enforcement staff is based on the number of assistant or deputy attorneys general in the states in 1948, as listed in the *Book of the States* (Chicago: Council of State Governments, 1949). They range from 1 in Vermont to 152 in Pennsylvania. The information is not available for Georgia, so that the number of states in Table V-4 is 47. The population base is 1950.

formal chances and the use of base office is slight, I conclude that the institutional explanation of base office is of minor importance.

TABLE V-4
Relationship between Chances to Be a Law Enforcement Official and the Law Enforcement Base

Legal Opportunities to Be a Law Official	*Number of States in Which the Law Enforcement Experience of Leaders Is*	
	High	*Low*
High	12	12
Low	11	12

The historical explanation, the differences in the times when the states' governments were established, is probably more relevant. In the history of American political institutions, the state legislatures have undergone a change in status. Within the highly restricted set of activities known as state government in the early nineteenth century, the legislature was dominant. The post-Revolutionary fear of the executive did not instill the framers of the states' constitutions with indestructible faith in the legislature; but the restraints imposed upon the executive gave the legislature greater relative strength. In the post-Civil War period, however, as the state legislatures became more active particularly in the area of economic regulation, the makers of state constitutions became concerned primarily with restricting legislative power. The long state constitutions date from this period and represent mostly an attempt to circumscribe legislative action. Over the past fifty years, the trend has been toward strengthening the executive as opposed to the legislature; or at least this has been the dominant theme of constitutional revisions and proposals for the reform of state government.[10]

From the historical point of view we would expect legislative office to be the most important base office in the opportunity structures of the states with the older legislatures. Voting patterns throughout the country demonstrate that traditional views of politics are significant; it is therefore quite possible that the politician's perspective of his state's legislature is traditional and historical in origin. We cannot document the esteem with which the legislature is held in Massachusetts, for example, as compared with the legislature in California or Arizona. But we

[10] On early constitutional revision, see James Q. Dealey, *Growth of American State Constitutions from 1776 to 1914* (Boston: Ginn, 1915); for more recent trends, see Charles Adrian, *State and Local Government* (New York: McGraw-Hill, 1960); and Duane Lockard, *The Politics of State and Local Government* (New York: Macmillan, 1963).

can speculate that the politically ambitious in Massachusetts would consider office in the legislature important while a similar group in Arizona would not. These differing views would reflect the legislature's long, though not necessarily honorable, history in Massachusetts, dating back to the days when the state legislature was the focal point in state politics; in contrast, Arizona's state legislature dates only from 1912, a period when reformers were already trying to reduce legislative power and were beginning to think in terms of strengthening the governor. The historical explanation of the use of the office of state legislator as a base office is probably relevant to the regional concentration of its use which I have pointed out.

On the other hand, I should point out that the historical explanation is not entirely adequate. Three of the states whose leaders have the lowest incidence of legislative experience are among the original thirteen states, Pennsylvania, Delaware, and New York; a fourth state, Kentucky, was the fifteenth state to be admitted to the Union. The historical influence, then, is not binding; but there is no reason to assume that it does not exist.

When we look to constitutional history for an explanation of the use of the law enforcement office as a base office, we should pay special attention to the historical differences in local government within the states.[11] State political leaders who use the law enforcement office as a base office most often use county legal posts. But the county as a unit of local government has had an uneven history. It has been least important in New England where it has been overshadowed by the town; Connecticut has, in fact, eliminated the county as a unit of government. The county has emerged as the focal point of local government in the midwest; in some areas of the midwest, outside of a few cities, it is the principal form of local government. In certain midwest and border states the country courthouse and its rings, famous in the literature of political organization, inevitably play up the county law enforcement officer and the judge. Indeed, in Texas and Missouri there is verbal identification of most county officials with the "court," in its oldest and most traditional sense, as the seat of government. Thus, the chief county officials are "judges," although they may not carry out any of the duties normally associated with the office elsewhere. The exceptionally low use of the law enforcement office as a base office in New England and its higher use in certain midwestern and border states may very well reflect the states' historical treatment of the county as a unit of govern-

[11] Paul Wager, *County Government across the Nation* (Chapel Hill: University of North Carolina Press, 1960).

ment. At the same time, there are enough states which do not fit this picture for us to conclude again that, while the historical explanation may be relevant to the use of base office by the states, it is not the conclusive explanation.

When we try to explain the states' use of different base offices by the different issues which spark their politics, we must be cautious. The proposition that men advance from offices which give them a chance to exploit the issues important in a given political system is plausible. But the issues in American state politics are often subdued, or, at least, frequently devoid of policy content. Base offices, then, may become a major step in political promotion not because they place the holder at the center of controversy over policy but because they keep him safe from notoriety. In a political system which subdues policy issues, the manner in which issues are treated, rather than their content, is most likely to affect advancement in office. In turn, the offices upon which the states' political leaders choose to build their careers probably have their impact upon the issues of state politics.

Unfortunately, the electoral studies of the role of issues in elections have not dealt with the constituencies of the state leaders with whom I am concerned; they have dealt either with the attitudes of restricted local communities in national elections or with national samples which give us only broad regional distinctions in attitudes. Nevertheless, the concepts used in these studies should be very revealing at the state level where the political careers of most national leaders begin. The efforts to identify the impact of the voter's perceptions upon the voting act, to distinguish his orientation to party, personality, or issue, to define the issues in terms of both position and style, are efforts which could be made for state politics with profit. One conclusion which the voting studies have reached which seems especially relevant to the states' politics is that the issues in American elections do not easily fit the generally accepted ideological dichotomy of *left* and *right*. Important issues in American politics, prohibition, for example, have arisen over a style of life.[12] Other issues, corruption for one, have produced no overt differences between the parties or among voters, all of whom are in vocal agreement on the goal of probity; nevertheless, the issue of corruption has played a major part in electoral decisions.

The differences among the states in their electoral reactions to the two major parties, which we noted in the discussion of party competi-

[12] B. Berelson, P. Lazarsfeld, and W. McPhee, *Voting* (Chicago: University of Chicago Press, 1954), Ch. 9; and D. Stokes, "Spatial Models of Competition," *American Political Science Review*, LVII (1963), 368–77.

tion, may be indicative of differences in their approach to the issues in politics as well. Discarding, along with the voting studies, a simple left-right dichotomy for American politics, I would suggest that two broad types of appeal characterize political contests in the states. These appeals determine the style of a state's politics and may well have an impact upon the structure of political careers and the use of base offices. One appeal is to the demands and to the status tensions of ethnic and geographical groups. When the parties balance their tickets ethnically or geographically, they make such an appeal. Although the effects of group demands upon the states' politics are complex, the most obvious effect is the representation of ethnic and geographical groups among public officials. The other appeal is to the middle-class desire for "good government." This appeal has many facets; it scorns political patronage, strong party organization, especially urban organization or "machines," everything which can be called corrupt by middle-class standards. Each of these appeals can, and often does, substitute for conflicts over policy within a state; but each is easily translated into a policy conflict if the groups seeking greater representation or the parties proposing better government also propose different policy goals.

While both appeals are made in every state, one or the other seems to dominate and give its style to a state's politics. In the southern states, for example, the suppression of the Negro is the central fact of political life.[13] In the New England states the division of politics on European ethnic lines is, as Lockard has shown, most prominent.[14] Similarly, in northern states of the midwest, Minnesota, Wisconsin, and the Dakotas, European ethnic groups, Swedes, Germans, and Irish, have provided much of the basis for local political conflict. On the other hand, the good government appeal, while found everywhere, finds its greatest strength in response to strong party organization, in New York and Illinois, in Missouri and Pennsylvania. It is found also in states touched by the progressive movement, states of the midwest and far west such as Oregon and California.[15]

From the standpoint of the shape of the states' opportunity structures, it is most interesting that the states' political styles tend to coincide with their use of base offices. Where the office of state legislator has been the dominant base office, status politics is often the dominant style.

[13] V. O. Key, Jr., *Southern Politics* (New York: Knopf, 1949).
[14] Duane Lockard, *New England State Politics* (Princeton: Princeton University Press, 1959).
[15] Richard Hofstadter, *The Age of Reform* (New York: Knopf, 1955); Russell Nye, *Midwestern Progressive Politics* (East Lansing: Michigan State University Press, 1951); George E. Mowry, *The California Progressives* (Berkeley: University of California Press, 1951).

Where the law enforcement office has been the common base for political careers, good-government politics often dominates. As we have seen, New England and the south are the regions which use leaders with legislative experiences most heavily. But in the southwest, the political leaders of New Mexico have also been conspicuous for their apprenticeship in the state legislature. It is certainly interesting that New Mexico is also the western state whose politics has been most affected by ethnic divisions, the tensions between "Anglos" and the Spanish-speaking population.[16]

The good-government appeal which has been more pervasive in American politics is not as easily identified with the career structures of individual states. In Wisconsin, Progressivism can be associated with the strong use of the law enforcement office as a base office; but in California, another Progressive state, political advancement has no special base. In Illinois, Missouri, and New York, politics has often been reform in style, because of the antagonism toward urban machines; in these states too, politicians with law enforcement experience are the most successful. But in Texas and Montana, the law enforcement official has also shown the most promise in state politics, while the corrupting influences are not political but economic, railroad, mining, and oil interests.[17]

Where an obvious relation does exist between a particular style of politics and a particular style of office career, why does it exist? There are a number of reasons why the state legislator should prosper in status politics. The geographical confines of the legislative district make it easier for groups to place their representatives in the legislature; this is true for both the ethnic and geographical groups concerned with status. But also, within state government it is the legislature which has generally intervened in status conflicts. Only within the past decade have the courts undertaken to provide the solution to ethnic struggles, most particularly those focusing on the problem of Negro status. Prior to that time, state legislatures in the south have been the principal instruments for the repression of the Negro, while in the north, state legislatures have often provided the best means for improvement of the Negro's status through such legislation as FEPC laws.

Finally, status politics must thrive in a strongly ordered society

[16] Charles B. Judah and Frederick C. Irion, *The 47th State* (Albuquerque: Division of Governmental Research, University of New Mexico, 1959); Thomas C. Donnelly, *Rocky Mountain Politics* (Albuquerque: University of New Mexico Press, 1940).

[17] On the particular relation between law enforcement positions and the politics of Texas and Montana, see Joseph A. Schlesinger, *How They Became Governor* (East Lansing: Governmental Research Bureau, Michigan State University, 1957).

where status has meaning. As we have seen, the legislative base is most closely associated with the older, eastern states and with the south, the regions of the United States where social stratification is strongest. In these regions the apparatus of the state undoubtedly has the greatest value; if the Irish and Italian immigrants find satisfaction in the election of their representatives to the legislature in Massachusetts, it is because the Yankees before them have found these posts to be desirable; if the rednecks of the hills of Mississippi seek to preserve their superiority to the Negro through legislative position, it is because the planter aristocracy of the delta first deemed legislative position worthy. The more the citizens value state government as an important part of society, the more the state is integrated with the community, the more well defined is its office hierarchy as a social hierarchy, and the more likely is it that appeal to status will be made by politicians and satisfaction in politics will be found in the representation which the state legislature can provide. This is, at least, a reasonable explanation of why status politics and the state legislator have flourished together in the states of New England and of the south.

Good-government politics is more elusive than status politics, its climate more difficult to define. As I have pointed out, it can arise in a variety of situations, in response to various types of corruption, political and economic. Nevertheless, there are two valid reasons for the relation between good-government politics and political careers launched in law enforcement offices. The good-government appeal puts its emphasis on expertise and procedure, along with the depoliticization of governmental decisions, an approach quite in keeping with the strong legal tradition which pervades American politics. In American politics the lawyer is the accepted expert and law enforcement is the procedural means of resolving issues. But good-government politics and law enforcement politicians also flourish in similar communities. Antipolitical, anti-the-organization, whether political or economic, both tend to spawn in and to foster in turn unsettled communities and fractionated politics. An atmosphere of lawlessness, whether in the large cities of the north or the sparsely settled areas of Texas and Montana, is most conducive to reform politics whose hero is the defender of the law.

THE IMPLICATIONS OF BASE OFFICE FOR THE POLITICS OF THE STATES

There are then a number of possible explanations of the use of different base offices by the states. But there are also important questions to be answered about the implications of the use of a particular base office in the politics of a state. Does it make any difference whether most of a state's leaders serve in the state legislature or in a law enforcement post, or have no common office experience? The answer in terms of social background is not readily apparent. If the typical road to advancement is through the law enforcement office, most of a state's leaders will be lawyers by training. Whether that fact in itself will lead them to behave differently in politics is highly dubious.

But, from the standpoint of political attitudes, the office background of a state's leaders is most pertinent. When the major political figures in a state rise from the legislature, the legislators, or an important segment at least, will have a statewide orientation and an interest in statewide political organization. If, on the other hand, the legislature is a political dead-end, or if it filters men to local office or sends them to the United States House of Representatives, then the concern of many legislators will be for these dispersed constituencies. And the use of the legislative base office provides a focus for political organization in another and more physical sense. A legislative session brings together many people with political interests—party leaders, lobbyists, civil servants, and newspapermen; it creates a political community. The election of political leaders from the legislature reinforces the communal ties and promotes the development of centralized organization.

In contrast, where the law enforcement office is at the base of a state's opportunity structure political discussion and presumably political organization will be dispersed. The law enforcement posts from which men advance are primarily local, the offices of county attorney, district judge, and the like. The organization which these offices create is also local, of the county-ring variety; where cooperative action is responsible for office advancement, it resembles most closely the temporary alliances of tribal chieftans. But, for advancement from a law enforcement position there need be no alliances at all. The use of the law enforcement base may simply reflect the potency of the candidate's own personality in a state's politics and the impotence of political groups to decide on candidates.

We expect that the states which use no base office will also be states whose political organization is dispersed. If we take a common office experience of 40 per cent of a state's leaders as the minimum requirement for a base office, we find eight states without any base office: California, Colorado, Delaware, Louisiana, Oklahoma, Washington, Indiana, and Pennsylvania. With the exception of Indiana and Pennsylvania, these states according to the folklore of politics are states with weak political organizations.

CONCLUSIONS

In this chapter I began to appraise the shape of the states' opportunity structures. But the base office alone does not give us their shape. Lack of a base office must, of course, mean that there is no rigid stratification of offices leading to the top political positions in a state; yet it is still possible to have distinct patterns of advancement. At the same time, the existence of a strong office base does not guarantee a hierarchy of offices leading to the top. To gain a clearer idea of the relation between the states' opportunity structures and their political systems, we must see if the structure of political opportunity has even sharper form.

CHAPTER VI

State Patterns of Opportunity: The Manifest Office

HAVING EXAMINED THE SIZE and the base of the states' opportunity structures, we turn now to their shape or the sequence of offices through which men advance. If a political system controls politicians' behavior through their ambitions, political careers must be orderly enough to direct and to guide the expectations of the politically ambitious. Turnover can be high or low in the governor's office, but the ambition to become governor has its maximum impact upon lesser officeholders when only a few have reasonable expectations of advancement to the governorship. If all members of the political community have equal expectations, the tensions generated by ambition are reduced until the political contest becomes a lottery. At the same time, political tensions are also reduced when certain officeholders are sure of advancement, for these officeholders as well as for those who know they have no chance. In a political system which uses the tensions of office ambitions as a control, therefore, a moderate degree of uncertainty about political opportunities must exist.

In this chapter, then, I am interested in defining the patterns of political advancement within the states by focusing upon the careers of governors and senators. First I shall search for common paths to these offices and develop measures of orderly movement. Then I shall try to determine to what extent the common or obvious paths are used in the individual states. Finally I shall relate the types of political careers within the states to the two aspects of their political systems which I have already examined, the size of the opportunity structures and the conditions of party competition.

THE MEASURE OF OFFICE SUCCESSION IN POLITICAL CAREERS IN THE STATES

To measure the successive use of offices in the states I have devised three indices of sequence: *first office,* or the first public office in a man's career; *office experience;* and *penultimate office,* the office held just prior to gaining the top office of governor or senator.[1] If a governor or senator has held only one prior office, that office fits all three categories. The more complex a governor's or senator's career, the more complex the sequence of offices. The offices which I have measured for sequence are reduced from the great multitude of offices in the states to seven office types: the four base offices used in the preceding chapter, *state legislative, local elective, law enforcement,* and *administrative office;* and, in addition, *statewide elective office,* a category including all of the offices elected by the state at large with the exception of the office of attorney general which is included with the law enforcement offices;[2] *congressional office* or the office of United States representative; and *no prior office,* a category which is self-explanatory.

I have laid out the sequential positions of the various office types in the careers of governors and senators in the form of frequency "trees." The tree is a device for summarizing visually what would otherwise be a complex series of tables. For the office of governor, see Figure VI-1. The branches of this tree show the frequency with which the 641 men, elected governor between 1900 and 1958, come directly from the various types of office, as well as their previous office experience and their first elective offices. The tree should, therefore, be read from right to left. Note, for example, in Figure VI-1, that 18.88 per cent of this sample of governors have had a legislative office as their penultimate position. Moving to the left (*Office Experience*), we find that, of this group, all (100.0 per cent) have, by definition, had legislative experience, but that 15.7 per cent have also had law enforcement experience, that none (0.0 per cent) have had statewide elective experience, and that very few (0.8 per cent) have been in Congress, while 14.1 and 17.3 per cent respectively have had administrative and local elective experi-

[1] This analysis is based on the careers of governors elected between 1900 and 1958 and senators elected from 1914 through 1958. Where any data deal with the careers of defeated major party candidates for the two offices, that is stated explicitly in text and tables.

[2] The statewide elective category, when used for governors' previous office experience, refers to the minor state elective offices such as lieutenant governor and secretary of state. With reference to senatorial careers, the category includes the office of governor as well, and, in fact, consists almost exclusively of governors.

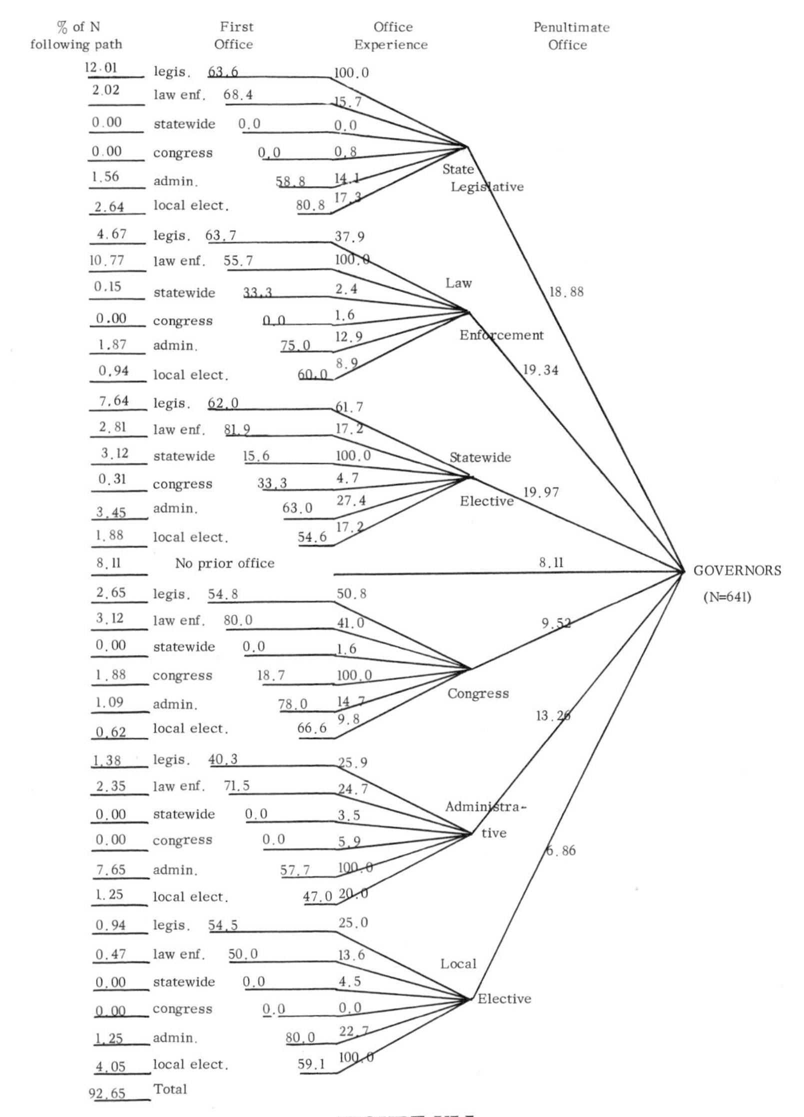

FIGURE VI-I
Prior Office Careers of Governors

ence. Moving still further to the left, we find in the *First Office* column the percentages of those who, having had experience in one type of office, also started their careers in that type of office. Thus, still looking at governors whose penultimate office has been in the state legislature,

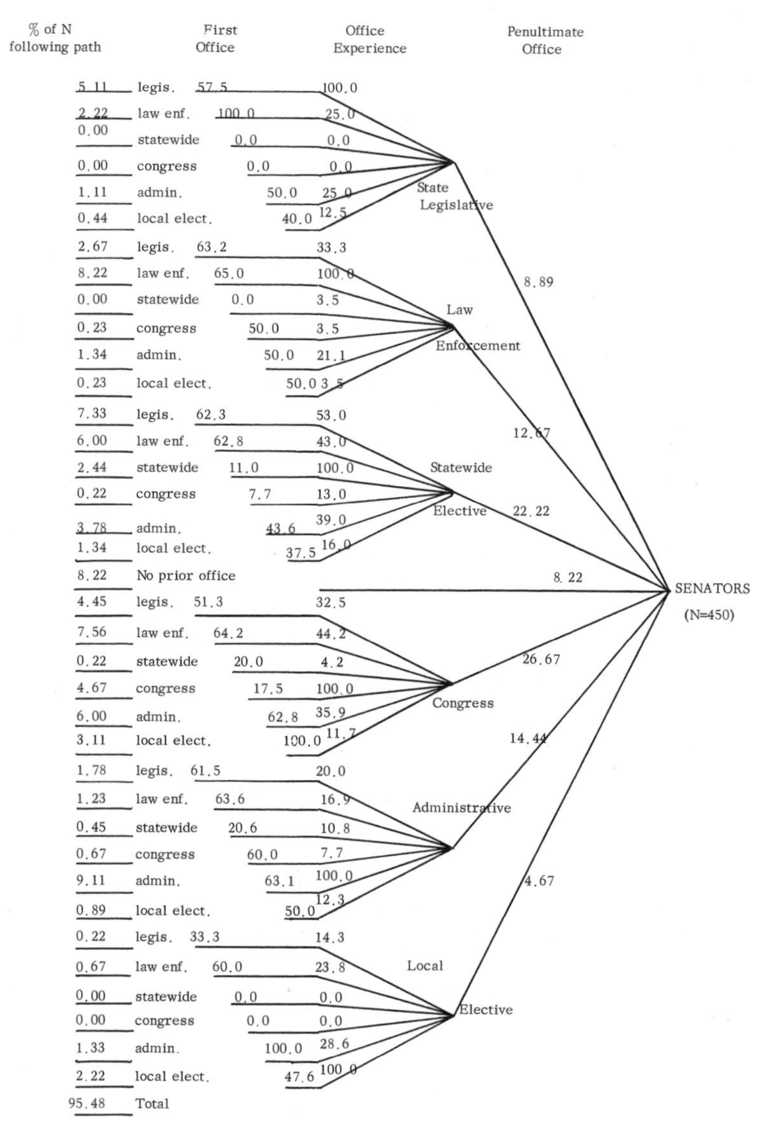

FIGURE VI-2
Prior Office Careers of Senators

we find that some 63.6 per cent started in the legislature. And of the 15.7 per cent who have also had law enforcement experience, 68.4 per cent started in a law enforcement position. We see, too, that some 80.8 per cent of those who have had local elective experience started there. The column on the extreme left records the percentages of all the gov-

TABLE VI-1
The Principal Lines of Advancement
(First to last comprising 2.5% and more of total)

First Office	*Percentage of All Governors*	*Last Office before Becoming GOVERNOR*	*Percentage of All Governors*
Legislature	12.01%	Legislature	14.65%
Local elective	2.64		
Legislature	4.67	Law enforcement	15.44
Law enforcement	10.77		
Legislature	7.64	Statewide	17.02
Statewide	3.12		
Law enforcement	2.81		
Administrative	3.45		
Legislature	2.65	Congress	2.65
Administrative	7.65	Administrative	7.65
Local elective	4.05	Local elective	4.05
No prior office			8.11
			69.57

First Office	*Percentage of All Senators*	*Last Office before Becoming SENATOR*	*Percentage of All Senators*
Legislature	5.11%	Legislature	5.11%
Legislature	2.67	Law enforcement	11.89
Law enforcement	8.22		
Legislature	7.33	Statewide	17.11
Law enforcement	6.00		
Administrative	3.78		
Legislature	4.45	Congress	25.79
Law enforcement	7.56		
Congress	4.67		
Administrative	6.00		
Local elective	3.11		
Administrative	9.11	Administrative	9.11
No prior office			8.22
			77.23

ernors who have followed each particular path.[3] (It is calculated by multiplying the three previous percentages by each other.) Thus, we see

[3] The columns on the extreme left of the trees do not add to 100 per cent because of rounding and, more importantly, because the data are not complete for each of the columns of the office sequence. The statistically observant reader will also notice that the column on the extreme right, which gives the percentages for penultimate office, also fails to add to 100 per cent. For governor, the total is 95.94, for senator, 97.78, for defeated governors, 97.76, and for defeated senators, 99.12. The reason is that I have not included an "other" category of penultimate office which consists primarily of such positions as member of state constitutional convention and presidential elector.

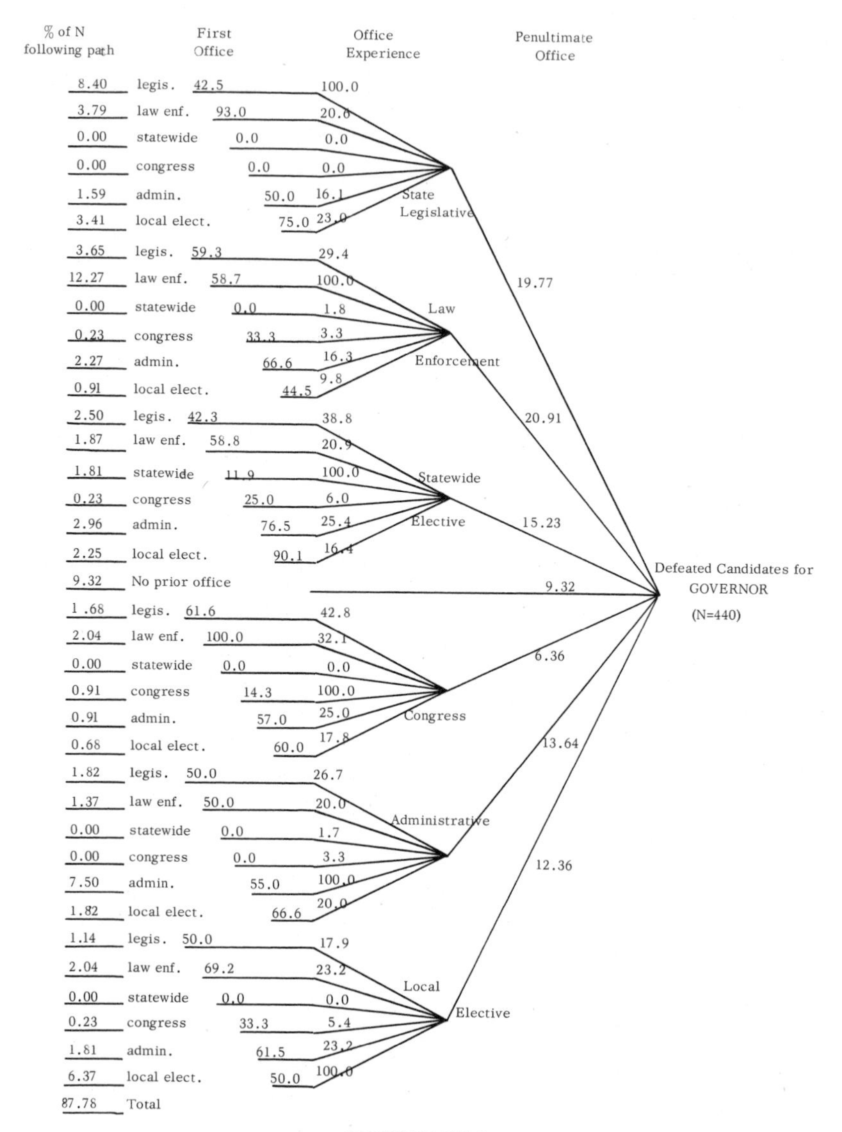

FIGURE VI-3
Prior Office Careers of Defeated Candidates for Governor

that 12.01 per cent started in the legislature and held a legislative office immediately before becoming governor; 2.02 per cent started in the law enforcement position and then advanced through the legislature, and so on.

The frequency trees which I have constructed for the offices of gov-

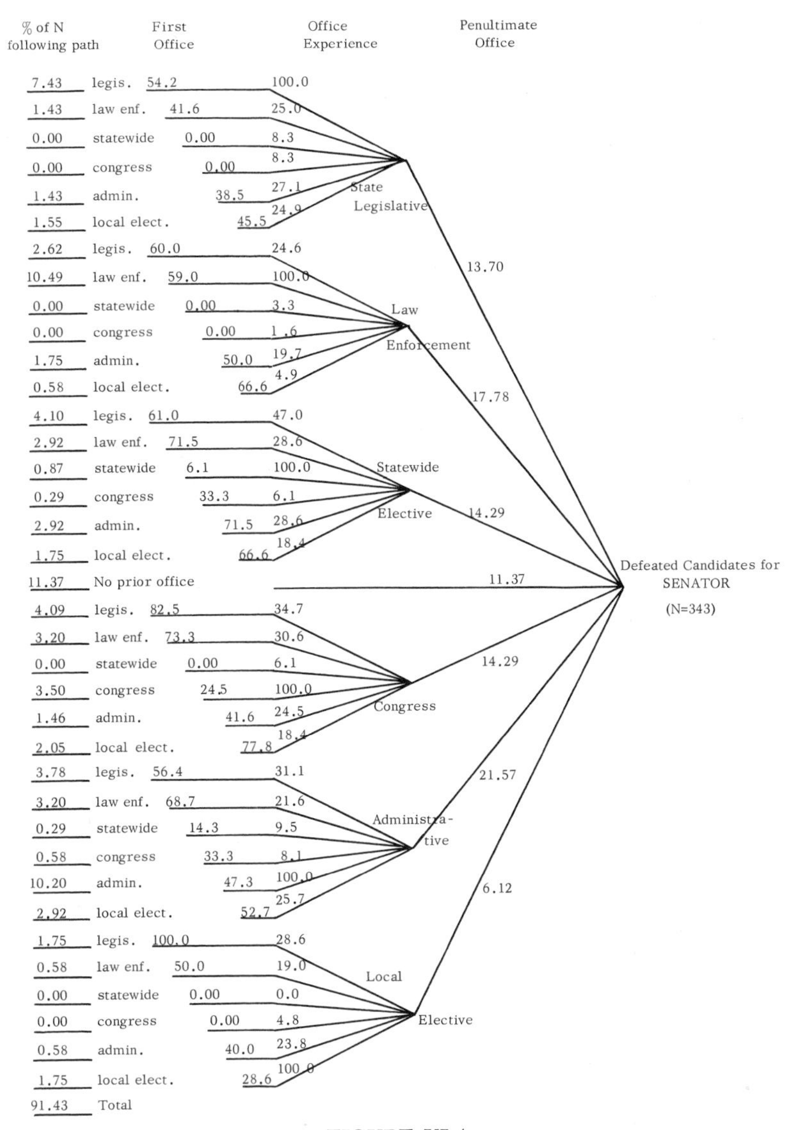

FIGURE VI-4
Prior Office Careers of Defeated Candidates for Senator

ernor and senator summarize a great deal of information about the career lines of the states' top elective leaders. Given the number of categories used, there are 37 routes to the governorship and to the office of senator, from first to penultimate office. Most of the states' leaders use relatively few of these routes. If we look for the routes followed by at least 2.5 per cent of the governors or senators, we find that 12 routes account for 70 per cent of the governors, and 13 for 70 per cent of the senators (Table VI-2). More than half the governors (52.41 per cent) have complex office careers, careers in which their penultimate offices differ from their first offices; even more (60.01 per cent) of the senators have complex careers.

To gain a still broader perspective of the career lines in American state politics, I have constructed frequency trees for the defeated candidates for governor and senator (Figures VI-3 and VI-4). These trees reveal fewer sequences in the careers of defeated candidates than in those elected to office. In the careers of defeated gubernatorial candidates, the lesser offices, state legislative and law enforcement, are the important penultimate offices. Defeated senatorial candidates have few penultimate offices in common, although 22 per cent obtain their nomi-

TABLE VI-2
Structure in the Office Careers of Governors, Senators, and Unsuccessful Major Party Candidates for Governor and Senator

	Use of Penultimate Office[a]			
Penultimate Office	*Unsuccessful Gubernatorial Candidates*	*Governors*	*Unsuccessful Senatorial Candidates*	*Senators*
Local elective	12.73%	6.86%	6.12%	4.67%
Legislative	19.77	18.88	13.70	8.89
Law enforcement	20.91	19.34	17.78	12.67
Administrative	13.64	13.26	21.57	14.44
Congress	6.36	9.52	14.29	26.67
Statewide elective	15.23	19.97	14.29	22.22

	Difference between Use of an Office as First and as Penultimate Offices (% Penultimate Office − % First Office)			
	Unsuccessful Gubernatorial Candidates	*Governors*	*Unsuccessful Senatorial Candidates*	*Senators*
Local elective	−2.71%	−4.52%	−4.47%	−3.56%
Legislative	+0.68	−10.41	−10.07	−12.67
Law enforcement	−2.97	−2.10	−4.04	−13.23
Administrative	−3.40	−3.61	+3.23	−8.23
Congress	+4.76	+7.33	+9.92	+20.88
Statewide elective	+13.42	+16.70	+13.13	+19.11
Total (sign ignored)	27.94	44.67	44.86	77.68

[a]The number of candidates who use each office is expressed as a percentage of the total number of candidates for senator and governor, successful and unsuccessful.

nations from administrative posts. Where they do exist, the relationships between types of first and penultimate offices are largely the same for defeated as for successful candidates.

When we add the defeated candidates to the successful candidates for the offices of senator and governor, we have four groups of political leaders whose careers give increasing evidence of advancement through office. Those leaders whose careers are most orderly and are characterized by the greatest movement from office to office are the successful candidates for the Senate. Those candidates whose political advance is the least well defined are the unsuccessful candidates for the governorship. Furthermore, there is somewhat less order in the careers of successful gubernatorial candidates than in the careers of defeated senatorial candidates. Table VI-2 points up the differences in the office careers of the four groups. Note that as we move from defeated candidates for governor to governors and from defeated candidates for senator to senators, there is a consistent decline in the use of the lesser office types, local elective, state legislative, and law enforcement offices, as penultimate offices and an increase in the use of the two more important offices, statewide elective and congressional office. Note also that the margin of difference between the use of each office type as a first office and as a penultimate office increases;[4] the difference is almost three times as large for successful senatorial candidates as for defeated candidates for the governorship.

The national results of the measurement of sequence in the careers of the states' leaders reveal, then, that systematic promotion to high office does exist in the states. Indeed, the higher the office, the more evidence there is of orderly advancement. Generally the office of senator ranks above the office of governor. My measures of sequence reveal that, although there are twice as many senators as governors, the route to the Senate is more sharply defined than the route to the governorship. Moreover, where there is any evidence of orderly advancement in the careers of the states' political leaders, the evidence is strong. That is to say, men who come to the office of governor and senator through the important penultimate offices of lieutenant governor or United States representative have more previous office experience than men who come from the lesser office of state legislator. Very few of the governors (11 per cent) who become senators start as governors; only 18 per cent of the United States representatives who become senators start in Congress. On the other hand, over half the state legislators, law enforcement offi-

[4] The percentage difference between the use of a type of office as a first and as a penultimate office is a useful measure of structure in political careers which we will use later in examining the impact of party upon structure.

cers, and administrators who reach the Senate have no previous office experience. A similar pattern is evident in the governors' careers.

Furthermore, the national results of the measures of office sequence reveal distinct career lines for the states' two major elective positions. These distinctions are related to the differences in the use of base offices which we considered in the last chapter. There is, on the one hand, a state career which starts in the state legislature and continues in statewide elective office. There is, on the other hand, a federal office career starting in a law enforcement position and continuing in the federal Congress. This is not to say that there are no mixed careers. The offices of governor and senator are important offices toward which men are bound to strive from many directions. Nevertheless, there are distinctive careers leading to each. For example, a higher proportion of governors than senators begin their careers in the legislature, while the reverse is true of the law enforcement positions. More significant is the fact that, regardless of their penultimate offices, a governor is more likely to have been in the state legislature while a senator is more likely to have held a law enforcement position (Table VI-3).[5] Thus, of the senators who come from the legislature, one fourth have also had some prior law enforcement experience, and of governors who come from a law enforcement post, some 40 per cent have also had some prior legislative experience. Over 40 per cent of both governors and senators who have penultimate positions in the United States Congress have had prior law enforcement experience, further strengthening the federal direction of the law enforcement base office.

TABLE VI-3

Prior Office Experiences[a] of Governors and Senators

Penultimate Office	*Law Enforcement Experience*		*State Legislative Experience*	
	Governors	*Senators*	*Governors*	*Senators*
Legislative	15.7%	25.0%	100.0%	100.0%
Law enforcement	100.0	100.0	37.9	33.3
Statewide	17.2	43.0	61.7	53.0
Congress	41.0	44.2	50.8	32.5
Administrative	24.7	16.9	25.9	20.0
Local elective	13.6	23.8	25.0	14.3

[a]These figures present the percentages of governors and senators in each category of penultimate office who have had law enforcement or state legislative experience.

[5] Note that in these calculations as well as in those of Table VI-2 the administrative office category does not behave as expected. The category is undoubtedly too broadly defined to reveal the differences expected here, including, as it does, all appointive posts except those in law enforcement, regardless of importance.

But there are also important differences in the penultimate offices which lead to the top positions of leadership in the states. There are two office types which most often lead directly to the governorship, statewide elective and state legislative office. The importance of statewide elective office is increased when we transfer the office of attorney general from the law enforcement category to the statewide elective category. Under this scheme, 26 per cent of the governors have held a statewide elective office as their penultimate office, 19 per cent the office of state legislator, and 13 per cent a law enforcement position. Relatively few governors come directly from the United States House of Representatives or from local elective office. Only 8 per cent have held no previous office. The same small percentage of senators have held no office prior to election. But for the senators the office of United States representative is an important penultimate office. Also important is statewide elective office, mostly for those seeking the governorship.

THE MANIFEST OFFICE

Having set forth the general data on the offices leading to the top leadership positions in the states, I shall now seek to make use of these findings within the framework of ambition theory. Since a theory of ambitions operates from a simple and obvious motive, we should also look for the simplest and most obvious explanations in the development of office careers. There are a number of obvious or *manifest* conditions which link offices together and make likely movement between them. The first is the logic of electorates. When two offices have the same or similar electorates, it is logical to expect movement from one to the other. Governors have to pass the same statewide electoral test as senators; for that reason alone, they are obvious candidates for the Senate. For the same reason, the minor statewide elective posts, the offices of lieutenant governor, attorney general, and secretary of state, which share the electorates of governors and senators, give their holders an advantage in the search for higher office. For similar reasons, the more homogeneous the electorate of a state, the more likely that officeholders with partial electorates, state legislators, congressmen, and county officers, will be able to move to offices with statewide electorates. By the same logic, governors and senators from the constituencies most similar to the presidential constituency enjoy an advantage over officeholders from less representative areas.

The second manifest tie between offices is the similarity of functions. The legislative function requires similar skills and talents whether in the city council or the federal Senate. Different demands are made upon judges and executives. I have already pointed out that different career lines lead to the national judicial and executive offices. But there are offices, the most obvious of which are the offices of Vice President and of lieutenant governor, that carry titles implying, even if they do not require, functions similar to those of the executives whom they follow in rank. For my purposes, it makes little difference whether similar functions lead officeholders to direct their ambitions at those higher offices for which they feel prepared or cause those who make the choices, including the voters, to look with favor upon officeholders' aspirations for offices with similar functions. Manifestly, the functional resemblance of offices is a condition which affects the course of political careers.

The third condition which leads overtly to movement between two offices is a shared political arena. A governor deals continuously with the legislature and the President with Congress. Whether the executive conflicts or agrees with the legislative body, it is natural that legislative leaders, in frequent contact with the executive, should think of themselves as potential executives and that observers should consider them among those available for the job.

These three factors, then, the electoral, the functional, and the environmental, condition the normal expectations about advancement in politics. When all three factors are present, as they are for the offices of lieutenant governor and governor, a high rate of promotion from the lesser to the higher office is expected. But the presence of any one of these conditions is sufficient to raise expectations that there will be some movement between the offices. Since these are normal expectations they do not really require an explanation; rather it is necessary to explain the failure of those in obvious places to win promotion. For example, we want to know why the Vice Presidency has been a dead-end precisely because it is obviously the office in line for the Presidency. We can explain the Vice Presidency itself readily enough by the way in which the Vice President is chosen, as part of the presidential compromise, not independently as the lieutenant governor generally is. But the Vice President is so obviously a man who wants to be President that our problem is to explain not his ambitions but his failure to attain them.

There is a simple rule which we can use to determine the manifest offices or the offices obviously in the line of promotion. We can ask which officials must usually confirm or deny their intentions to run for higher office when there is an opening. The manifest relationship between offices is of course circular. Because others have used a particular office as a steppingstone, observers assume that it will be used in the same manner again. Ambitions and expectations, therefore, interact and reinforce each other, and politicians, of necessity, treat their colleagues as though each had the ambitions appropriate to his office. As a result, even though the personal ambition of an officeholder may on occasion be weak or even non-existent, his position in an office which is manifestly in the line of succession forces us to consider not only his personal ambitions but the ambitions associated with his office in order to understand the attitudes of other politicians toward both the office and its holder. The senator is wary of the popular governor of his home state; the governor is wary of his personable lieutenant governor; such wariness is built into the career system.

The concept of manifest office is, therefore, useful in accounting for some of the order in American political careers. The concept has the virtue of simplicity; it has the virtue also of not requiring us to search for hidden influences upon the destinies of politicians. It equates appearances with reality. But, in saying that the means to advancement in American politics is the open and observable route, the concept does not predicate a perfect or rigid use of manifest office for advancement. My position, of course, is that political opportunities in the American states are largely open. For such highly valued offices as the office of governor and senator, the strivings of many men offset the advantages of the manifest officeholders in the American states. But the breakdown in the use of manifest office need not direct our attention to external forces impinging upon the attainment of political office. Both competition and personal idiosyncrasies are enough to prevent perfect use of manifest offices. Some manifest officeholders will choose to retire for personal reasons; others will be obviously disqualified for higher positions. Herbert Lehman, the Jewish governor of New York from 1933 to 1942, has been the only elected governor of New York in recent history not to be considered seriously for the Presidency. The manifest office concept, then, leads us to expect only that some, but by no means all, politicians who advance to higher office will take the obvious routes.

The concept of the manifest office leads me to formulate *a manifest office hypothesis* about the states' opportunity structures. I propose that the states which deserve our closest attention are those which depart from the norm, using manifest office either very infrequently or almost exclusively for political advancement. When the offices obviously in the line of succession do not comprise the route to political advancement in a state, we must ask whether chance and personal idiosyncracy alone are the reasons, or whether organizations outside the office structure, partisan or otherwise, control the careers of officeholders. In other words, the manifest office hypothesis is primarily a device for ferreting out the existence, within a state, of organizations which stand apart from the organization of officeholders provided by the state's office structure. If, on the other hand, there is an overuse of manifest offices in a state, we are led to suspect that political organization is primarily an officeholders' organization and that the impact upon the opportunity structure of other political organizations, parties or interest groups, is weak. The manifest office hypothesis suggests only that a moderate degree of succession in office is normal; by itself it tells us nothing about a state's politics.

The Manifest Office Hypothesis and the National Data

What constitutes normal use of manifest office by the states can, of course, come only from an arbitrary judgment. To arrive at an empirical definition of the norm, I have gone back to the national averages for the use of penultimate offices. As I have already pointed out, two types of penultimate office lead most frequently to the governorship, the lesser statewide elective posts and the office of state legislator. All these offices satisfy at least some of the conditions for a manifest relationship with the office of governor. The lesser statewide elective offices have electorates congruent with the governor's; their functions are similar, their governmental arena the same. Of the statewide elective offices, the office of lieutenant governor best satisfies the conditions for a manifest relationship. Not only does the lieutenant governor actually succeed to the office of governor when the governor can no longer carry out his duties[6]; the mere title of lieutenant governor implies succession to the governorship. While the state legislator does not have a manifest electoral or functional relationship with the governor, both share a common political arena. The legislature is the branch of government with which the governor has the closest contacts, and questions inevitably arise as to whether legislative leaders in particular are possible governors. Together, state legislative and statewide elective offices account for the penultimate offices of almost one-half the governors in the period 1900–1958; the penultimate offices of the remaining governors are scattered among the other five office types.[7] I consider, then, a state's use of manifest office

[6] My figures do, however, exclude lieutenant governors who may have succeeded to the governorship but were not subsequently elected in their own right. Similarly the figures do not include among the senators those who may have been appointed but who were not subsequently elected.

[7] For the purposes of this discussion of manifest offices, the position of attorney general has been included among the statewide elective offices. This transfer reduces the law enforcement category as penultimate office leading to governor by 6.4 per cent and to senator by 1.1 per cent.

for the governorship to be normal if 50 per cent of its governors have come from statewide elective or state legislative office or both.

For the office of senator, there are also two prominent types of penultimate office, statewide elective and congressional office. Both types satisfy some of the conditions for a manifest relationship with the office of senator. The statewide elective offices enjoy a congruent electorate; they form an obvious pool of men expecting to advance in politics. Certainly the speculation about a sitting governor is almost universal: will he or will he not make a try for the Senate? For a United States representative, advancement to the Senate is also a logical promotion; congressional office shares a functional relationship with the office of senator. Together, congressional offices and statewide elective offices account for the penultimate offices of 49 per cent of our senators. Fifty per cent, then, is also a good definition of the normal use of manifest office for promotion to the senate.

The Use of Manifest Offices in the States

According to this definition of normal, i.e., the use of manifest office by 50 per cent or more of a state's governors and senators, there are extreme variations among the states in the use of manifest office. The range for the governorship goes from 14 per cent in Nevada to 80 per cent in Iowa; the range for the office of senator, from 11 per cent in New Mexico to 86 per cent in Mississippi. Table IV-4 gives the distribution: the use of manifest offices for the governorship is somewhat less than for the office of senator; the state distribution for the governorship skews down, the distribution for the office of senator skews up. The distribution supports our assertion that the office of senator is more important, and that the more important or the higher the office, the more likely will the careers which precede that office show progressive advancement in office.

For my purposes the most important thing to note in Table VI-4 is the positive relation between the use of manifest office for each of the states' top elective positions. The relationship is far from perfect (the correlation coeffiicent is 0.24, and significant at the level of 10 per cent), but it does exist. It is not built into the office categories. Therefore, the tendency for both senators and governors of a state to use manifest offices to somewhat the same degree provides the strongest support for my manifest office hypothesis.

The manifest office hypothesis asserts that the use of obvious prior offices for political advancement is in itself an independent quality in

TABLE VI-4
The Use of Manifest Offices in the States for Advancement to the Offices of Governor and Senator

Percentage of All Governors Who Use Manifest Offices for Each State	*Percentage of All Senators Who Use Manifest Offices for Each State*							
	80–89	*70–79*	*60–69*	*50–59*	*40–49*	*30–39*	*20–29*	*10–19*
80–89				Iowa				
70–79	Vt.							
60–69		Ga.	S.D.	Mass. R.I.				
50–59	Miss.				Calif. La.	Idaho Minn. Wis.	Ore.	
40–49		Kan.	Ala. S.C. Conn. Me.	Ariz. Mich. Fla. Neb. Ky. N.D. W.Va.		N.C.	Utah	
30–39		Ark.	N.H. Va.	Ill. Wash.	Colo. Md.	Del.	Mo. Mont. N.J.	
20–29		Ohio Tex.		Tenn.	Pa. Wyo.		Ind.	
10–19				Nev. Okla.	N.Y.			N. Mex.

the political systems of the American states. The use or non-use of the obvious offices for advancement, therefore, ought to be consistent throughout a state's opportunity structure. If officeholders control the political life of a state, their control should manifest itself in the orderly advancement from office to office for both the governorship and the Senate. If, on the other hand, other organizations compete with the officeholder for control of the governorship, they should compete for the office of senator as well.

What are the other organizations which compete with officeholders for control of the states' opportunity structures? Party organization is one. A classic conflict in democracies is the conflict between party officials inside and outside the government. We expect an effective party organization which is not entirely the creation of its officeholders to exercise some independent discretion in the choice of candidates for office. Unfortunately we have no measures of party organization in the states. One factor, however, which involves both party organization and the opportunities for office is the nominating system. Today, only four states retain the convention for the nomination of governors and senators, Connecticut, New York, Delaware, and Indiana. In Table VI-4 three of these states fall in the bottom right-hand quadrant, while Connecticut is more centrally located. Certainly it is not merely a matter of chance that the states using the convention for nominations are less likely to use manifest offices.

We have, then, come upon what appears to be an important consequence of the direct primary. The primary makes more likely the promotion of men from manifest offices and reinforces the officeholders' control of political organization. The reasons for this are much the same as the reasons why the primary system magnifies the importance of money, fame, and newspaper support. Primary voters lack party direction in their choice; substitute directives, therefore, have great impact. When a candidate for nomination holds an office manifestly in line for the office he is seeking, he gains an advantage in the direct primary which is reduced within the confines of the convention, composed as it is of the more politically sophisticated who are, at the same time, subject to greater organizational influence from without the office structure.

In addition to the method of nomination, another factor pertinent to the states' use of manifest office is their social and economic environment. In varying degrees, the states' economic and social structures provide alternative routes to political distinction. In the more rural states, state government itself is the largest aggregate of power, wealth, and prominence, and by this token state officials are most likely to attract popular attention. But in the urban industrial states, many aggregates of wealth and power—industrial corporations, the major outlets of the press, radio, and television, and important educational institutions—provide bases from which to build up popular support. In Illinois, strong party organizations have gone outside the ranks of those whose claims are based simply on office to advance such men as Frank Lowden from business, Paul Douglas from the university, and Adlai Stevenson from the federal government as well as an inherited position of prominence within the state. In Michigan, the automobile industry has provided one senator (James Couzens), one governor (George Romney), and one near-senator (Henry Ford). In New York, Nelson Rockefeller's advancement to the governorship is conspicuously not through long apprenticeship in state office. Government as such may be bigger in the large industrial states, and officeholders in these states may have more formal power than their colleagues in the rural states; but the officeholder is more likely to dominate the structure of political opportunity in the rural than in the industrial state.

Support for my proposition about the relevance of external organization, political, economic, and social, to the use of manifest office lies in the distributions shown in Table VI-4. The states which overuse the manifest offices for both governor and senator are Vermont, Mississippi, Georgia, and South Dakota. These states are in different regions and have different party loyalties; but within their regions they are the most rural states. At the other extreme, the states which make the least use of manifest office for the governorship and the Senate are New Mexico, Indiana, New York, New Jersey, Montana, and Missouri. Except for Montana and New Mexico, these are complex urban states which also enjoy a reputation for strong party organizations.

New Mexico is an instructive case. I have already pointed out that its constitution has a unique rule which prevents any state official from running for another state office immediately following his first term. This readily explains the state's failure to use manifest offices for the governorship, but, since New Mexico also makes least use of manifest offices for promotion to the Senate, it is likely that more than constitutional prescription reduces the importance of manifest officeholders in the state. Moreover, New Mexico is a state where party organization was able to resist the adoption of the direct primary until 1938, well after most states had adopted the system,[8] and it has been conspicuous in other contexts too. I have speculated that its unusually advantaged position in the national leadership corps is due to strong party organization, unusual in the region. Now, using an entirely different measure, I am led to make the same inference. Thus, New Mexico also supports my proposition about the relation between strong extra-office organization and the use of manifest office.

While in most of the states the relation between the use of manifest office for the governorship and for the Senate is positive, in some states there are marked discrepancies. Oregon and Wisconsin use manifest offices heavily for the governorship but make little use of the manifest offices for the Senate. On the other hand, Ohio, Texas, Oklahoma, Arkansas, and Nevada make little use of the manifest offices for the governorship but use them frequently for the Senate. The explanation of these aberrations is more difficult. The concentration of four of the states in the southwest suggests a regional phenomenon. In these states the very disorder which characterizes advancement to the governorship and which is enhanced by the lack of any powerful external organization may well strengthen the position of the manifest officeholder with respect to the Senate.

The concept of manifest office is, of course, a gross measure of the shape of the states' opportunity structures at the top. It combines office

[8] Thomas C. Donnelly, *Rocky Mountain Politics* (Albuquerque: University of New Mexico Press, 1940), pp. 237–44.

types and hides what may be an even stronger preference among the states to use particular offices for promotion to high places. To correct this failing, I have again classified the states according to their use of penultimate offices, this time taking the use of a single office type by at least 30 per cent of a state's governors or senators to be indicative of shape at the top of the state's opportunity structure. Table VI-5 shows us that only a minority of the states failed to meet this more rigorous measure of shape. In a few states a single office type is used as a penultimate office by more than 50 per cent of the state's governors or senators. In many states at least 40 per cent of the governors or senators use a single office type as the steppingstone to higher office. In some states 30 per cent or more of the governors or senators use one office type as a penultimate office, 30 per cent or more another; in 6 states this is true for the office of governor, in 14 for the office of senator. In 27 states there is a concentrated use of penultimate offices for both the governorship and the Senate. In only one state, Delaware, are the paths to office so diverse that no single penultimate office is used by at least 30 per cent of either the governors or senators.

TABLE VI-5

Patterns of Penultimate Offices Leading to Governor and Senator[a]

	Number of States Which Use the Following as Penultimate Office:						
	No Office	*Law Enforcement*	*State Legislative*	*Statewide Elective*	*U.S. Congress*	*Administrative*	*Local Elective*
Percentage elected GOVERNOR							
50% plus		1		2			
40–49	1	3	2	3		2	
30–39		10	9	5	1	3	1
Percentage elected SENATOR							
50% plus				2	5		
40–49				4	7	2	
30–39	1	5	2	12	7	7	

[a]Number of states without a 30 per cent pattern for governor: 11; for senator: 9.

The 30-per-cent standard for the states does not cause me to alter drastically my manifest office hypothesis. For the office of governor, the statewide elective offices are still the significant penultimate offices; for the office of senator, the governorship and the office of United States representative. The only change occurs in the prominent use of the law enforcement office for the governorship. But in this analysis, in order to emphasize the distinctions between office types, I have returned the office of attorney general to the law enforcement category.

The distribution in the use of the various office types as penultimate offices is to some degree regional. The use of statewide elective office, primarily the office of lieutenant governor, is distinctly a New England phenomenon, although the pattern is also used by some states in the midwest and the far west. Law enforcement office is used as the prominent penultimate office for the governorship in the border and mountain states, along with administrative office. The use of the office of state legislator for the governorship is less of a regional phenomenon, although the trend is strongest in New England and in the south, where it complements the frequent use of legislative office as a base office in these regions. The use of specific penultimate offices for the Senate is much less a regional matter than it is for the governorship.

MANIFEST OFFICE, BASE OFFICE, AND THE SHAPE OF THE STATES' STRUCTURES OF POLITICAL OPPORTUNITY

In Table VI-6, using both penultimate office and base office as the measures, I have classified the states according to the clarity of the shape of their opportunity structures. The table shows the characteristic careers of both governors and senators.[9] Category I includes the 11 states whose opportunity structures are most clearly formed: there are definite career lines leading to both the governorship and the Senate which include the use of manifest statewide elective and congressional offices at the top. In these states, when an opening occurs in either of the top elective positions, relatively few high officials can expect to fill them. Categories II and III include the 24 states which have a definite pattern of advancement for one or the other of the two top positions. Category IV includes the 13 states which have either no patterns of advancement or whose patterns are composed of the broadly defined office types encompassing many officeholders: the state legislature, administrative offices, and law enforcement offices.

I. The Clearly Marked Structures of Political Opportunities

In 11 states the routes for political advancement are clearly marked. Specific patterns of advancement lead to both the governorship and the Senate. These patterns, for the most part, combine the use of the principal base offices discussed in the preceding chapter with the

[9] Note that in Table VI-6 the first column, or base office, is constructed from the careers of all the major party candidates as discussed in Chapter V. The penultimate office columns are based on the careers of the successful candidates only.

TABLE VI-6

Types of Opportunity Structure in the States

	Base Offices (*Held by 40% or more of the candidates for governor and senator*)	*Penultimate Offices Leading to* *GOVERNOR* (*Held by 30% or more of the successful candidates. Offices in capitals are held by at least 40%*)	*SENATOR*
I. Highly Structured States			
A. Principal Patterns Lie within the State			
Iowa	Legislature	STATEWIDE	Governor
Rhode Island	Legislature	STATEWIDE	Governor + Law Enforcement
B. Bifurcated between State and Federal Patterns			
Vermont	Legislature + Administrative	STATEWIDE	Governor + CONGRESS
Connecticut	Legislature + Law Enforcement	STATEWIDE	Governor + Congress
Maine	Legislature + Local Elective	LEGISLATURE	Governor + Congress
Michigan	Administrative + Law Enforcement	Statewide	Congress
Massachusetts	Legislature	STATEWIDE	CONGRESS
New Hampshire	Legislature	Legislature	Congress
Illinois	Law Enforcement	Statewide + Law Enforcement	Congress
Louisiana	None	Statewide + Law Enforcement	Congress
Ohio	Administrative	Law Enforcement + Congress	GOVERNOR

TABLE VI-6—Continued

	Base Offices	*Penultimate Offices Leading to* *GOVERNOR*	*SENATOR*
II. States with Diffuse Paths to the Governorship but Structured for Senate			
A. Senate Pattern from the Governorship			
Georgia	Legislature	Legislature	GOVERNOR
Florida	Legislature + Law Enforcement	Legislature	Governor + Administrative
North Dakota	Legislature	Legislature + Law Enforcement	Governor
Colorado	None	Law Enforcement	Governor + Administrative
Maryland	None	Law Enforcement	Governor + Administrative
Virginia	Legislature	No Pattern	GOVERNOR + ADMINISTRATIVE
Wyoming	Legislature + Administrative	Administrative	GOVERNOR + Administrative
South Dakota	Legislature	No Pattern	Governor
Kansas	Legislature	No Pattern	GOVERNOR
North Carolina	Legislature + Law Enforcement	No Pattern	Governor
South Carolina	Legislature	No Pattern	GOVERNOR
B. Senate Pattern from Congress			
Mississippi	Legislature + Law Enforcement	Legislature	CONGRESS
Texas	Law Enforcement	Law Enforcement	Congress
West Virginia	Law Enforcement	Administrative	CONGRESS
Alabama	Legislature + Law Enforcement	Legislature	CONGRESS
Arizona	Law Enforcement	Legislature	CONGRESS + Law Enforcement
Nebraska	Legislature	No Pattern	CONGRESS
Tennessee	Legislature + Law Enforcement	No Pattern	CONGRESS + Law Enforcement
New York	Law Enforcement	No Pattern	Congress + Administrative
Oklahoma	None	No Pattern	CONGRESS
Washington	None	No Pattern	CONGRESS
Arkansas	Legislative + Law Enforcement	Law Enforcement	CONGRESS + Governor

TABLE VI-6—Continued

	Base Offices	*Penultimate Offices Leading to* *GOVERNOR*	*SENATOR*
III. States Diffuse for Senate, but Structured for Governors			
California	None	Statewide	No Pattern
Minnesota	Legislative	Statewide	No Pattern
IV. States Diffuse for Both Governor and Senator			
Delaware	None	No Pattern	No Pattern
Idaho	Legislative	Local Elective	No Pattern
Kentucky	Law Enforcement + Administrative	Law Enforcement	No Pattern
Nevada	Law Enforcement + Administrative	Law Enforcement	No Pattern
Montana	Law Enforcement + Administrative	LAW ENFORCEMENT	No Pattern
New Jersey	Legislative + Administrative	Legislative + Administrative	No Pattern
Utah	Legislative	LEGISLATIVE + ADMINISTRATIVE	No Pattern
Wisconsin	Law Enforcement	Law Enforcement	Legislative
Oregon	Legislative	Legislative	Legislative + Administrative
Indiana	None	NO OFFICE	Law Enforcement
Missouri	Law Enforcement	LAW ENFORCEMENT	Law Enforcement
Pennsylvania	None	Law Enforcement	Administrative
New Mexico	Legislative + Law Enforcement	ADMINISTRATIVE	ADMINISTRATIVE

manifest statewide elective and congressional offices described earlier in this chapter. Regionally, the states with highly developed structures of opportunity are mostly New England states. In addition, there are the midwestern states of Ohio, Michigan, Illinois, and Iowa. Note that I have included Maine and New Hampshire, although their principal penultimate office for the governorship is the office of state legislator. Neither of these states has minor statewide elective officials; they appear, instead, to groom legislative leaders for the governorship. They seem to have an abbreviated version of the pattern of advancement used by the other four New England states in this category.

Within the states in Category I there is a strong tendency to keep distinct the career lines leading to each of the top elective positions. While state office plays the most prominent role in the careers of the governors, congressional office is especially important in the careers of the senators. In only two of the states, Iowa and Rhode Island, does the pattern of advancement for both the governorship and the Senate consist entirely of state offices. Only in Ohio is congressional office important for the governorship, while statewide elective office, the office of governor, is most important for advancement to the Senate. In Vermont, Connecticut, and Maine, the manifest offices of governor and United States representative are equally important in leading directly to the Senate. In the five remaining states, congressional office is the most prominent penultimate office for the Senate.

II and III. The Modified Structures of Opportunity

These categories include the states whose routes for political advancement are obvious for one or the other of the top leadership posts. But note that in Category III, devised for those states with a distinct pattern of advancement for the office of governor but none for the office of senator, there are only two states, California and Minnesota. All the other states which have definite career patterns for the governorship also have definite patterns of advancement to the Senate, bearing out our earlier assertion that the higher the office, the more clearly defined the career lines.

In Category II we find the 22 states which have definite modes of advancement to the Senate but none for the governorship. These states divide evenly between those which use the manifest office of governor, mostly in combination with the base office of state legislator, and those which use the office of United States representative, often in combination with a law enforcement office as a base office. Regionally, these states are mostly in the south and west. Those states which most frequently promote governors to the Senate are in the southeast: Maryland, Virginia, the Carolinas, Georgia, and Florida. In addition, there are the sparsely populated states of the extreme midwest and the west, the Dakotas, Kansas, Wyoming, and Colorado. The states which conspicuously promote United States representatives to the Senate are border and southern states, West Virginia, Tennessee, Oklahoma, Texas, Arkansas, Alabama, and Mississippi.

IV. Weak Structures of Opportunity

The 13 states in this category have no clear pattern of advancement for either the governorship or the Senate. The extent to which political opportunities are diffuse varies. But even those states which use a particular office type to some degree use those office types which include large numbers of officials, the legislative, administrative, and law enforcement categories. Only in Delaware is there no semblance of order in political advancement; neither base nor manifest offices are used. Regionally, the states in this category are mid-Atlantic states, Pennsylvania, New Jersey, and Delaware, and western mountain states, Montana, Idaho, Oregon, Nevada, Utah, and New Mexico.

THE RELATION OF BASE OFFICES TO MANIFEST OFFICES

The relationship between base office and the general shape of a state's structure of opportunities can be seen in Table VI-6. There is a positive relation between the state legislative base and the ordering of opportunities; 7 of the 11 states in Category I have a legislative base. Also there is a close relationship between the state legislative base and a focus on state offices. Of the 11 states in Category II which use the office of governor for promotion to the Senate, 9 have such a base. Of the 27 states with a legislative base, 18 have some degree of structure, and for 17 it is focused on state office.

The use of the law enforcement office as a base office is most characteristic of those states which use congressional office as a manifest office or of the states which use no special penultimate office. In Category II, 8 of the 11 states which use the manifest office of United States representative for promotion to the Senate use the law enforcement office as a base office. In Category IV, 6 of the 13 states which have weak opportunity structures use the law enforcement office as a base office. Only 5 of the 19 states with a law enforcement base have structures focused on state office; the rest are either diffuse or focused on Congress.

These results strengthen the inferences we have made in the preceding chapter about political styles and the use of base offices. The legislative base office is associated with orderly promotion from office to office; it is also characteristic of a certain professionalism in a state's politics. In contrast, the use of the law enforcement office as a base office is compatible with volatile politics not only in theory; in practice it is associated with diffuse opportunities for higher office.

THE SHAPE OF THE STATES' OPPORTUNITY STRUCTURES AND THEIR SIZE

Thus far I have treated the size and shape of the states' opportunity structures as independent properties. Yet the frequency with which offices become available to new men must certainly have its effect upon the possibilities for an orderly system of political advancement. The most reasonable inference is that regular movement from office to office requires a moderate rate of turnover in personnel. Very high turnover in office generates high expectations; in the most extreme situations, revolution destroys all orderly procedures for filling political office. On the other hand, when turnover in elective office is greatly limited, when the most desirable positions in a state are, in effect, career posts, orderly progression in office is again difficult. When a Senate or a congressional seat becomes available after 20 years, men from many directions will undoubtedly contest with each other. Certainly no one will be likely to observe the propriety of waiting his turn. If, under such conditions, patterns of advancement do emerge, it will be because they work to the advantage of certain officeholders, e.g., the governor or county prosecutors. If, then, there are to be guidelines for political advancement, there must be some movement from office to office to focus ambitions, but neither too little nor too much.

Table VI-7 shows the extent to which the data support the above proposition. The table relates the states' general rate of opportunity, as defined in Chapter III and adjusted to population, to the shapes of the states' opportunity structures as laid out in Table VI-6. From Table VI-7 it is evident that the most highly developed opportunity structures are compatible with neither very high nor very low opportunity rates. Nine of the 11 states in Category I fall in the middle quartiles with respect to their opportunity rates. Half of the states whose opportunity rates are highest are in Category IV; that is, they are states with weak opportunity structures. The states whose opportunity rates are the lowest fall mostly in Category II; they have definite patterns of advancement for the Senate but none for the governorship. Again we have indicated the career stature of the office of senator. The size of the states' opportunity structures does, apparently, have some impact upon the order or form which political opportunity takes in the states.

TABLE VI-7

General Opportunity Level within a State and Degree of Structuring in Careers of Governors and Senators

	Number of States with the Following Structural Types:					
Opportunity Levels (by Quartiles)[a]	*Highly Structured*		*Diffuse for Governor, Structured for Senator around*		*Diffuse for Senator, Structured for Governor*	*Diffuse for Both Governor and Senator*
	A (State Focus)	*B (Dual Ladder)*	*A (Governor)*	*B (Congress)*		
Highest (I)		1	4	1		6
(II)	2	3	1	4		2
(III)		4	2	3	1	3
Lowest (IV)		1	4	3	1	2

[a] Based on Table III-4.

THE SHAPE OF THE STATES' OPPORTUNITY STRUCTURES AND PARTY COMPETITION

There is another factor whose impact upon the shape of the states' opportunity structures should be considered. In Chapter IV, I have discussed the relation of party competition to the size of the states' opportunity structures and concluded that a state's opportunity rate is more often than not independent of the level of party competition in the state. I have come to a similar conclusion about the relation of party competition to the shape of the states' opportunity structures. There is of course some relationship. If a state's party system is highly competitive for all offices, it is not likely that a party will be able to groom and promote candidates through succession in office.

Eleven of the 13 states in Category IV, those with diffuse structures, have a relatively high level of party competition for the governorship or the Senate or for both offices. In contrast, 18 of the 20 states which can be classified as one-party for both the offices of governor and senator fall in Categories I and II; that is, their opportunity structures are either clearly formed or moderately well defined.[10] But it is still

[10] The competitive level for governor and senator is that defined in Joseph A. Schlesinger, "The Structure of Competition for Office in the American States," *Behavioral Science,* V (1960), 197–210.

possible to combine a relatively high degree of party competition with patterns of advancement. It is true that the manifest offices for the Senate are used more in states where the manifest offices themselves are not very competitive. But the relationship is not striking. Thus, while a high level of competition for the office of governor makes it less likely that governors will be promoted regularly to the Senate, a low level of competition does not guarantee that the governorship will be the final stop on a well-marked route to the Senate.

AMBITION THEORY AND THE SHAPE OF THE STATES' OPPORTUNITY STRUCTURES

My rationale for seeking order in American political careers derives from the inference that, if progressive ambitions are to act as a control upon the behavior of politicians, there must be some focus or pattern in political careers. Thus far I have found no patterns of advancement so clearly outlined that one can predict with relative accuracy the next governor or senator of a state. But I did not expect to find such patterns, nor does the concept of progressive ambitions require anything approaching certainty in order that the concept be valid.

In what ways, then, do my findings about the shape of the states' opportunity structures clarify the concept of progressive ambitions? The finding that patterns of advancement become clearer as we go up the office hierarchy implies that progressive ambitions will also become more focused and more intense as we approach the top elective positions. State legislators, county prosecutors, and hundreds of other assorted local officials may have progressive ambitions, but my evidence suggests that such ambitions cannot be directed at specific offices on the basis of experience. The lesser statewide elective officials and some congressmen are much more likely to feel the specific tensions of realistic expectations for higher office; this is even more true of governors. Progressive ambitions as a control over the behavior of politicians must, therefore, operate from the top. Politicians in the higher offices are more likely to consider or respond to constituencies beyond their own. Congressmen, or at least those congressmen in a position to advance, are more likely to take a broad perspective on policy matters than state legislators. The reason is not simply that congressmen come from larger constituencies; it is also because their career lines are in better focus. Governors, more often than not, will have even clearer perspectives, not only because they cannot make a career of their office, but also because their opportunities for advancing have been more sharply outlined by the experiences of their predecessors. Progressive ambitions affect the behavior of lesser officials, then, mostly to the extent that those in higher office seek to realize their ambitions by influencing the behavior of those beneath them.

At the same time, the finding that federal and state office careers are often distinct modifies the interrelationship of offices which the concept of progressive ambitions implies and has an important bearing upon the operation of the federal system. While my data show that state and federal careers are sometimes intertwined, they also reveal distinct routes to the states' two major elective positions: the state-office route for governors, the federal-office route for senators. Moreover, the frequent use of different base offices for the two positions demonstrates that, even within the states, the officials drawn to federal careers are frequently different from those drawn to careers in state office. It is possible, then, for office ambitions to contribute to the states' political independence. But if the only opportunities for higher office are at the national level, if all state and local offices lead only to national office, the states' opportunity structures will merely reinforce federal domination of the states' political systems.

Nevertheless, the finding of most importance for the premises of ambition theory is that order is present in American political careers and that progressive ambitions can have their focus. From the standpoint of ambition theory, it is not particularly important to know why a certain type of order exists—why, for example, congressmen and governors move to the Senate. It is, however, important to ask why there *is* order, so that we may determine whether political careers are the product of independent planning or one of the unanticipated consequences of other plans and constitutions. In bureaucratic organizations such as the civil service, the industrial corporation, or the university, we take for granted career planning or patterns of advancement. But in the elective office structure of the American states such planning or patterning is by no means obvious. Although there are positions which are highly prized, no legal prescriptions bestow advantages upon the lesser officials in the office structure who may aspire to these positions. It is easy to assert, therefore, that any order which does emerge in the states' office structures must be the result of planning by external organizations, by parties or interest groups. But I have tried to demonstrate that the order and regularity in American political careers is more often than not the product of the states' office structures themselves and the rules for gaining office.

CONCLUSIONS

My examination of the shape of the states' opportunity structures has revealed certain characteristics about office careers in the United States which reinforce the assumptions of an ambition theory of politics. My findings about the use of manifest offices and the use of base offices in conjunction with manifest offices point to the conclusion that American political careers do not proceed chaotically. There are patterns of movement from office to office; as the office becomes more conspicuous, the patterns become clearer. The basic assumption of ambition theory is that politicians are guided by the possibilities for advancement; here we have evidence that the political systems of the American states provide guidelines for the politician's ambitions.

CHAPTER VII

Ambition, Opportunity, and the Party System: A Theoretical Discussion

MY ANALYSIS OF political opportunities in the United States thus far would undoubtedly fail to satisfy the ambitious politician. I have treated political parties only as a side issue and mostly to demonstrate that political opportunities are often independent of the party system. But the politician seeking elective office knows that all the major hurdles in running for office are related to his political party. Certainly to win the states' highest offices, he must win as a Republican or a Democrat. The politician, therefore, sees his chances for gaining office in partisan terms, and rightly so. His chances are circumscribed not only by the states' opportunity structures and the competitive relations of the two parties which I have already discussed; they are restricted also by the opportunity structures which determine his chance of gaining the nomination within his party. The party is, after all, the most conspicuous organization whose primary purpose is the control of the opportunities for public office. Any analysis of political opportunity and political ambition must give parties their proper due.

My concern, however, has been to define the proper role of political parties. I have found, for example, that the number and arrangement of political opportunities in the states is often independent of party competition. But I do not intend to write off the relevance of political parties to political opportunity with that conclusion. I mean only to point out that the parties do not affect opportunities primarily by their competitive relations. I would say that they do so primarily by their organization. It is, of course, true that party organization is influenced by the party's competitive status and by its expectations. But I would suggest that organization is also affected by the independent opportunity structures which I have described. That is why I have postponed my discussion of political opportunity and political parties until now. Now we cannot assume that opportunity is entirely a party matter, and we must look for interaction between the parties and the structure of opportunities in the nation and in the states.

In this chapter I am concerned with the theoretical problem of relating the states' opportunity structures, party competition, and the opportunity structure of each party. For a theory about party opportunities and organization, I have drawn on the concepts of ambition theory as well as party theory. Both ambition theory and party theory have as their object the explanation of the behavior of politicians in office and in their contests for office. Both theories seek to explain that behavior as the product of the tensions which parties or politicians undergo as they attempt to gain or to retain office. The difference is that party theory assumes only what I call static ambitions, the desire to govern, while the basic assumption of ambition theory is the existence of varied office drives and varied outlets. Only when we introduce potentially diverse goals do we introduce the possibility of conflict as well as cooperation among the politically ambitious of the same party. We introduce at the same time the problem of organization or the need to develop lines of cooperation among officeseekers.

My purpose now is to demonstrate theoretically how party organization emerges both from the concepts of party theory about the competitive relations of parties and the concepts of ambition theory which have led me to construct a hierarchy of ambitions and opportunities. In turn, I also want to demonstrate in theory that party organization can have its impact upon party competition. In effect, I would suggest that democratic electoral politics produces two types of tension which work upon each other: (a) the tensions of party relations or the party system, the strategic problems which each party faces in trying to win office in competition with other parties; (b) the tensions of party organization which drive members of a party together or apart, or which induce cohesion or factions within a party.

The tensions of party organization, I would maintain, arise not only from the immediate electoral needs of the candidates, which play a prominent part in party theory, and which I call static and discrete ambitions. Tensions arise also from the long-run goals of politicians, or what I call progressive ambitions. Organizational tensions, therefore, do not necessarily pull a party all in one direction, as simple party theory implies. To correct this implication I will first examine what party theory tells us about party behavior. Then I want to add to party theory what I consider the essential influences upon party behavior: first, in the immediate electoral situation which is the concern of party theory, the tensions generated within the parties by diverse electoral constituencies; secondly, the long-range tensions deriving from progressive ambitions and the states' structures of opportunity.

PARTY THEORY: SIMPLE (OR TEAM) THEORY

The central problem of party theory is the explanation of the behavior of political parties, in particular of the policies they choose, both in contesting for office and in carrying on the government. But the democratic governing party does not behave independently; it is only one participant in a competitive contest for the control of government. Its responses reflect, therefore, the strategy necessary to win that contest. Essential to that strategy is the number of competitors, since it determines whether or not the parties must form coalitions in order to govern. The critical distinction in democratic party systems is between two or more than two parties. Since only the two-party situation guarantees that a party can govern without recourse to coalitions, I shall restrict my attention to it.

Most political scientists have concluded that in a two-party system both parties tend to converge and take similar stands on public policy. Both Great Britain and the United States, the most prominent examples of the two-party system, appear to support this proposition. Despite their different ideological origins, the British Labor and Conservative parties, most observers agree, have moved toward each other on major issues of policy in much the same way as the Democrats and the Republicans in the United States. The parties distinguish themselves ideologically and by marginal positions aimed at showing up their differences.[1]

While there is little disagreement that in a two-party system the parties do tend to converge, observers have yet to agree upon the reasons. Leaving aside those analysts on the right as well as on the left who see agreement as a conspiracy by the established elite,[2] most observers seek their explanations in the electorate and in the nature of the two-party contest. Since only one party can win, each party must appeal to some of the same voters, whether they are independents or supporters of the opposite party. Since such voters are most likely to stand some-

[1] For a recent discussion, see Samuel H. Beer, *British Politics in the Collectivist Age* (New York: Knopf, 1965).

[2] For a right-wing interpretation of American politics as an elite conspiracy, see Phyllis Schlafly, *A Choice Not an Echo* (Alton, Illinois: Pere Marquette Press, 1964). On the left there is C. Wright Mills, *The Power Elite* (New York: Oxford University Press, 1956).

where between the policy positions of the two parties, both parties must use some of the same policy weapons.[3]

This argument, as developed by party theorists from Schattschneider to Downs, rests upon the assumption that with respect to policy the voters form a continuum which goes from left to right or from radical to conservative. If the voters divide along this continuum according to the normal curve, with many more at the center than at either extreme, the argument about convergence is reinforced. The normal distribution means that every policy shift by a party toward the center or mode gains it more votes than it would lose. Each party, therefore, quickly zeroes in on the policies favored by the voters located at the center. Thus Downs concludes that not only does the distribution of voters bring the parties together, but it is also the basic cause of the development of a two-party system.[4]

The difficulty is that empirical studies of American voting, while not refuting the convergence of the two parties, provide little support for the party theorist's view of the distribution of voters. According to these studies, very few voters respond to the parties or to issues in ideological or left-right terms; those voters who do are among the least likely to change their votes.[5] Indeed, Stokes has argued that a great many issues which have been important in American elections do not submit to a spatial distribution; they are not issues on which the voters have divided to any significant degree.[6] The great issues of the 1952 presidential campaign—corruption, Communist infiltration into government, and the Korean war—were not issues which allowed us to classify the voters in divergent groups. No significant group of voters could be found in favor of corruption, Communists, or war. Similarly, the issue of prosperity which cost the Republicans dearly from 1929 on was hardly one which divided the voters. The important issue of the 1960 campaign, the state of American prestige, was another issue which could not be expected to divide voters. Even in 1964, when the Republican presidential candidate, Barry Goldwater, sought to provide a clear ideological choice, much of his campaign consisted of appeals for law and order and against "moral decay," neither of which were issues on which there was significant disagreement among the electorate. In effect, neither the

[3] The argument is stated most explicitly in E. E. Schattschneider, *Party Government* (New York: Rinehart, 1942); and Anthony Downs, *An Economic Theory of Democracy* (New York: Harper, 1957).
[4] Downs, *Economic Theory,* pp. 117–32.
[5] A. Campbell, P. Converse, W. Miller, and D. Stokes, *The American Voter* (New York: Wiley, 1960), Chs. 9 and 10.
[6] D. Stokes, "Spatial Models of Party Competition," *American Political Science Review,* LVII (1963), 368–77.

parties in stating the issues nor the voters by their response act as though the voters constitute a left-right continuum.

Instead, both parties and voters act as though the parties are responsible for a general state of affairs. Each party, therefore, seeks to appear in a favorable light, to be perceived as the party most likely to bring peace, prosperity, high prestige, law and order, and moral uplift. From this point of view, the voters' experiences of government by each party would seem to have much more to do with their decisions than platforms and policy promises.

The evidence of the voting studies, then, does not invalidate and, indeed, clarifies the proposition that in a two-party system the parties converge as they compete. The studies suggest reasons other than those proposed by party theory for convergence and agreement. The conclusion that much of the issue content of electoral contests does not concern goals or even policies but the choice of that party which is the best instrument to achieve similar goals and policies reinforces the assumption of convergence. In fact, the distribution of voter attitudes need not even fit the normal curve; it can be bimodal or multimodal and therefore divisive in terms of the spatial model. The important consideration is that, if the dominant issues are conceived of and phrased in terms of consensus, then the parties will be under tension to seek consensus.

In effect, the voting studies confirm an older assumption about government. The assumption is that governing parties are restricted by the facts of political life, that the responsibilities of government or of having a good opportunity to govern restrict a party in its policy choices to that which is immediately possible. The two parties in their appeals to the voters and the voters in their response to the parties would seem to be already aware of what philosophers and theorists are coming to recognize as the normal process of political decision-making—except in revolutionary circumstances, decision-making is incremental and exploratory and not according to grand designs or theories.[7] The character of decision-making is more apparent in a two- than in a multiparty system because each party is, under the conditions of competition, a responsible party. Nevertheless it is probably true of all government.[8]

Aggregate and survey analyses of American voting have brought to our attention additional evidence of significance for party theory. Even in a two-party system, the parties do not necessarily compete on equal

[7] On incremental decision-making, see David Braybrooke and Charles Lindblom, *A Strategy of Decision* (New York: Free Press, 1963).
[8] For a discussion of the limitations on governmental decision-making, see T. C. Sorenson, *Decision-Making in the White House* (New York: Columbia University Press, 1963).

terms. As we have noted in Chapter IV, in many of the American states and their lesser constituencies, one party dominates. But even nationally this is true: the historical evidence shows that in presidential politics the Republicans were the dominant party at least from 1896 until 1932, when the Democrats entered upon a period of dominance which has not yet ended. The surveys made since 1948 reveal consistently that about two-thirds of the voters willing to identify with a party identify with the Democrats.

In terms of party theory, we can only conclude that the Democrats prior to 1932 and the Republicans thereafter failed to behave rationally by not providing the inducements to the voters necessary to maintain the competitive balance. We can account for some of the parties' irrational behavior or inertia in failing to make their appeals competitive in terms of the historical and group attachments of certain voters to the parties. I will argue subsequently that the different constituencies with which the parties must deal provide organizational tensions which also make it difficult for the parties to respond rationally in terms of party theory. At this point, however, the existence of one-party domination within the two-party framework leads me to reexamine the argument for convergence which party theory states.

When a party enters an electoral contest with a majority of the voters committed to its general position, its strategic problem is quite different from that of its opponent. There is no reason for the dominant party to seek convergence. For the dominant party all of the advantages lie in playing up the differences between party labels. It is the minority party which is under pressure to converge, to give the impression that the party distinction is irrelevant to the choice before the voters. Again the presidential campaign of 1964 is instructive. According to the thesis I have just stated, the Republicans in their choice of an ideological candidate behaved irrationally. As the minority party, they ought to have played down their differences from the Democrats, while the Democrats emphasized the differences.[9] But leaving aside the irrationality of their original choice, the Republicans as well as the Democrats behaved rationally in the 1964 campaign, in accord with this thesis. The Democrats in the campaign attacked as sweeping and different Goldwater's proposals to alter the social security system and to give field commanders control over nuclear weapons. In response Goldwater was thoroughly rational. He spent much of his time defending himself against the charge that his proposals would bring about drastic change. Indeed, on the issue of nuclear weapons he ended up arguing that the Democrats

[9] Aaron Wildavsky, "The Goldwater Phenomenon, Purists, Politicians, and the Two-Party System," *Review of Politics,* XXVII (1965), 386–413.

were already doing in secret what he was proposing, an argument which must have led some voters to wonder why he had raised the issue in the first place. The condition of dominance, then, within the two-party system introduces different kinds of tensions for the two parties. The tension to converge exists primarily for the minority party. The majority party seeks instead to differentiate itself from its competitor.

Here I should point out that Downs does argue that the two parties are always seeking to differentiate themselves in order to give the voters some reason for their choice.[10] But we need not assume, as Downs does, a spatial dimension to differentiation in the liberal-conservative sense. Differentiation may take the form of vague distinctions in style or of "valence" and need not involve disagreement over goals. Or it may involve broad ideological distinctions which are discounted by the electorate because in practice the two parties choose similar policies. In either case, we can say that the two parties in fact approach each other. The alternative is that the two parties may in fact diverge, with or without ideological differences. They may choose different concrete policies: one party may support the labor unions, while the other pushes for legislation restricting union activities; one may seek a progressive income tax, while the other rejects the tax entirely; in foreign policy, one may pursue coexistence, while the other favors a more aggressive course of action. Both convergence and divergence in policy, then, are possibilities, but not necessarily, as party theory would have it, in left-right terms. I would suggest that convergence or divergence depends on whether the two parties are responding to the same or to different voter attitudes, however defined.

PARTY THEORY AND COMPLEX CONSTITUENCIES

Party theory has directed our attention to the central problem of democratic politics: how does competition for office influence the parties' policies? The answer which party theory provides is true for a simple competitive two-party system: the two parties are drawn toward the middle ground of agreement and thereby to similar policies. But the statement of the problem and the answer given by party theory oversimplify greatly modern democratic party systems, particularly the system of the United States. Even if we set aside for the moment progressive ambitions for office, we still cannot define the American political contest as a zero-sum game in which one party governs and the other opposes. The offices are too varied: a party may win the Presidency while losing the Congress, win the governorship while losing the office of secretary of

[10] Downs, *Economic Theory*, Ch. 7.

state. In the United States, control of government means a different thing to the President, to the party chairman, to the governor, and to the mayor, even though they are all members of the same party. All these officials seek their offices independently. That is not to say that they are independent of each other, but some are more dependent than others. The needs of varied officeholders and the tensions which they undergo lead us to revise simple party theory.

Three conditions are essential to the development of a complex two-party system; without any one of these conditions we have the simple two-party model. (1) Some officials must be elected independently of others, that is to say, there must be a separate choice, even if it is by the same electors. This condition makes possible different electoral fates for candidates of the same party. In contrast, the Vice President is not elected independently, nor is the lieutenant governor in New York and Michigan. The electoral dependence of these candidates, who must share the same fate as the President and the governor, forces them to act as part of a team, thereby fulfilling the conditions of a simple competitive two-party system. (2) There must be independent nominations for each office; in other words, no single group or central party committee can select all of the nominees. Otherwise, all of the nominees would presumably be chosen in accord with the goals of the central group, again satisfying the conditions for the team of the simple two-party model. (3) The electorates for some offices must react differently from those for other offices. This is a crucial condition, for if the electorate for office A reacted in partisan terms exactly as the electorate for office B, then the two candidates of the same party would be drawn together by their prospective electoral fates, despite their independent nominations and elections. Once again we would have the simple party team.

Given the three conditions necessary for the complex two-party system, I would suggest that any model of that system and of party organization within the system should begin with a single office and the efforts aimed at attaining that office.[11] The cooperative efforts aimed at attaining a single office I call a party *nucleus;* the nucleus is the party team of simple party theory. The party nucleus exists only in those constituencies where the party has some expectations of victory. We know that a party's chances vary greatly, from situations where it is dominant and its offices are safe, to places where its chances are non-existent.

[11] I have discussed the organization of the party nucleus, the content of its activities, and their interrelationships more fully in the chapter entitled "Political Party Organization," in James G. March, ed., *Handbook of Organizations* (Chicago: Rand McNally, 1965).

Only where the party is dominant or competitive can we expect men to organize for the purposes of capturing office. One-party constituencies, therefore, will have but a single party nucleus; competitive constituencies will have two. This does not mean that there will be no active members of the minority party in constituencies where the minority's chances are hopeless. In such constituencies the minority may even run candidates for the offices which they have no expectation of winning. But the purpose of these activities will be to assist those party nuclei which do have a chance to win, and the payoffs to the minority activists will have to come from the competitive nuclei. The minority organization whose cause is hopeless I call a *mock nucleus.*

Electoral Relations in Complex Party Theory

While simple party theory derives from the simple assumption that parties behave in response to their need to amass enough votes to win elections, a complex party theory must assume complex relations among the electorates for different nuclear offices. These relations will vary in the following ways. When two offices are elected at different times, they have different electorates: the political conditions and the reactions of the voters are not identical; the turnout and, therefore, the composition of the electorate must also vary. But even in elections held at the same time, there are discrepancies in the electorates for different offices; there is usually a variation in the number of the voters for each office. Most important, however, for many offices, no matter what the electoral timing, the potential composition of the electorates cannot be the same; their electoral constituencies are different under law.

For the purpose of constructing a complex two-party model, I would suggest three types of electoral relationships among nuclear offices. (See Figure VII-1.) (1) The electoral constituencies of the offices may be *congruent,* that is, the offices have the same potential electorate. The constituencies of governors, senators, and minor statewide elective officials normally have this relationship, as do the constituencies of county officials. (2) The constituencies of nuclear offices may be *disjoint,* that is, their electorates are entirely different. In Figure VII-1, (X, Y), (X, Z), and (Y, Z) are the examples. The governor of one state has none of the same voters as the governor or any other official of another state. Within a state, congressional districts are disjoint, as are most state legislative districts, with the exception of multimember districts. In the American political system, the constituencies of most nuclear offices are disjoint. (3) Finally, the constituencies of some nuclear offices are *enclaved,* that is, one constituency is part of another. In

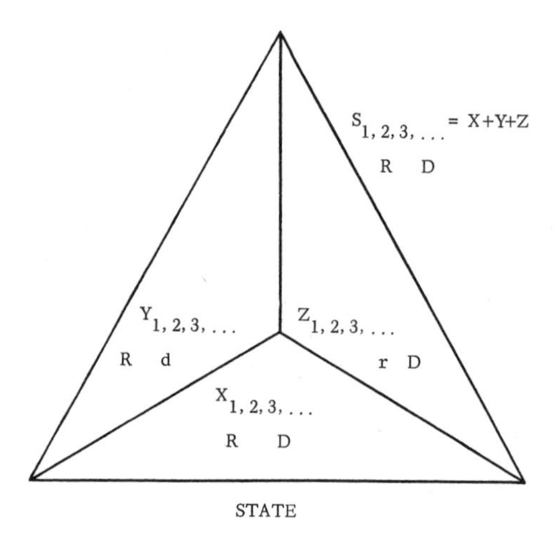

Key to Symbols

S, X, Y, Z : Constituencies
1, 2, 3, . . . : Offices
R: Republican nucleus
D: Democratic nucleus
r: Republican mock nucleus
d: Democratic mock nucleus

Explanation

Competitive Relations:
S and X: competitive
Y: Republican dominant
Z: Democratic dominant

Constituency Relationships:
A. Congruent
$(S_1, S_2, S_3, \ldots S_n)$
$(X_1, X_2, X_3, \ldots X_n)$
$(Y_1, Y_2, Y_3, \ldots Y_n)$
$(Z_1, Z_2, Z_3, \ldots Z_n)$
B. Disjoint
(X, Y) (X, Z) (Y, Z)
C. Enclaved
(S, X) (S, Y) (S, Z)

FIGURE VII-1
Model of a State Political System

Figure VII-1 (S,X), (S,Y), and (S,Z) are the examples. Within a state all constituencies which do not encompass the state are enclaves of those which do; every nuclear office in the country is an enclave of the presidential constituency.

The type of relationship which the constituency of one nuclear office has to another will, of course, be relevant to party behavior only if the behavior of the voters in each constituency differs. If each party has precisely the same chance of winning in every constituency, then all party nuclei will draw together. But in the three types of constituency relationships which I have described, the likelihood that voters will react differently is strong. Of the three, electoral results will probably be most similar in congruent constituencies, and consequently the behavior of the candidates within each party most alike. Nevertheless, I have already pointed out that even for offices with congruent electorates the results in the states are often diverse. The most diverse electoral behavior can be expected in disjoint constituencies; the "safe" states which belong to each party and, within the states, the safe legislative districts are one consequence of disjoint constituencies. Enclaved constituencies will have the most complex electoral relations. It is not only possible but likely that the constituencies of many nuclear offices, competitive and non-competitive, will be within a broader constituency which may be competitive or dominated by one party. Since I am most concerned with amplifying party theory through the application of ambition theory to party behavior, and since progressive ambitions are most likely to involve movement from an enclave to the larger constituency, I will be concerned primarily with the consequences of enclaved relationships for party theory.

In my analysis of enclaved constituencies I shall ignore one possibility for the minority party, that its leaders ally themselves with the majority party for division of political spoils. This has occurred in the United States in various places and times. For example, Fenton points to the existence of a Bi-Partisan Combine which exerted influence in eastern Kentucky during the 1920's.[12] In Illinois, the multimember legislative district and cumulative voting, combined with strong party organization, have invited such connivance between the Chicago Democratic machine and the minority Republicans in the city. But note that such agreements become intolerable within a competitive nucleus. In the elections of 1964, when the state's failure to reapportion forced an election at large for the Illinois legislature, the Republican gubernatorial candidate, Charles Percy, not only felt it necessary but was able to purge the Chicago Republicans from the party list. In effect, a statewide election produced a single nucleus, making the local arrangements untenable or at least subject to purge.[13]

Enclaved Constituencies and the Electoral Tensions upon the Parties

Since party theory depends upon the distribution of voter attitudes, let us now examine the effect of enclaved constituencies upon the parties' problem of winning office. To observe the problem, I have constructed a simple model of enclaved constituencies: a state (S), which constitutes

[12] John Fenton, *Politics in the Border States* (New Orleans: Hauser, 1957), pp. 47–57.
[13] *The New York Times,* May 31, 1964.

the greater electorate, choosing the governor, and three enclaves (X,Y,Z) which choose state legislators (Figure VII-1). In each of the three enclaves relations between the two parties differ: X is highly competitive; Y is dominated by the Republicans; and Z is dominated by the Democrats. The state at large is also competitive. Accepting my assumptions about nuclear organizations, we should expect to find active nuclei of both parties in the state and in constituency X (SR,SD,XR,XD), an active Republican nucleus in constituency Y (YR), and an active Democratic nucleus in constituency Z (ZD). Mock nuclei may also exist, for the Democrats in their weak constituency (Yd) and for the Republicans in theirs (Zr). I have assumed that the enclaves are equal in size, each representing, therefore, a third of the state's potential electorate.

What does the complex distribution of party strength in our model imply about the tensions arising from party competition? Here it is important to note that there are no implications, unless they arise from organizational transfers or the impact of organizational activity in one nucleus on the chances of another. From the standpoint of the state nucleus, in a competitive situation it is a matter of indifference how the votes are distributed spatially, as long as each vote has the same value. True, both parties have inverse electoral bases, the Republicans' votes coming from districts Y, X, and Z in that order, while the Democratic votes are in Z, X, and Y. But the marginal votes are crucial, regardless of their location. In effect, then, if we ignore organizational tensions in our model, the competitive nuclei (SR, SD, and XD, XR) will move toward convergence or try to play up the similarities of their positions, while the dominant nuclei (YR and ZD) will seek divergence or the maximum distinction.

The distribution of party strength in the various constituencies takes on significance only if we make two assumptions: (a) organizational efforts have some effect on voting results, and (b) there is some transfer of effect from one nuclear organization to another. While the literature of politics is full of implications about both assumptions, there is very little hard evidence about the effects of organizational activity on elections.[14] By activity I mean all of those things which go into a party

[14] The best systematic studies of the impact of organizational activity locally on voting are those by P. Cutright and P. H. Rossi, "Grass Roots Politicians and the Vote," *American Sociological Review*, XXIII (1958), 171–79; and D. Katz and S. J. Eldersveld, "The Impact of Local Party Activity upon the Electorate," *Public Opinion Quarterly*, XXV (1961), 1–24. On the transfer effect of activity in one nucleus to another, there is the literature on "coattails." See, for example, C. Press, "Voting Statistics and Presidential Coattails," *American Political Science Review*, LII (1958), 1041–50.

organization, from working in precincts and spending money to nominating candidates and presenting the party's stand on issues. But if such activities do affect votes and if they are transferable from one nucleus to another, whether purposefully or not, they introduce organizational tensions which may or may not reinforce the tendencies to converge or diverge produced by the state of party competition.

The organizational tensions arise from the fact that the four nuclei of each party in our model have different needs and resources. In the immediate electoral situation, the nuclei in the competitive constituencies (SR and SD, XR and XD) will seek all the votes they can. Presumably they will make payoffs in terms of policy or other resources in order to obtain their majorities. On the other hand, the dominant nuclei (YR and ZD), are assured of election and need make no concessions. Both Yd and Zr, having no hopes of winning the election, exist, if at all, on the hope of getting something from those nuclei which can win. Their needs, therefore, are entirely dependent upon those of the other nuclei and for that reason they can exert no independent pressures. As enclaves, however, whatever contributions they make are more likely to be to the state nucleus than to those nuclei with which they have a disjoint relationship.

Organizational needs, however, are not necessarily the same as organizational resources. The state nuclei will obtain their votes primarily from the areas of dominance (YR and ZD), and it is likely that much of the other materiel of party organization, workers, money, and potential candidates, will also come from the areas of disproportionate strength. Of course the fact that resources exist does not necessarily mean that they will be organized and used. While the evidence is not entirely clear,[15] the reasonable inference is that effective organization emerges under competitive conditions and tends to disappear under one-party conditions. Therefore, while the dominant nuclei will have more resources in our model, the competitive nuclei are most likely to have the effective organizations.

Let us now examine the composite picture of tensions within each party. First there are those tensions which arise from the need to cooperate, from the existence of competition. The state nuclei, which are com-

[15] The evidence about the relationship between competition and organization is unclear, I suspect, because of the failure of students to examine the total context. V. O. Key, Jr., in both his *Southern Politics* and *American State Politics,* provides clear evidence that party organization develops with active interparty competition. On the other hand, in a study of Pennsylvania legislative districts Frank Sorauf found little relationship; see *Party and Representation* (New York: Atherton, 1963).

petitive and need all the help they can get, can expect cooperation from the enclaved nuclei in the following rank order:

	Republicans	Democrats
1	X	X
2	Z	Y
3	Y	Z

On the other hand organizational resources including votes and other materiel will come to the state nuclei from the enclaves in the following order:

	Republicans	Democrats
1	Y	Z
2	X	X
3	Z	Y

Note the conflicting pressures in these two arrangements. The nuclei in the state and in the competitive (X) constituency are under pressure to converge. The cooperative tensions above, then, tend to push the two parties together in terms of policy. The distribution of resources, however, plays up the divergent tensions found in the Y and Z constituencies.

Lacking any precise measure of the relative value of organizational activity in elections, it appears reasonable to conclude that in our model state the organizational pressures of the enclaved nuclei upon the larger state nucleus of each party will tend to cancel each other. The nuclei in constituency X push the state nuclei toward convergence, while the nuclei in constituencies Y and Z bring pressure to diverge. The nuclei in X are likely to be active and to cooperate with the state nuclei. On the other hand, the nuclei in Y and Z control a greater share of the contribution in votes and are likely to have command of more of the resources of organization. The mock nuclei exert no independent influence; they exist as extensions of the state nuclear organizations. Since the organizational pressures exerted by the enclaved nuclei cancel each other, the needs of the state nuclei will tend to decide their actions. Since the state nuclei are competitive, the two parties will tend to converge, as they would in simple party theory.

There is little reason to assume, however, that most states fit the simple model. We have already seen in Chapter IV that relatively few states can be called competitive. Certainly within the states, electoral districts tend to favor one or the other party. As the one-party districts (Y's and Z's) begin to outnumber the competitive districts (X's), the electoral substructure of the state introduces divergent tensions in party organization.

AN EMPIRICAL ILLUSTRATION: THE STATES OF INDIANA AND MICHIGAN

In reality, under the cover of a competitive statewide situation, it is possible for relations between the two parties to vary considerably in the subconstituencies. Two competitive states which illustrate this proposition are the neighboring midwestern states of Indiana and Michigan. Both states can be described as competitive since the 1930's. In the gubernatorial elections of 1960 the Democratic candidates in each state won by slim margins, less than 1 per cent of the vote. But if we look beyond the statewide contests at the types of constituencies from which the parties drew their votes, we find marked differences between the two states. In Indiana most of the subconstituencies were, like the state, competitive. (See Figure VII-2.) In the gubernatorial election of 1960 well over half the votes of both parties in Indiana came from counties in the middle range, those where neither party received more than 55 per cent of the vote. In contrast, both parties in Michigan relied little upon competitive counties. The curve for both Michigan parties in the 1960 gubernatorial election goes down in the middle and up at the extremes. In Michigan, locally, little fighting took place on middle

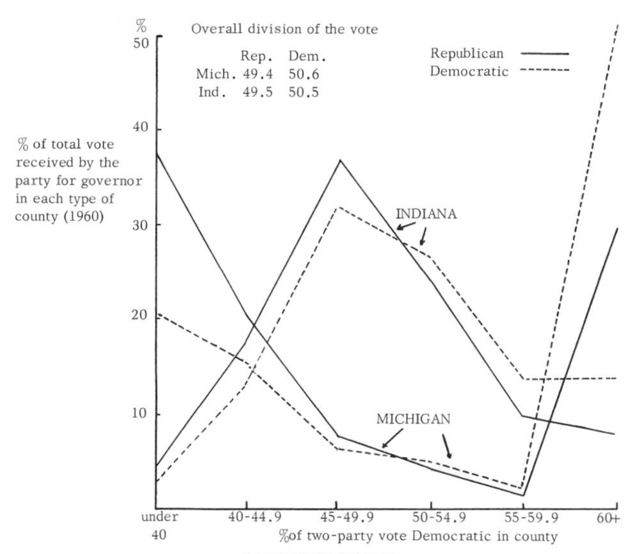

FIGURE VII-2
The Substructure of Politics in Two Competitive States

ground. Most of the subconstituencies were in the camp of one party or the other.

The theoretical significance of the different patterns of competition in the two states concerns the parties' organizational substructures. The even distribution of the two-party vote throughout Indiana and the uneven distribution in Michigan tell us nothing directly about the postures of the two parties. It is very likely that the situation in Michigan indicates cleavages among the voters which do not exist in Indiana, but the geographical dispersion of voters is not in itself an adequate index of their attitudes. It is certainly possible that the attitudes of Indiana Republican voters are as far removed from those of the Democrats as is the case in Michigan, even though in Indiana voters of both parties tend to live in the same counties.

But the differences in the distribution of the vote do determine the types of constituencies in each state according to our model. Indiana consists mostly of the X constituencies of our model. In Michigan the two parties must deal with districts similar to Y and Z. In Indiana, then, each party is most likely to consist of active nuclei drawn toward the nuclei of the other party by their need to appeal to the same voters. In turn the interdependence between the local nuclei and the state nucleus within each party is maximized. In Michigan the reverse is likely to be true. Lacking competition for most offices except those elected by the state at large, the two parties are likely to be made up of local nuclei under no pressure to draw closer to their opponents locally nor to aid their own statewide nuclei. The influence of the local nuclei within each party, therefore, is to drive the parties apart, even while the statewide nuclei are drawn together by competition.

The above analysis of the distribution of party votes in Michigan and Indiana uses the county as the unit. But the differences revealed are relevant for all party nuclei. Congressional districts as well as state legislative districts must be carved from a given geographical distribution of party strength. Quite apart from the question of apportionment according to population, the distribution of party votes affects the party system within each district. In the congressional elections of 1960 Michigan and Indiana differed sharply also in the number of the congressional districts which were competitive (see Table VII-1). Gerrymandering and malapportionment can account for these differences between the two states. But the fact remains, as the distribution of electoral strength in Figure VII-2 reveals, that gerrymandering was far more difficult to accomplish in Indiana than in Michigan; in Michigan gerrymandering was often automatic, because of the distribution of partisan voters.

TABLE VII-1
1960 Elections for Congress in Michigan and Indiana

	Proportion of District Elections in the State Won by the Following Margins of the Two-Party Vote:			
	50–54.9%	*55–59.9%*	*60% and over*	*Number of Districts*
Indiana	54.5%	27.3%	18.2%	11
Michigan	11.1	27.8	61.1	18

I have used the example of Indiana and Michigan to demonstrate the effect of constituency relationships upon internal party organization and the relations between the two parties. But in so doing I have considered only the immediate electoral needs of the various nuclei and the kinds of tensions these needs produce. There are, however, other pressures which influence parties. Ideology may affect party behavior, although I suspect not to the extent that many observers would like to believe. Moreover, political parties serve more than immediate political ends. They make social and economic contacts which may well generate tensions independent of the pressures provided by the distribution of party strength which I have discussed. But even if we retain as our basic assumption the view that parties are primarily office-seeking instruments, more than immediate electoral interests are involved. For another major influence upon party organization and party systems, I shall now turn to ambition theory.

AMBITION THEORY: THE SECOND ORDER OF ORGANIZATIONAL TENSIONS

Ambition theory allows me to introduce additional organizational tensions. Thus far I have discussed only the organizational tensions generated within the immediate electoral situation by the immediate needs of each nuclear organization in quest of its own office. In terms of ambition theory, then, I have accounted for the impact of only two types of office ambition upon party organization, discrete ambitions and static ambitions. It remains for me to examine the tensions produced by progressive ambitions or the hopes for future office.

Progressive ambitions can reach out in various directions, each of which may bring a different kind of pressure to bear upon policy decisions. Very important to the behavior of party nuclei are the ambitions for offices only indirectly in the control of the electorate and obtained by agreements and coalitions among officeholders. I shall call the pressures exerted by such ambitions the second order of organizational tensions.

Such ambitions are mostly characteristic of legislators. The parties themselves organize the legislatures and distribute the positions of legislative leadership and influence. The most important positions go to the majority party, including the offices of speaker, majority leader, and usually of committee chairmen. All legislators of the majority party, therefore, including those from safe districts, are under tension deriving from the hope for higher office within the legislature to insure the party's legislative majority. In other words, although safe nuclear organizations are under no immediate electoral pressure to aid their colleagues in competitive constituencies, as we have already noted, the desire for legislative influence and positions of leadership encourages aid. This second order of organizational tensions occurs between popular elections, in the governmental phase of party behavior.

The pressures to cooperate, generated by ambition for positions of legislative leadership, depend, of course, on the existence of meaningful competition between the two parties for control of the legislature. If one party has safe majorities in the legislature, its leaders or senior members will be less concerned about the fate of party members in competitive districts. By the same token the minority party's leaders will be less concerned with its marginal needs and more concerned with internal wants. Dominated by the members from safe seats, the minority leaders will tend to keep those positions of importance within their control for themselves.

Here it is important to point out that progressive ambitions of the second order, i.e., for positions of legislative leadership and influence, may produce a tension in the constituency party counter to that we might expect from simple party theory. If the party organizations in the legislature are non-competitive and therefore divisive, the parties' candidates, even in competitive constituencies, will be under divergent tensions. For this reason, attempts to test the adequacy of party theory by examining the behavior of legislators from competitive constituencies are inadequate.[16] The goal of each party is not solely the winning of an

[16] There is by now a substantial literature on the relationships between constituencies and legislative voting. An early discussion of the problem in relation to party theory is Samuel Huntington, "A Revised Theory of American Party Politics," *American Political Science Review,* XLIV (1950), 669–77. See also Duncan MacRae, "The Relation between Roll-Call Types and Constituencies in the Massachusetts House of Representatives," *American Political Science Review,* XLVI (1952), 1046–55; Lewis A. Froman, "Inter-Party Constituency Differences and Congressional Behavior," *American Political Science Review,* LVII (1963), 57–61; W. J. Keefe and M. Ogul, *The American Legislative Process* (Englewood Cliffs, N.J.: Prentice-Hall, 1964), pp. 284–92; and T. A. Flinn, "Party Responsibility in the States: Some Causal Factors," *American Political Science Review,* LVIII (1964), 60–71.

election in a particular constituency; it encompasses progressive ambitions as well.

In the United States the common legislative practice of constructing constituencies to protect parties and legislators from the winds of electoral change builds into the system districts reflecting forces quite different from statewide or national constituencies. Gerrymandering and malapportionment, particularly the kind which assembles a high proportion of voters attached to one party in a single district, intensifies the divisive tensions upon party nuclei. Legislators of both parties may purposefully cooperate to create such districts, preferring safe constituencies to the more even distribution of party votes with its greater potential for improving party strength in the legislature.[17] Such safe constituencies reduce the tensions generated by competition for the two parties to converge, and, through the internal structure of influence in the legislative groups, this has its impact upon competitive constituencies as well.

THE THIRD ORDER OF ORGANIZATIONAL TENSIONS: PROGRESSIVE AMBITIONS FOR ELECTIVE OFFICES

In addition to the organizational tensions generated by progressive ambitions for party-controlled offices, the progressive ambitions for elective offices, whose course we have been charting, produce significant tensions within political parties. These ambitions also exert long-run pressures upon nuclei of the same party to draw together. Electorally, the normal lines of advancement are, first, from the enclaved constituency to the larger political arena, as when a state legislator becomes governor or a representative, senator, or, secondly, from a lesser office to a higher office whose constituencies are congruent, as when a governor becomes senator. The smaller or lesser nuclear organization, therefore, is under tension to behave in a manner also befitting the larger nucleus. If the larger nuclear organization is competitive and drawn toward the opposition, men in the enclaved nuclei with ambitions for higher nuclear office will also tend to converge upon the opposite party.

The moderating effect or the pressure for convergence exerted by progressive elective ambitions depends, then, upon the competitive conditions which more often characterize the larger constituencies than their enclaves. But this contrast is not inevitable. It is certainly more

[17] On the legislators' perception of the districting process as a private matter, see G. Steiner and S. Gove, *Legislative Politics in Illinois* (Urbana: University of Illinois Press, 1960), Ch. 4.

likely that the broader constituencies encompassing more varied areas and groups will have livelier competition between the two parties than the smaller constituencies which are likely to be more homogeneous. But it is possible, as in Texas and Virginia, for states dominated at the state level by one party to develop competition in congressional districts. Similarly, there are a number of states which are more competitive than the national electorate which is committed in a general way by a sizeable majority to the Democratic party.

The majority's commitment to the Democratic party nationally puts the presidential nucleus of each party under different tensions. For the Democrats, the advantage lies in pointing up the differences between their party and the Republicans. Consequently, in terms of policy the Democratic party is drawn toward the one-party constituencies from which its national majority emerges. Republicans with presidential ambitions, on the other hand, tend to pull their party toward the Democrats and away from the constituencies where the Republican party is dominant and to play down policy differences.

The two parties, therefore, are subject to very different organizational stresses. The presidential nucleus of the Democratic party is most responsive to the goals of its one-party urban areas, while the Republican presidential nucleus is drawn toward the party nuclei in competitive constituencies. Of the two, the tensions within the Republican party present the more difficult organizational problem. The officeholders, possessed of all of the organizational advantages which come from officeholding, are pitted against those who, more often than not, have only the hope of office working for them. The Republican party faces a serious dilemma: the presidential nucleus must either make itself attractive to the national electorate and therefore less appealing to areas of Republican organizational strength or appeal to these areas at the cost of national electoral strength. The Democratic problem of national organization is simpler, for the goals of the presidential nucleus coincide with those of its nuclei most likely to be in office as well.

Within the Democratic party organizational problems arise mostly from the party's dominance of the south. The groups and the appeals which have made the Democratic party the dominant national party since 1932 are not the same as those which have made the party dominant in the southern states. The Democratic presidential nucleus, therefore, reflects mostly the characteristics of its northern urban one-party constituencies, as the Democratic candidates for President and their appeals demonstrate. On the other hand, the southern faction has been able to exert organizational pressures of the second order through congressional positions of power. But, even here, the increasing ability of northern Democratic congressmen to build up seniority is likely to reduce the south's dominance of congressional Democratic organization. The Democratic party, then, must rely for its organization on two types of one-party constituencies, one of which is far more compatible with progressive ambitions for the Presidency. As a result, the presidential nucleus is most likely to move toward the needs of the northern urban constituencies at the expense of the southern constituencies. The Republican party does not face this particular problem of organization; the constituencies where it is dominant are much the same.

ORGANIZATIONAL TENSIONS AND THE PARTIES' STRUCTURES OF OPPORTUNITY

The careers of the candidates of the two parties for national office reflect the different organizational tensions which exist within each party. The Democratic candidates emerge notably from the party's northern areas of strength, New York, Chicago, Boston, rather than from the southern areas of dominance. In contrast, the Republican candidates come mostly not from areas where the party is dominant but from areas where the situation is competitive. The emergence of the Senate as the principal repository of Democratic presidential hopefuls reflects the Democratic dominance of that body. In contrast, most of the Republican potential candidates are either in state houses or outside the ranks of officeholders.[18]

I suggest, therefore, the following proposition: the more similar the career lines of the candidates of the two parties, the greater the pressure for the parties to converge on policy. In Chapters V and VI I looked for the typical careers of governors and senators. Now, by examining these careers in party terms, I can measure and compare the structure of opportunity within each party. If the Republican candidates for the offices of governor and senator enter politics and come to the nomination through much the same routes as the Democratic candidates, then we can conclude that the tensions arising from progressive ambitions are much the same in each party. If, for example, the office of state legislator is the base office for the leaders of both parties, then the legislative members of each party are under pressure from the larger nuclei toward whose offices legislative ambitions are directed. If, on the other hand, the leaders of one party advance through law enforce-

[18] This is not to say that there are no potential presidential candidates for the Republican party in Congress, but rather that those who do emerge there are likely to represent those areas and attitudes where the Republican party is dominant and, therefore, least competitive with the Democrats.

ment offices and the leaders of the other party advance through the state legislature, the tensions to converge are reduced and the tensions generated by progressive ambitions work for the divergence of the two parties.

The similarities and differences between the opportunity structures of the two parties do reflect to a large degree the disposition of party strength for the nuclear offices of a state. If the state as a whole is not competitive, we cannot expect the parties' nominations to be equally attractive, nor can we expect each party to control the same or similar congruent or enclaved nuclear offices. The minority party, then, cannot have lieutenant governors or attorneys general seeking advancement; even if it controls some state legislative and congressional districts, the officeholders of these districts will not find a hopeless nomination for senator or governor especially desirable.

At the same time, competitive statewide constituencies do not guarantee the same opportunity structures for both parties. As we have seen, the electoral substructures of competitive states can be very different. These differences make it possible for the two parties to have divergent opportunity structures in competitive states. Where the opportunity structures of the two parties are different, the tensions deriving from progressive ambitions will reinforce the pressures for divergence which, as we have already deduced, will come from static or immediate electoral ambitions.

I have described the three orders of organizational tensions in different time settings—the immediate electoral situation, the governmental phase between elections, and the projection of future elections. But all three types of tension exist at a single point in time. A party's organization for a single election, involving agreements among nuclear organizations and the transfer of organizational materiel, is the product of all these pressures. In turn, the policy stands of the two parties in elections, state or national, and their convergence or divergence on policy are affected by the organizational tensions which I have described.

When we consider, then, whether the parties are likely to come together or pull apart in a particular party system, we must take into account the full implication of political ambitions and the kinds of tensions which they generate. If one party controls a nuclear office such as the Presidency or a state governorship, we expect the tensions of the first order to cause the dominant party to diverge, to seek to distinguish itself from the opposition. If, on the other hand, the office is competitive, we expect both parties to converge for electoral reasons. At the same time, the pressure to converge in a competitive situation may be offset by the existence within the larger constituency of one-party enclaves. In other words, before we can predict whether or not the two parties will converge, we must consider the competitive status of the parties not only in the larger constituency but in each of the lesser or enclaved constituencies. Competitive nuclear organizations will not necessarily draw the two parties together if these organizations are dependent for their support on nuclei in one-party constituencies. Moreover, the pressure to converge may or may not be reinforced by the parties' opportunity structures or by organizational tensions of the second and third order. When the career opportunities for the ambitious in each party differ, the pressure for the two parties to converge or to agree on policy is reduced.

CONCLUSIONS

In this chapter I have examined party theory in the light of a theory of ambitions and argued that together they provide a more realistic view of the two-party system and its relation to political opportunity. While I have only touched on the problem of party organization, I have pointed out that party organization will be affected by the pressures which the immediate and the long-run ambitions of politicans produce. I have also demonstrated that long-run ambitions as well as the complex relations of electoral constituencies make possible a variety of results within a two-party system, a variety which simple party theory does not lead us to expect. In the next chapter I shall consider the implications of party theory as amplified by ambition theory for political opportunity in the states.

CHAPTER VIII

Opportunity and the States' Party Systems: The Organization of State Parties

IN THE PREVIOUS CHAPTER I sought to demonstrate in theory that the states' structures of opportunity, their party systems or the competitive relationships of the two parties, and the parties' internal organizations were interdependent. In other words, in the American states political parties organize to satisfy men's ambitions for office according to political opportunities which are clearly defined. In part the opportunities for office are determined by the turnover in office and the prominence of certain offices for advancement within the states; in part political opportunities are determined by the nature of party competition in each constituency. Together the states' opportunity structures and the states' party systems define the potential and actual lines of office advancement for each party or the basis for active party organization. In turn, active party organization generates tensions which affect the parties' competitive relations and which cause the parties to converge or pull away on policy. In this chapter I am concerned with identifying the opportunity structures of American state parties. I am also concerned with the implications of state party organization for the states' party systems.

THE OPPORTUNITY STRUCTURES OF AMERICAN STATE PARTIES

In Chapter IV I have concluded that we can identify in the American states a structure of political opportunity which is independent of the party system or the competitive relations of the two parties. I have pointed out, for example, that the opportunities for the offices of governor and lieutenant governor are high regardless of the rate of party competition, while the opportunities for the offices of senator, congressman, or secretary of state are generally low. But each state's parties are also entities within which ambitious politicians seek advancement; only after obtaining the nomination of one or the other major party are significant offices obtained. The distribution of party nominations, therefore, the turnover of nominations within each party and the kinds of experience leading to these nominations, allow us to define the opportunity structures of state parties in much the same way we have defined the opportunity structures of the states. As with the states, we are also interested in the extent to which opportunities within the parties are dependent upon the parties' competitive standings and the extent to which they are determined by internal rules of organization.

My analysis of the structure of opportunities within American state parties is based on the careers of the Republican and Democratic nominees for the offices of governor from 1900 through 1958 and for senator in the period 1914–1958. My findings about the parties' approach to nominations for office, therefore, are limited. They can give us soundings on the role of officeseeking in party organization in the American states, but only further empirical research which includes numerous other offices can give us a complete picture of the relation between public office and party.

THE SIZE OF THE OPPORTUNITY STRUCTURES OF THE STATES' PARTIES

In the aggregate, the turnover rates for gubernatorial and senatorial nominations within the states' parties are noticeably high. (See Table VIII-1.) In more than half the elections under consideration

TABLE VIII-1
Turnover Rates for Party Nominations[a]
(1914–1958)

	Republican	*Democratic*
Governor		
(32 states)[b]	65.9	69.2
Senator		
(36 non-southern states)	55.3	64.6

[a] The percentage of elections in which the party has nominated a candidate different from the one nominated in the preceding election. For this purpose the two senatorial lines are kept distinct.
[b] Non-southern states permitting the reelection of incumbents.

the candidates for both offices differ from their predecessors. Turnover among Democratic candidates is slightly higher than turnover among

TABLE VIII-2

Opportunity Rates[a] for Nominations for Governor and Senator Combined (12-Year Generation)

State	*Republican*	*Democratic*	*Party Difference (R−D)*	*Party with Majority of Victories (1914–1958) for Governor*	*Senator*
North Dakota	4.52	8.68	−4.16	R	R
Iowa	4.28	8.06	−3.78	R	R
New Hampshire	5.84	8.74	−2.90	R	R
Vermont	6.08	8.58	−2.50	R	R
Maine	5.30	7.76	−2.46	R	R
Nebraska	5.48	7.66	−2.18	R	R
Idaho	3.05	5.05	−2.00	R	R
Minnesota	6.02	7.82	−1.80	R	D[b]
Kansas	5.42	6.18	−1.76	R	R
Wisconsin	5.58	7.28	−1.70	R	R
South Dakota	5.54	7.12	−1.58	R	R
Michigan	5.50	6.84	−1.34	R	R
Pennsylvania	5.00	6.32	−1.32	R	R
Delaware	4.07	5.13	−1.06	R	R
Washington	3.92	4.95	−1.03	R	D
New Jersey	6.16	7.04	−0.88	D	R
Indiana	4.61	5.45	−0.84	R	R
California	4.61	5.33	−0.72	R	R
Oregon	4.61	5.28	−0.67	R	R
Nevada	3.22	3.86	−0.64	D	D
Illinois	4.52	5.06	−0.54	R	R
Massachusetts	5.84	6.26	−0.42	R	R
West Virginia	4.61	4.88	−0.27	D	D
Connecticut	3.98	3.96	0.02	R	R
Utah	3.95	3.92	0.03	D	D
Kentucky	5.46	5.40	0.06	D	D
Ohio	5.54	5.30	0.24	D	R
Missouri	5.84	5.36	0.48	D	D
Colorado	7.04	6.32	0.72	D	D
New York	4.85	3.62	1.23	D	D
Wyoming	4.77	3.52	1.25	D	D
Maryland	4.77	3.26	1.51	D	D
New Mexico	7.58	5.96	1.62	D	D
Rhode Island	7.20	4.94	2.26	D	D
Montana	5.17	2.65	2.52	D	D
Arizona	6.42	3.64	2.78	D	D
Tennessee		5.42			
Arkansas		5.06			
Texas		4.94			
North Carolina		4.88			
Oklahoma		4.88			

TABLE VIII-2—*Continued*

State	Republican	Democratic	Party Difference (R−D)	Party with Majority of Victories (1914–1958) for Governor	Senator
Louisiana		4.88			
Mississippi		4.24			
Florida		4.10			
Alabama		3.96			
South Carolina		3.80			
Virginia		3.76			
Georgia		3.50			

[a] For a discussion of the opportunity rate, see Chapter III. Briefly, it is the frequency with which a nomination becomes available for a new man within a 12-year period.
[b] Farmer-Labor included with the Democrats.

Republican nominees. In both parties, the turnover among the nominees for governor is slightly higher than the turnover among senatorial nominees.

To compare the opportunity rates of the states' parties for major office I have used the 12-year generation devised in Chapter III to allow for the discrepancies in terms between offices. Table VIII-2 shows the combined chances for nomination in each state party for the three major state offices, the governorship and the two Senate seats, over a 12-year period. As is apparent from the table, there are marked variations among state parties with respect to the number of opportunities for nomination. The chances for nomination to major office are lowest in the Democratic party of Montana, where a new man's chances of obtaining the Democratic nomination are a little over 2.5. In the Democratic party the best chance for a major nomination is in New Hampshire: in a typical 12-year period there are more than 8 new nominations for the three offices. The Republican range is somewhat narrower, from a low of 3.05 chances in Idaho to a high of 7.58 in New Mexico. But, on the whole, marked differences in opportunities among the states' parties are the exception. In most state parties the opportunity rate for the three offices ranges between 4 and 5 chances for a new man in a 12-year period. Even in the dominant parties the rate seldom falls below 4 chances. In other words, a new man has a chance at a major state party nomination at least once every three years. In only 17 state parties are the opportunities less frequent; in 22 state parties the chances for nomination are more frequent, once in every two years and more often.

The opportunity rates in the states' parties, then, are impressively high, indicative of a great deal of fluctuation at the very top of the pyramid within state parties. While the data indicate that the less valuable nominations are easier to obtain, the noteworthy fact is that the opportunities for nomination are good even in party structures where nomination is tantamount to election. Note that for most of the southern Democratic parties the opportunity rate is four or better, a consequence of high turnover in the governor's office. In these parties an equilibrium of opportunities has apparently developed; a high rate of opportunity has come about for the governorship to offset the limited opportunities for the other two major state offices, the Senate seats.

At the same time, the relationship between the size of a party's opportunity structure and its competitive position is clear. With few exceptions, the majority parties in the states have lower opportunity rates than their opponents, indicating the importance of incumbency. Furthermore, the discrepancies between the opportunity rates of the two parties within a state are greater according to the degree of dominance of one or the other party. The rankings of the states in Table VIII-2 are, therefore, also a good measure of Republican-Democratic strength; in those states where the difference between the opportunity rates of the two parties is less than one, the parties are also most competitive.

The positive relationship between party competition and the size of the parties' opportunity structures, however, by no means precludes the impact of the states' opportunity structures. To determine whether or not the structure of opportunity within the states has an independent impact upon party nominations, I have examined the parties' behavior with respect to each office. One way to test the impact of office as such upon party nominations is to correlate the turnover in nominations for the two parties by states. If the competitive position of the parties is the major factor affecting turnover, then the correlation should be negative. In other words, the party which wins elections will have incumbents and will tend to renominate them because of their demonstrated vote-getting capacity, if the party is making its nominations in response to its competitive needs. The losing party, with fewer demonstrated winners, will have a higher turnover, again only if it is nominating in response to electoral needs. In Table VIII-3 we do find a negative correlation for the office of senator (-0.58), which accords with our earlier findings that party competition is a major factor in determining opportunities for the Senate (see Chapter IV).

On the other hand, if the office as such determines the turnover in nominees, we should expect either no correlation at all between the

TABLE VIII-3
Correlation Between Turnover Rates in Nominations for Governor and Senator (1914–1958)

	Republican and Democratic Party Nominations
Governor (32 non-southern states permitting reelection of incumbents)	+0.30
Governor (36 non-southern states)	+0.56
Senator (36 non-southern states)	−0.58

nomination turnover rates of the two parties or a positive relationship. There is, in fact, a positive correlation between the turnover rates of the two parties for gubernatorial nominations. These results are also in accord with my earlier findings that party competition is least relevant to the opportunities for the office of governor. In contrast to the office of senator, incumbency is not a critical factor in determining the chances for a gubernatorial nomination. Indeed, with respect to gubernatorial nominations the parties tend to imitate rather than to complement each other; for the governorship the minority party tends to repeat its nominations to about the same degree as the majority party.

In effect, then, the parties' distinctive handling of the nominations for governor and senator reflects the different positions of the two offices in the states' opportunity structures. The imitative tendency with respect to gubernatorial nominations is most suggestive; it indicates that the force of incumbency may carry over to the defeated candidates of the opposition. There is also evidence that the same situation may exist for congressional nominations. In a study of congressional elections for a single year, Ackerman points out that as many as one-eighth of the races are between the same contestants as in the previous election.[1] In our earlier discussion we have characterized the office of congressman as a career office; it appears that one can make a career of being a defeated candidate for Congress as well.

The size of the parties' structures of opportunity reflects both the competitive standings of the parties and the standings of the offices in the states' opportunity structures. To the extent that the two parties dispense their nominations in opposite fashion, that the successful party honors its incumbents, while the minority party seeks out fresh talent, we have evidence that party competition is the critical factor in determining the number of political opportunities within the party framework. When, however, the parties do not behave as mirror images in

[1] Donald H. Ackerman, Jr., "Significance of Congressional Races with Identical Candidates in Successive District Elections," *Midwest Journal of Political Science*, I (1957), 173–80.

their handling of nominations for a particular office but, in fact, tend to imitate each other, we have evidence of the independent impact of the states' structures of opportunity.

Whether the parties, as Democratic or Republican organizations, differ in their approach to political opportunity is also relevant. In Chapter IV I have discussed the reasons for the differential treatment of offices within the states, but I did not consider a partisan explanation. I have, however, found in my analysis of the national office hierarchy partisan differences in the approach to the Presidency, the Cabinet, and the Supreme Court. We also know that the restraints imposed by the Twenty-Second Amendment upon presidential tenure are the response of a Republican-dominated Congress to a four-term Democratic President.

TABLE VIII-4
Correlation between the Percentage of Victories for the Party (1914–1958) and the Party's Nomination Turnover Rate

	Republicans	*Democrats*
Senators (36 states)	−0.64	−0.85
Governors (32 states)	−0.14	−0.63

One way to test the partisan approach to political opportunities is to correlate by states the percentage of victories for each party for the governorship and the Senate with each party's nomination turnover rates for these offices. In effect, we are testing for the force of incumbency which experience indicates should play a major part in nominations, thereby giving a negative correlation, i.e., the greater the proportion of victories for a party, the lower the turnover in its nominations. While Table VIII-4 does give us only negative correlations, there are significant differences. For both offices, incumbency appears to carry much greater weight with the Democrats. The value of incumbency for Republican governors is extremely low (-0.14), indicating that incumbency plays no particular part in the Republicans' treatment of that office. It appears, therefore, that the Republican party is the more effective instrument in limiting the career potentialities of the governor's office.

There are, however, important qualifications to my findings of partisan distinctions, qualifications which strengthen the conclusion that the states' opportunity structures have an independent impact upon the number of opportunities provided by political parties. First, the correlation for the office of senator is higher in both parties than it is for the governorship, reflecting the greater value of incumbency for senatorial office. Furthermore, Table VIII-4 is based on 36 states and excludes the south. But it is the Democratic-dominated south which has typically placed constitutional restraints upon the governor's tenure. This suggests that party dominance, rather than the parties as such, produces conditions which permit the state's structure of opportunities to have its maximum impact. In a competitive or minority situation, the needs of the party for candidates who can win office enhances the importance of the successful candidate and his ability to gain renomination.

My conclusions about the availability of political opportunities within the state parties' framework underline two important facets of party organization. First, they indicate that over and above the pressures generated by party competition, the tensions created by the position of a particular office in the state's opportunity structure will affect the interdependence of nuclear office organizations within parties. Thus, no matter what the competitive conditions, we should expect the organizations surrounding the offices of governor and lieutenant governor to be more inclined to seek alliances and means of cooperating with other nuclear organizations than the organizations of congressmen, senators, and secretaries of state. High turnover in personnel, in addition to the attraction of the office for men with progressive ambitions, makes the governorship an unlikely office around which to build an independent political organization.

Secondly, my conclusion about the difference in tenure among party nominees is relevant to the definition of the power base within party organizations. Again, if we consider the competitive factor as constant, the longer the tenure of a party nominee, the more likely that he will develop influence within the organization surrounding his office. Brief tenure, on the other hand, lends itself to the emergence of less overt influences, men within the party organization but outside the officeholding ranks and external interests or pressure groups. My findings, then, point to the existence of largely personal organizations surrounding congressional and senatorial office, while strong extra-office organization is quite compatible with frequent changes in local government.[2] On the other hand, despite the ephemeral governor, strong extra-office organizations have not been conspicuous at the state level, probably for much the same reasons that the movement for the strong governor has lagged behind that for the strong mayor; the need to pro-

[2] There is remarkably little literature on party organization in congressional districts. On the personal character of congressional district organization, see Charles Clapp, *The Congressman* (Washington: Brookings Institution, 1963), pp. 330–92. See also Avery Leiserson, "National Party Organization and Congressional Districts," *Western Political Quarterly,* XVI (1963), 633–49.

vide effective government at the state level has been less pressing than the needs of local government.

The Shape of the Parties' Structures of Opportunity

In my discussion of the states' opportunity structures I have pointed out that not only the number of office opportunities, but also the ordering of opportunities, is relevant to our understanding of American politics. Similarly, to understand American party organization we should ask not only about the number of opportunities available within each party, but also about their distinctive pattern or course. As is the case with the size of the parties' opportunity structures, the competitive standings of the parties are bound to affect the way in which the parties order political opportunities. A party, after all, can promote men only from offices which it controls. But no rules require office promotion. The competitive standings of the parties can, therefore, limit the use of certain offices; they do not necessarily determine the pattern which the parties impose upon political opportunities.

One measure of shape which I have employed earlier is the use, by at least 30 per cent of a state's governors or senators, of a particular penultimate office. Applied in partisan terms to the 36 non-southern states, this measure reveals a gubernatorial nomination pattern in 32 of the Republican state parties and 25 of the Democratic parties (Table VIII-5). The situation is similar for the office of senator (Table VIII-6).

The differences between the two parties in their use of penultimate offices for the governorship are not striking. While the Republicans tend to use the minor statewide offices for promotion more often than the Democrats, this reflects mostly their dominant position in many of the states. Eleven of the Democratic parties make conspicuous use of law enforcement offices; but this reflects in part their strength in regions where the use of law enforcement offices is strong. The use of law enforcement offices is also characteristic of minority parties in general; they are used by the Democrats in California, Connecticut, Wisconsin, and North Dakota; they are valuable offices for minority Republicans in Missouri and Kentucky. Only minority parties make significant use of local office, an indication that in minority parties nuclear organizations often exist realistically only at the local level.

With respect to senatorial nominations also, the Republicans tend to make greater use of the statewide elective offices as penultimate offices, the Democrats of law enforcement offices. Promotion from the governorship to the Senate is exclusively the practice of dominant par-

TABLE VIII-5

Party Nominations—Last Office Patterns for Governor

Per Cent	No Office		Legislature		Law Enforcement		Statewide		Congress		Administrative		Local	
	R	D	R	D	R	D	R	D	R	D	R	D	R	D
30–39	Ariz.[a] Del. Ind.		Mont.[a] N.H. N.D. W.Va.[a]	Minn.[a] Pa.[a] R.I.	Colo. Ill. Mo.[a] Wis.	Calif.[a] Conn.[a] Md. Mo. Nev. N.M. Wis.[a]	Colo. Ill. Wyo.	Del.[a]		Ohio	Utah.[a]	Del. Nev.	Md.[a]	Mich.[a] Wis.[a]
40–49			Idaho Iowa Neb. N.J. N.M.[a] Ore.	S.D.[a] Utah	Pa.	Ill.[a] W.Va.	Calif. Iowa Mich. Minn. R.I.[a]	Wyo.			N.J. W.Va.[a] Wyo.	N.M.		
50 and over			Me.	Ore.[a] Vt.[a]	Ky.[a] N.Y.	Mont. N.D.[a]	Conn. Mass. Vt. Wash.	Ky.		Wash.		Mich.[a]		Me.[a]

[a] Minority party.

TABLE VIII-6
Party Nominations—Last Office Patterns for Senator

Per Cent	*No Office*		*Legislature*		*Law Enforcement*		*Statewide*		*Congress*		*Administrative*		*Local*	
	R	*D*	*R*	*D*	*R*	*D*	*R*	*D*	*R*	*D*	*R*	*D*	*R*	*D*
30–39	Colo. Conn. Del.			Minn.[a]	Ky.[a]	Ind.[a] Mo. Mont. N.M. N.Y. Pa.[a]	Calif. Idaho Iowa Minn. N.H. Ohio S.D. Vt.	Ky. Me.[a] Md. Ohio	Mass. Mich. Nev.[a] S.D. W.Va.[a]	Calif.[a] Conn.[a] Mich.[a] R.I. W.Va.[a]	Ky.[a] Mich. Mo.[a] N.J. N.Y. Pa.	Md. Mont. N.M.		
40–49			Ind.	Wis.[a]	Wash. Wis.		Conn.		Ill. Me. Neb. Vt.		Md.[a]	Iowa[a] Wyo.		
50 and over	Utah[a]			S.D.[a] Vt.[a]		Ariz.	Kans.	Colo. R.I.	N.H. Wyo.	Ariz. Utah Wash.	Ariz.[a] Ore.			

[a] Minority party.

ties, with the exception of the Democrats of Maine where cyclical control of the governorship makes the practice possible for minority nominations. Promotion from the United States House of Representatives is characteristic of either dominant or competitive parties, although it is practiced moderately (for less than 40 per cent of a party's senatorial nominees) by viable Democratic minority parties in California, Connecticut, and Michigan, and by the minority Republican parties of Nevada and West Virginia. Use of the state legislature as a source for senatorial nominees is exclusively a minority party practice, with the interesting exception of the Republicans of Indiana.

It is also worth noting that only Republican state parties make a practice of selecting nominees for both the governorship and the Senate outside the ranks of officeholders. Even among Republicans the practice is not conspicuous. On the other hand, it does agree with our national findings that opportunities for non-officeholders are generally greater within the Republican than within the Democratic party.

The use of penultimate offices is, however, only one measure of order within state parties, and not the most refined one. It does not measure the complexity of the careers leading to a partisan nomination. But it is the complexity of political careers, their stages of advancement, which is most likely to focus political ambitions and to produce the career tensions which affect party organization. One measure of complexity is the difference between the offices in which partisan candidates begin their public careers and their last offices before nomination. I have, therefore, calculated for each state party the distribution of first offices held by the nominees for governor and senator and the distribution of their penultimate offices. These percentage distributions are then arrayed against each other and the differences calculated and totalled.[3]

[3] An example of the way in which the profile differences have been calculated is the following for the Vermont Republican party. Here we are concerned with measuring internal structure.

	First Office	*Penultimate Office*			
Office Type	*Governor and Senator Combined* *A*	*Governor* *B*	*Profile Difference* *(A−B)*	*Senator* *C*	*Profile Difference* *(A−C)*
No office	3%	4%	1%	0%	3%
Legislative	45	22	23	0	45
Law enforcement	16	0	16	0	16
Statewide	0	52	52	33	33
Congress	0	0	0	44	44
Administrative	26	17	9	22	4
Local elective	10	4	6	0	10
	100	99	107	99	155
	(N=31)	(N=23)		(N=9)	

The possible range in this profile difference is from 0, (which indicates that the offices at the time of nomination are the same as those at the beginning of the nominees' careers), to 200 (which indicates that they are completely different). A profile-difference score of less than 100 indicates that the penultimate offices are more like than unlike the first offices; a score of more than 100 indicates that they are more unlike. In effect, then, we have a measure of the degree of structure in careers.

Tables VIII-7 and VIII-8 present the general distribution of structure in careers among the state parties. The range is considerable, from hardly any differentiation in the careers of the Democratic candidates for governor of Wisconsin who score a mere 26, to the highly structured careers of Republican senatorial nominees in Wyoming who score 173.[4] But the tables also show that careers leading to senatorial nominations in both parties are more complex than those leading to gubernatorial nominations, a finding which allows us to conclude that the states' opportunity structures have their impact upon the shape as well as the size of the parties' opportunity structures.

TABLE VIII-7
Party Differences in the Degree of Structure in Careers Leading to Nominations for Governor and Senator

Profile Difference, First Office to Last Office	*Republican Nominees for*		*Democratic Nominees for*	
	Governor	*Senator*	*Governor*	*Senator*
	(Number of States' Parties)			
25–49	4	2	11	0
50–74	14	9	10	17
75–99	10	11	11	11
100–124	4	6	3	6
125–149	2	3	1	1
150+	2	5	0	1
	36	36	36	36

At the same time, the effect of party competition upon the shape of the parties' opportunity structures appears to be only partial. It is true that the Republican office careers are more complex than those of the Democrats, a reflection of Republican dominance in the north for most of the period under study. Then too, minority status for both parties is generally related to simple office careers. On the other hand, dominance does not necessarily assure a complex pattern of office promotion.

[4] See Appendix B for data indicating the degree of structure within parties, based on the profile differences.

TABLE VIII-8

The Degree of Structure in Careers Leading to Nominations for Governor and Senator, According to Competitive Status of Party[a]

Profile Difference, First Office to Last Office	*Nominees of Dominant Parties for Governor*	*Nominees of Dominant Parties for Senator*	*Nominees of Competitive Parties for Governor (Per Cent)*	*Nominees of Competitive Parties for Senator (Per Cent)*	*Nominees of Minority Parties for Governor*	*Nominees of Minority Parties for Senator*
25–49	5.3%	0.0%	17.6%	2.9%	42.0%	5.3%
50–74	42.0	15.8	38.3	29.4	26.3	68.4
75–99	31.6	26.3	23.5	38.3	26.3	21.0
100–124	15.8	26.3	8.8	20.6	5.3	0.0
125–149	5.3	10.5	5.9	5.9	0.0	0.0
150+	0.0	21.0	5.9	2.9	0.0	5.3
	100.0	99.9	100.0	100.0	99.9	100.0
	(N = 19)		(N = 34)		(N = 19)	

[a] The assignment of dominant, competitive, and minority status to state parties is based on the diagrams in Joseph A. Schlesinger, "The Structure of Competition for Office in the American States," *Behavioral Science,* V (1960), 197–210. States are assigned status according to their general position for most offices.

Dominant Parties R		*Dominant Parties D*	*Minority Parties*	*Competitive Parties R and D*		
Vt.	S. D.	Ky.	are	Mass.	Utah	Del.
Me.	Calif.	R.I.	the opposite	Idaho	Ohio	N.J.
Kan.	N.D.	Ariz.	of the dominant	Conn.	W.Va.	N.Y.
Iowa	Ore.	Nev.	parties	Colo.	Ill.	Ind.
N.H.	Wis.	N.M.	in each state	Wyo.	Mich.	Wash.
Neb.	Pa.	Mo.		Minn.	Md.	
		Mont.				

Competitive parties tend to reveal as strong a pattern of office promotion as dominant parties.

The absence of orderly promotion in minority parties is readily explained; a party must win offices at several levels of government before it can develop the practice of office promotion. When dominant parties, however, fail to develop such practices, when they ignore the offices within their control for purposes of advancement, we have an indication of another and different aspect of party organization worthy of examination. Let us take, therefore, one further measure of the shape of the parties' opportunity structures, their use of manifest offices.

Manifest Office and Party Organization

In Chapter VI I advanced the proposition that we can detect important organizational relationships within a political system by the overuse or underuse of offices obviously in the line of promotion to high place. Similarly, the parties' handling of what I have called manifest offices should give us insights into their organizations. Using the data on party nominations for the offices of governor and senator, I have examined the parties' use of manifest offices. As is the case with the partisan pattern of office careers, the parties' competitive standings are an obvious factor in their use of manifest offices (Table VIII-9). The dominant parties use the manifest offices more than competitive parties, and both the dominant parties and the competitive parties use manifest offices more than minority parties. But, as is the case with the parties' career patterns, the control of office alone does not assure its use for promotion; the dominant parties vary greatly in their use of manifest office. In Kansas 86 per cent of the Republican senatorial nominees come from the manifest offices of governor and congressman; but in Oregon Republicans choose only 10 per cent of their senatorial nominees from these offices. In Iowa 77 per cent of the Republican nominees for governor come from the manifest offices of state legislator and statewide elective official; but in Pennsylvania Republicans choose only 14 per cent of their gubernatorial nominees from these offices. Factors other than the competitive standings of the parties, then, determine the use of manifest offices.

The evidence suggests that the quality of party organization itself determines the use of manifest office. In general, senatorial nominees are more likely to come from manifest offices than gubernatorial nominees. Nevertheless, there is a direct and positive relationship between the use of manifest offices for the Senate and its use for the governorship. Moreover, the relationship is most conspicuous in dominant par-

TABLE VIII-9

The Use of Manifest Offices by State Parties for Nominations for Governor and Senator, According to Competitive Status

Percentage of Nominees from Manifest Office	*Nominees for Governor*			*Nominees for Senator*		
	Dominant	*Competitive*	*Minority*	*Dominant*	*Competitive*	*Minority*
70%+	15.8	2.9	0.0	26.3	2.9	0.0
50–69	21.0	17.6	21.0	31.6	44.2	5.3
30–49	31.6	38.2	21.0	26.3	17.6	31.6
Under 30	31.6	41.2	58.0	15.8	35.2	63.2
	100.0	99.9	100.0	100.0	99.9	100.1
Number of state parties	19	34	19	19	34	19

[5] See Appendix B, Table B-2, for the distribution of the use of manifest offices by state parties.

TABLE VIII-10
Correlations among the Use of Manifest Offices by State Parties in Making Nominations for Governor and Senator

19 Minority parties	−0.16
34 Competitive parties	+0.12
48 Democratic parties	+0.17
36 Republican parties	+0.29
19 Dominant parties	+0.44

ties, those parties most capable of using manifest offices at will. (See Table VIII-10.) The tendency for the dominant parties to approach both major offices in a similar fashion, when there is no formal reason to do so, supports the assumption that organizational factors are at work.

One way to examine the factors involved is to look more closely at the state parties at the extremes, parties, dominant in their states, which overuse or underuse manifest offices for both their senatorial and gubernatorial nominations. In Vermont, the Republicans are heavy users of manifest office; 74 per cent of their gubernatorial nominees and 77 per cent of their senatorial nominees come from manifest offices. In Kentucky, the Democrats choose 64 per cent of their gubernatorial nominees from the manifest offices and 61 per cent of their senatorial candidates. At the other extreme are the Democrats of Missouri and Indiana Republicans. In Indiana, the dominant Republicans choose only 23 per cent of their gubernatorial candidates and 14 per cent of their senatorial candidates from manifest offices; in Missouri, the Democrats as the dominant party nominate only 29 per cent of their gubernatorial candidates and 16 per cent of their senatorial candidates from manifest offices.

The Overuse of Manifest Office: The Examples of Vermont and Kentucky

The concept of manifest office assumes that American parties are controlled by their officeholders, their most conspicuous officeholders. In the contest for office advancement, therefore, those already in offices close to the top positions of elective leadership ought to have an advantage which is demonstrated by their statistical prominence among the nominees for leadership positions. When, however, their prominence is overwhelming, we are led to suspect that something more than the advantage of conspicuous office is at work, that there is, in effect, an organized effort to utilize the advantages of conspicuous office. In other words, the ties of party organization are stronger than when manifest officeholders have some advantage but not the consistently decisive advantage. On the other hand, the overuse of manifest office does not indicate as strong an organization as does the ability of a dominant party to ignore its manifest officeholders. We should expect, therefore, that manifest office will be used heavily by political organizations which are either dominated by officeholders or characterized by the overt use of the power of office to choose and advance successors rather than by organizations where the power is covert and non-elective politicans or non-political interests are the dominant influences. This assumption is prompted also by my earlier finding that the environment which tends to foster the overuse of manifest offices is the one-party rural and homogeneous state.

The states of Kentucky and Vermont demonstrate my proposition about the overuse of manifest offices. In Kentucky, of the twelve men whom the Democrats have nominated for governor between 1914 and 1958, seven come from the manifest statewide elective offices, five are lieutenant governors, one a state auditor, and one a former governor. Moreover, the remaining five are also public officeholders: three are United States representatives, one is a circuit court judge, the other the chairman of the state highway commission. For the Senate, the Kentucky Democrats have chosen eight of eleven nominees from manifest offices, five from the governorship, and three from the House of Representatives. Of the remaining three, two are also officeholders, one a state legislator, the other the chief justice of the state court of appeals. Vermont Republicans make even heavier use of manifest office: of their nine senatorial nominees, four are United States representatives, three governors; of all the states, Vermont promotes lieutenant governors to the governorship most frequently.[6]

In both Vermont and Kentucky one party dominates the political system, but it is by no means always assured of winning office. The competitive standings of the parties make possible, then, the use of manifest office by the dominant party and, at the same time, encourage cooperation among its nuclei. The distinguishing characteristic of the dominant parties in both these states is the conspicuous role of officeholders in determining office promotion. In both states the governor or the state administration is expected to support a successor. This practice is aided considerably by regularized turnover in the governor's office. In Kentucky regular turnover is assured by a constitutional one-term limit; in Vermont there is a traditional restriction, a one-term

[6] For discussion of the careers leading to the office of governor in Vermont, see Joseph A. Schlesinger, *How They Became Governor* (East Lansing: Governmental Research Bureau, Michigan State University, 1957).

tradition until 1928, a two-term tradition thereafter. In addition to the traditional term limit, Vermont Republicans have also established a clear line of office succession from the state legislature, through the office of lieutenant governor, to the governorship.

In Vermont, then, Republican organization is, to all intents and purposes, synonymous with the state's opportunity structure. In Kentucky, the patronage of the governor's office is perhaps a more blatant force in the state Democratic organization. But the organization is still conspicuously dominated by officeholders, not only by the governor who is capable of influencing the selection of his successor, but also by senators like Alben Barkley and Earle Clements who, faced with stronger competition from Republicans than the governor has to face, have found it worthwhile to maintain organizational ties with other state nuclei. Indeed, in Vermont as well as in Kentucky, there is an overt relationship between the holding of state office and the opportunity for a senatorial career. In both states an active minority party is one factor in bringing the nuclear organizations of both offices close together. In Vermont, the existence of a single congressional district, making the congressional and senatorial constituencies congruent, undoubtedly encourages the movement from the House of Representatives to the Senate.[7]

The peculiar electoral arrangements in Kentucky illustrate well the impact of electoral structure on party organization. The Democratic domination of state politics rests upon the election of the governor in odd-numbered years. The Republicans, on the other hand, can compete effectively for the Senate during national election years when there is a larger turnout and national political sentiments are aroused. Thus, we see in the Democratic party very strong ties between the senatorial and gubernatorial nuclear organizations, since the latter provides the former with its principal advantage in facing Republican opposition. The Republican senatorial nucleus, however, has little in the way of an effective state office base so that it has been drawn, as in the case of such senators as Thruston Morton and John Sherman Cooper, towards strong ties to the national Republican presidential nucleus.

In both Vermont and Kentucky the picture of party organization which emerges is not at all like the stereotype of a party machine. In both states one party is dominant, but its organization is openly controlled by officeholders who allow factionalism of a continuous sort. Fenton speaks of a three-party system in Kentucky, two Democratic

[7] On Vermont politics, see Duane Lockard, *New England State Politics* (Princeton: Princeton University Press, 1959). For Kentucky, see J. Fenton, *Politics in the Border States* (New Orleans: Hauser, 1957).

factions and a Republican party. On occasion, the dominant government faction associated with men such as Barkley and Clements has been challenged by the forces of A. B. "Happy" Chandler. Lockard speaks of a similar situation in Vermont; a dominant Republican faction associated with the conservative Proctors has been challenged successfully on occasion, as it was in the 1940's by Ernest Gibson.

The Democratic party of Kentucky has more often been characterized as a machine organization than the Republican party of Vermont. Kentucky Democrats have been credited with extensive use of the perquisites of office, the use of patronage and kickbacks, to keep organization effective. But stronger minority competition and the more flamboyant character of Kentucky politics may be enough to account for the less complete reliance on regular office promotion as the backbone of Democratic party organization. Nevertheless, the Kentucky Democratic party is only a somewhat less pure example of the type of officeholders' organization perfected by the Republicans of Vermont. Both organizations have developed in states where rural and conservative business interests have created the homogeneous economic and social environment conducive to the existence of a firm and secure political class.

The Underuse of Manifest Office: The Examples of Missouri and Indiana

The underuse of manifest offices for senatorial and gubernatorial nominations by parties capable of using these offices indicates the less important role of its officeholders within the party organization. That is, within the party, officeholders play a lesser role than their title and position would presumably allow them. Others are effectively organized to allow the promotion of men without the advantages of public elective position.

The Democrats of Missouri demonstrate this proposition. In Missouri, the Democrats are the dominant party, although not to the exclusion of all opposition. Yet, unlike the Democrats of Kentucky, for the most part they pass over the obvious public officials for promotion. In Missouri, Democratic gubernatorial nominees come from a variety of sources: two have held no public office at all, three have held some type of local office in St. Louis, one is a circuit judge, another a former United States attorney, two are United States representatives; five have come from offices manifest in varying degrees: one is a lieutenant governor, one an attorney general, one a state auditor, one chairman of the state public service commission, and one a former state representative.

The party has scattered its senatorial nominations about in similar fashion. One senatorial nomination has gone to the mayor of Kansas City, one nomination to a county judge, one to a circuit attorney, one to a state attorney general, and two to state representatives; one nomination went to a federal Cabinet member, one to a sub-Cabinet member, one to a former employee of the federal Congress; only two nominations have gone to men who had held manifest offices; one to a United States representative, one to a former governor who had gone on to federal legal service.

One explanation of the Missouri Democrats' disregard of manifest officeholders for senatorial nominations is the strong tie between the national and state party organizations. In Chapter II I have pointed out that Missouri is highly advantaged in the presidential office complex. Among Missouri's Democratic senatorial nominees, there are an unusual number with federal administrative experience. Among those who have received the senatorial nominations are Stuart Symington, Secretary of the Air Force (nominated and elected in 1952), Breckenridge Long, Third Assistant Secretary of State (nominated but defeated in 1920), Joseph W. Folk, the chief council for the ICC and a former governor (nominated but defeated in 1918), and Bennett Champ Clark, son of the one-time Speaker of the House whose only public office had been parliamentarian of the United States House of Representatives (nominated and elected in 1932).

One explanation of the Democratic disregard of manifest officeholders for the governorship of Missouri is that it is an organization in which non-elective politicians play a dominant role, unlike the Democratic party of Kentucky. Fenton has described the situation in Missouri as follows: "Unlike West Virginia and Kentucky, Missouri does not have a tradition of strong executive leadership. In the absence of leadership by the governor, party control has tended to drift into the hands of strong political leaders such as Tom Pendergast or combinations of local political leaders and representatives of powerful interest groups."[8] It is interesting to note, therefore, that the Missouri Democratic party's selection of manifest officeholders for its gubernatorial nominations dates almost entirely from the 1940's and the onset of the decline of the Pendergast machine.

Another instructive example of the underuse of manifest office is the Republican party of Indiana. Of the state parties we have examined, the Indiana Republican party is the only one which operates within the framework of the convention system of nominations for major

[8] Fenton, *Politics in the Border States*. pp. 134–35.

statewide elective officials. In Indiana, therefore, the non-elective politician has formal machinery to balance the assets of manifest officeholding. It should be made clear that the convention does not automatically work to the disadvantage of the manifest officeholder; in Conneticut manifest officeholders are successful within the framework of the convention. But the very simple advantage which manifest officeholders have, that of being in an obvious steppingstone position, is less likely to affect the convention delegate than the primary voter.

In Indiana another formal political groundrule, the one-term limit for governor, also helps to weaken the organizational role of the manifest officeholder. We have noted that Kentucky has the same formal limitation on the governor's powers, but, associated with the primary and strong patronage, tenure restriction does not preclude the development of an effective officeholding organization. In Indiana, however, tenure restriction along with the convention aids both the non-elective politician and the representatives of at least one powerful interest group, the American Legion, which has its national headquarters in Indiana. Gordon Craig was nominated and elected governor in 1952 after much organizational experience with the Republican party and service as national commander of the Legion, although he had never held public office. Glen R. Hillis was nominated governor in 1940 with only minor experience as a county prosecuting attorney; but, more importantly, he had been state commander of the Legion. Another whose advancement came essentially from organizational work was Homer Capehart, nominated and elected senator in 1944.

Another politician aided within the Indiana Republican party by the convention system has been the state legislator. Two speakers of the lower house of the legislature, Harry Leslie in 1928 and Hobart Creighton in 1948, were nominated for governor. The Republican floor leader in the state senate, Arthur Robinson, was appointed to the United States Senate in 1925 and was subsequently nominated and elected; William Jenner, in 1944, became senator from the same position. Indiana is one of the few states where party organization around state legislative districts has not atrophied, despite the use of the direct primary for legislative nominations. V. O. Key attributes the persistence of organized local efforts in Indiana to the use of the convention for nominations to major state office, because the convention provides a framework within which local organization can and does receive direct payoffs from the state office organization.[9]

With respect to the character of Republican organization in In-

[9] V. O. Key, Jr., *American State Politics* (New York: Knopf, 1956), Ch. 6.

diana, it is also worthwhile to recall the nature of political competition in the state. In the preceding chapter, I have described the exceptionally narrow range of competition in all elections, despite Republican dominance. The slight discrepancy in party votes in both enclaved and congruent constituencies favors and encourages close-knit party organization. Aided by the convention machinery and the formal restrictions on state elective leadership, party organization as such plays a prominent role in the nominating process of the Indiana Republican party and is capable of weighting the attributes of others against the manifest officeholder.

THE PARTIES' STRUCTURE OF OPPORTUNITIES AND PARTY THEORY

In my theoretical discussion of the parties I have suggested that the career lines of the parties' major nominees can provide an index of the force of ambition within party organization. I have suggested further that the comparison of the career lines of the two parties within a state can provide a measure of the extent to which office ambitions draw the parties together or pull them apart. My discussion of the parties' opportunity structures now permits us to take that measure.

TABLE VIII-11
The Similarity between the Parties within the States

(Rank order correlation between proportions of Republican and Democratic leaders in 36 non-southern states.)

The First Political Office Held by Party Leaders:	
Law Enforcement	+.61
State Legislative	+.50
Local Elective	+.38
Administrative	+.24
The Last Office Held before Nomination for Governor:	
Law Enforcement	+.39
Legislative	+.21
Administrative	+.19
Local Elective	+.09
Statewide Elective	+.03
The Last Office Held before Nomination for Senator:	
Statewide Elective	+.19
Congress	+.04
Administrative	+.02
Law Enforcement	−.02

The overall data on the parties' gubernatorial and senatorial nominees indicates that the opportunity structures of American state parties are more alike than unlike. This is especially true at the base of the parties' opportunity structures (see Table VIII-11). The rank order correlations for the first offices in the careers of both parties' gubernatorial and senatorial nominees reveal a strong positive relation in each office category. The parties' nominees are most similar in their use of the law enforcement offices (.61) and the office of state legislator (.50) as first office. These results support my earlier analysis of base office; party competition is not the significant determinant of the type of office in which the states' elective leaders begin their political careers.

The higher the office in the parties' opportunity structures, the less positive is the relationship between the careers of the parties' nominees. At the same time, the relationship is, for the most part, positive. The positive relationship between the penultimate offices of the parties' gubernatorial nominees is significant in the law enforcement and state legislative office categories; the relationship is only somewhat less strong between the penultimate offices of the parties' senatorial nominees, except in the law enforcement office category, where the correlation is negative but insignificant (–.02). We conclude, then, that, overall, the opportunity structures of the states' parties generate greater pressure to bring the parties together than to pull them apart.

We can measure the similarity between the parties' opportunity structures more precisely by calculating the profile differences between the two parties in each state for their nominees at each stage in their careers. The profile difference is similar to that we used earlier; an index of less than 100 indicates that the offices of both parties' nominees at a given stage are more similar than different; an index of over 100 indicates that the office careers of the parties' nominees have taken different paths. Table VIII-12 gives the profile differences for the 36 non-southern parties: the party differences in the first offices for the senatorial and gubernatorial nominees combined, and the differences in the penultimate offices of the gubernatorial and senatorial nominees presented separately. At each stage, the average profile difference reflects what the rank order correlations have revealed; with respect to first office, the average difference is 59.9, i.e., the parties are more alike in their use of base office than different. The range goes from an index of 25 in North Dakota to an index of 98 in Nebraska, but in no state are the base offices of the parties' candidates more different than similar. With respect to penultimate office, the similarity between the parties is still present but not as strong. The average difference between the penultimate offices of the parties' candidates for the gubernatorial nomination is 97.9, for the senatorial nomination, 97.4. Moreover, the range is much greater than for the first offices. The index of difference in penultimate office for gubernatorial candidates ranges from a low of

TABLE VIII-12
Party Profile Differences

	First Office	*Office Penultimate to Office of Governor*	*Office Penultimate to Office of Senator*
I. States where parties are similar			
Missouri	26	50	60
Nevada	67	52	46
Idaho	35	50	85
Ohio	35	74	71
New Jersey	52	86	58
North Dakota	25	98	74
New York	41	77	83
Utah	54	65	98
Pennsylvania	47	79	97
Illinois	74	79	77
Nebraska	98	86	84
II. States where parties are most dissimilar			
Washington	61	177	120
Vermont	46	118	162
Wyoming	71	119	149
Kentucky	58	149	109
Maine	54	142	120
Massachusetts	61	126	110
California	67	111	113
Wisconsin	51	119	116
Connecticut	44	101	116
Minnesota	28	112	105
III. States where parties are similar for governor but diverge for senator			
Arizona	70	80	150
New Hampshire	95	62	130
South Dakota	43	89	149
Rhode Island	84	69	111
Kansas	65	52	111
Indiana	43	67	106
Colorado	46	37	108
IV. States where parties are different for governor but converge for senator			
Michigan	87	160	76
Delaware	90	129	95
Iowa	95	126	73
New Mexico	63	117	86
Maryland	96	103	60
Montana	69	101	83
West Virginia	68	152	25
Oregon	46	109	89
Average	59.9	97.9	97.4

37 in Colorado to a high of 177 in Washington; for the parties' senatorial nominees, the range goes from 25 in West Virginia to 162 in Vermont.

The theoretical significance of the measure of similarity in the parties' opportunity structures lies in the tensions upon the parties which the measures reveal. The reader should keep in mind, however, that I am now attempting to isolate only one kind of tension which affects political parties. I have already pointed out that party competition generates tensions which cause the parties to converge. Even if the states' parties have divergent career lines, therefore, they can be pulled together at the state level by common competitive needs. But it is also possible that the two parties, pulled apart at the state level by the domination of one, move toward each other because of the similarity of their opportunity structures.

The measure of similarity of the parties' opportunity structures allows us to categorize the states according to the effect of career tensions upon the states' party systems. Using the measure of similarity, I have grouped the states in four categories: (1) In eleven states the parties' office profiles are similar at every stage, i.e., at each stage the index of difference is less than 100. (2) In ten states the parties' profiles, while similar for base office, diverge for the penultimate offices leading to both the gubernatorial and senatorial nominations, i.e., the index of difference for both nominations is more than 100. (3) In seven states the index of difference is under 100 for the gubernatorial nominees, over 100 for the nominees for the Senate. (4) In eight states the index of difference is under 100 for the senatorial nominees, over 100 for the nominees for governor.

The eleven states in category I are those where the progressive ambitions of the parties' leaders theoretically worked most effectively to draw the parties together. In those states the careers of the parties' nominees are similar at all three points. In contrast to these states are the states in Category II. In the states where the major nominees of the two parties follow different careers, progressive ambitions working on different types of officeholders presumably tend to pull the parties apart. But the states of Categories III and IV demonstrate that career tensions do not operate uniformly. In some states only the careers of gubernatorial candidates work to bring the parties together; in others only the careers of the senatorial nominees. If the differences in the parties' career lines have everywhere been greater for the Senate than for the governorship, we could infer that this is due to the more rigid stratification of senatorial careers. As it is, we must infer that the differences in career lines are related also to the electoral substructures of the states whose effect I have discussed in the preceding chapter.

For the states in Category III there are several possible and compatible explanations. The parties' profiles for the gubernatorial nominations may be similar because there is little order or structure in the careers of the candidates for either party. Then again, the parties may have similar career structures because their electoral substructures are similar, as is the case in Indiana. The differences between the parties with respect to their senatorial nominees, on the other hand, may reflect only the element of order associated with senatorial careers.

The eight states of Category IV are more difficult to explain, representing as they do greater similarity between the parties in their senatorial careers than in those of their candidates for governor. One explanation is that stronger competition for the office of senator within a state breaks down patterns. Another is that, in states such as Michigan, competition at the state level masks, as we have seen, broad differences in party strength beneath that level. Attainment of the gubernatorial nomination, therefore, is achieved in each party by different means; but in both parties competitive conditions at the state level favor for the senatorial nomination those officials who have demonstrated their appeal to the statewide electorate, in turn reinforcing the tendency of the two parties at the state level to converge. In support of this explanation, note that, of all the states, those in this group are most unlike, not only with respect to the penultimate offices of the parties' gubernatorial candidates, but also with respect to the first offices of the nominees as well.

In those states where the similarity between career lines of the two parties is not consistent, we must conclude that the effect of progressive ambitions upon the party system is mixed. Of course, the degree of similarity or difference is not in itself adequate to define the force of progressive ambitions. The direction of the officeholder's ambitions must be reinforced by order or structure.

The Cumulative Tensions Working upon Party Systems

We now have both a theory of the role played by ambitions in American state parties and measures of the tensions generated by ambitions which, however crude, permit us to characterize the party systems of the American states. I have posited, in theory, that American parties face three orders of tensions arising from political ambitions. The first order of tension arises from the conditions of party competition; the more competitive the electoral situation, the more likely the two parties are to converge. In Chapter IV I have assessed the competitive standings of the parties by states, and these standings can now serve as a measure of the force of party competition at the statewide level, although it is a crude measure because it does not penetrate to the electoral substructure. The second order of tensions arises from the distribution of offices only indirectly controlled by the electorate; the more favored both state parties are in their national organizations, the more likely are they to converge. Here my crude measure of what is a complex situation is the index of advantage for federal appointments developed in Chapter II. Finally, the third order of tensions are those arising from the parties' internal opportunity structures; the more like their opportunity structures, the greater the pressure for convergence. These I have measured in this chapter.

Let us now relate these various tensions in order to assess their cumulative effect. All three may work consistently in one direction or the other. The two parties may be drawn together at the same time by the force of competition, by their ties to the national party nuclei, and by similar structures of opportunity. Or they may work in the opposite direction. Then again, it is not only possible but likely that the tensions may conflict with each other.

To compare the cumulative effect of the three orders of tension upon the states' party systems, I have assigned a positive or negative value to each order and totaled the values for each of the 36 non-southern states. (See Table VIII-13.) To the first order of tensions, those tensions generated by party competition, I have assigned a value of +1.0 or —1.0. For this purpose I have used the least rigorous test of competition for the period 1914–1958; only states where one party has won 70 per cent of the elections for both governor and senator are considered non-competitive. My measure of the second order of tensions, the relative position of each state party in the presidential complex, is assigned only a positive or convergent value; I do not consider that the parties' failure to receive national recognition necessarily drives them apart. If both parties in a state are advantaged in the presidential office complex, therefore, I have assigned a full value of +1.0; if only one party is advantaged, the state is assigned a value of 0.5 (Table II-3). For the third order of tensions, those arising from the parties' opportunity structures, I have used the measure of the parties' career profile differences. If, according to Table VIII-12, the parties' profiles are similar, I have assigned a value of +1.0 for each nomination; if they are dissimilar, I have assigned a value of —1.0. If the tensions in either direction are reinforced by a high degree of structure in both parties, as demonstrated by the differences between the first and penultimate offices (see Appendix B), I have added a value of 0.5 to the value for direction.

The maximum possible range of cumulative tensions is from +5.0 to —4.0. The actual values go from a total of +5.0 in Ohio, the

TABLE VIII-13
The Cumulative Impact of Ambition Tensions on the Party Systems of the States

State	*First Order Tensions*[a]	*Second Order Tensions*[b]	*Third Order Tensions*[c] *A Governor*	*B Senator*	*Total*[d]
Ohio	+1.0[e]	+1.0	+1.5	+1.5	+5.0
Utah	+1.0	+1.0	+1.0	+1.5	+4.5
Illinois	+1.0	+0.5	+1.0	+1.5	+4.0
Missouri	+1.0	+1.0	+1.0	+1.0	+4.0
Nebraska	+1.0	+0.5	+1.5	+1.0	+4.0
New York	+1.0	+1.0	+1.0	+1.0	+4.0
Idaho	+1.0		+1.0	+1.5	+3.5
Iowa	+1.0	+1.0	−1.0	+1.0	+3.0
Nevada	+1.0		+1.0	+1.0	+3.0
New Jersey	+1.0		+1.0	+1.0	+3.0
New Mexico	+1.0	+1.0	−1.0	+1.0	+2.0
Rhode Island	+1.0	+0.5	+1.5	−1.0	+2.0
West Virginia	+1.0	+0.5	−1.0	+1.5	+2.0
Colorado	+1.0	+0.5	+1.5	−1.5	+1.5
Indiana	+1.0	+0.5	+1.0	−1.0	+1.5
Michigan	+1.0	+0.5	−1.5	+1.5	+1.5
North Dakota	−1.0		+1.0	+1.5	+1.5
Pennsylvania	−1.0	+0.5	+1.0	+1.0	+1.5
Delaware	+1.0		−1.0	+1.0	+1.0
Maryland	+1.0		−1.0	+1.0	+1.0
Montana	+1.0		−1.0	+1.0	+1.0
Arizona	−1.0		+1.5	−1.5	−1.0
Kansas	−1.0	+0.5	+1.0	−1.5	−1.0
Kentucky	+1.0	+0.5	−1.5	−1.0	−1.0
Massachusetts	+1.0	+0.5	−1.0	−1.5	−1.0
New Hampshire	−1.0		+1.0	−1.0	−1.0
Oregon	−1.0	+0.5	−1.5	+1.0	−1.0
South Dakota	−1.0		+1.0	−1.0	−1.0
Wyoming	+1.0	+0.5	−1.5	−1.0	−1.0
Connecticut	+1.0	+0.5	−1.5	−1.5	−1.5
Washington	+1.0		−1.5	−1.5	−2.0
Vermont	−1.0	+0.5	−1.0	−1.0	−2.5
Minnesota	−1.0	+0.5	−1.0	−1.0	−2.5
California	−1.0	+0.5	−1.0	−1.5	−3.0
Wisconsin	−1.0		−1.0	−1.0	−3.0
Maine	−1.0		−1.0	−1.5	−3.5

[a] Party competition is +1 if there is competition (neither party's victories are more than 70 per cent of the total in the period 1914–1958) for both governor and senator, and −1.0 if one party dominates both offices.
[b] Position within the presidential party is based on Table II-3 in Chapter II. + tensions only have been counted. Scores are +1 if a state is advantaged in both the Republican and Democratic parties, +0.5 if it is advantaged in one party only.
[c] Degree of similarity in career lines leading to nominations for governor and senator (Table VIII-12) are scored as follows:
For both Governor and Senator: +1.0 = more similar than dissimilar
−1.0 = more dissimilar than similar
These values are increased by 0.5 in either direction if the career pattern is highly structured for *both* parties (i.e., over 70 per cent—see Table B-1).
[d] The total is the balance of values for the four columns.
[e] + = a CONVERGENT tension
− = a DIVERGENT tension

state where all three orders of tensions work for convergence of the parties, to a total of −3.5 in Maine, the state where the three orders of tensions for the most part work to drive the parties apart.

It is important to keep in mind the limitations of my quantitative evaluation of the effect of ambition tensions upon the states' party systems. First, the data cover only the period 1914–1958; the results, therefore, are predictive of the parties' relations only within that period; beyond that period they are useful only if the conditions have remained the same. Secondly, the three orders of tensions are considered to be equal in value; I have not attempted to consider whether it is valid to assign the same value to the effect of party competition and the effect of the parties' opportunity structures. My quantitative evaluation, based on the theory of tensions generated within parties by political ambitions, can only give us the broad characteristics of the states' party systems.

Whether or not even my broad characterizations of convergence and divergence are accurate must await better tests than we now have of party relations. Recent political history, at least, indicates that party politics is less divisive in the states at the positive extreme of my scale than in those at the negative extreme. Ohio, for example, has sometimes been described as a state of sharp ideological divisions because it produced such strongly conservative Republican senators as John Bricker and Robert Taft. At the same time, no Democrat has so muted party differences as Ohio's Frank Lausche, first as governor, then as senator; among Republicans, party chairman Ray Bliss is one of the principal proponents of reorganizing the Republican party so that it can compete effectively in urban areas. Similarly, in states such as Illinois and New York, the tendency has been strong for the gubernatorial and senatorial candidates of both parties to come together and do battle in similar fashion. On the other hand, states at the divergent end of the scale, such as Wisconsin and Minnesota, have been conspicuous for sharp ideological cleavages between the parties.[10]

CONCLUSIONS

In this chapter I have measured the parties' structures of opportunities and related structure to party organization. I have also attempted to characterize the relations of the parties within the state by considering

[10] John Fenton, in *Midwest Politics* (New York: Holt, Rinehart and Winston, 1966), classifies Ohio, Illinois, and Indiana as "job-oriented" states and, presumably, ones where there is little distinction between the parties; Minnesota, Wisconsin, and Michigan are classed as "issue-oriented" states, or ones where party distinctions are clear.

the effect of the parties' opportunity structures, as well as the effect of party competition and the parties' positions in the national office hierarchy. While I have by no means made exhaustive tests of the theory of ambition tensions, I have attempted a crude measure of their existence and their direction.

CHAPTER IX

Political Opportunities and the Politician's Life-Cycle

My picture of political opportunity in the United States has been drawn from the aggregate careers of numerous individuals who have achieved some degree of prominence in American politics. But if my findings are to be useful in terms of ambition theory, we must know more about the individual politician. Thus far I have been most concerned with the politician's office and his movement from one office to another. But I know that a man's opportunities in politics, his chances for advancement, are dependent upon more than his present position.

In my concern to measure the neglected area of political opportunity in the United States, I have ignored the relevance of social opportunity. Yet observation, well supported by serious studies, tells us that social opportunity is most relevant to political advancement in the United States.[1] In the United States the opportunities to advance have been best for white Anglo-Saxon Protestant males. Before assigning progressive ambitions to the particular officeholder, therefore, we should consider the restrictions facing women and Jews and Negroes and Puerto Ricans. Women's ambitions are most realistically directed

[1] On the non-representativeness of the American political elite, there is C. Wright Mills, *The Power Elite* (New York: Oxford University Press, 1956), and D. M. Matthews, *The Social Background of Political Decision Makers* (Garden City, N.Y.: Doubleday, 1954). See also William C. Mitchell, "The Ambivalent Social Status of the American Politician," *The Western Political Quarterly,* XII (1959), 683–98, for a discussion of the more general problem of relating the ways in which politicians are perceived to their behavior.

at the House of Representatives, and more realistically directed at the Senate than the Presidency. The progressive ambitions of the Jewish governor, even of a large and competitive state, are more realistic in terms of the Senate than of the Presidency. Of course the success of John F. Kennedy in 1960 demonstrates that restrictions based on religion, race, and sex may be only temporary. Nevertheless, before we assign progressive ambitions, it is certainly relevant to ask if the politician has not only the proper political credentials for advancement within his state but the proper social credentials as well.[2]

I have also largely ignored the vast subject of personality traits, yet I consider personality relevant to political opportunity.[3] I have taken some pains to demonstrate that all offices are not treated equally, that longevity in office is allowed some types of officials and denied to others. If these differences are based on different perceptions of the proprieties associated with one office as opposed to another, it must follow that a person considered fit for one office may not necessarily be considered fit for another. An emotionally unstable man may hold a minor office successfully but find the road to higher and more conspicuous office blocked. Some personal distinctions have been given relevance in political folklore. Nelson Rockefeller's divorce did not prevent his reelection as governor of New York, but it effectively cut off his chances

[2] It is also evident that political office has been a major means of social advancement for members of lower status groups. See Robert M. Rosenzweig, "The Politician and the Career in Politics," *Midwest Journal of Political Science,* I (1957), 163–72; and Heinz Eulau and David Kopf, "Occupational Mobility and Political Career," *Western Political Quarterly,* XV (1962), 507–21. While many groups are certainly inadequately represented in American politics, the extent to which elective politics does provide avenues of influence for them is also remarkable. For example, while there are only six Negroes in the 89th Congress, they have managed to hold down 10 per cent of the committee chairmanships in the house, which is about their proportion in the population. White non-southerners, on the other hand, have held down only 25 per cent of these posts.

[3] A large body of literature on leadership personality exists, but there is very little systematic application to politicians. One survey is John B. McConaughy, "Certain Personality Factors of State Legislators in South Carolina," *American Political Science Review,* XLIV (1950), 897–903. A thoughtful discussion of the problem of selection and personality is Harold Lasswell, "The Selective Effect of Personality on Political Participation," in R. Christie and M. Jahoda, eds., *Studies in the Scope and Methods of "The Authoritarian Personality"* (Glencoe, Ill.: Free Press, 1954). Lewis Edinger, "Political Science and Political Biography," *Journal of Politics,* XXVI (1964), 423–39, 648–76, presents a vigorous case for the inclusion of personality variables in the study of political leadership. Good surveys of the literature on leadership are those by Alvin Gouldner, ed., *Studies in Leadership* (New York: Harper, 1950); and Cecil A. Gibb, "Leadership," in G. Lindzey, ed., *Handbook of Social Psychology* (Cambridge: Addison-Wesley, 1954). An interesting application of many of the generalizations posed by social psychologists about leadership to a significant political leader is James M. Burns, *Roosevelt: The Lion and the Fox* (New York: Harcourt Brace, 1956).

for the presidential nomination. Personal and social considerations, then, also determine the structure of political opportunities.

Unfortunately the systematic analysis of most personal and social considerations is beyond the scope of this study. But there is one personal characteristic with which I can readily deal and which is most pertinent to the study of political opportunity—the politician's age.[4] The age cycle also restricts a man's political chances. A man's reasonable expectations in one period of his life are unreasonable at another time. A man can fail to advance in politics as much because he is the wrong age at the wrong time as because he is in the wrong office. All governors of large, competitive states and all Senate leaders do not have the same chance at the Presidency, not only because some lack the proper social qualifications but also because some are outside the likely age limits. The individual politician, therefore, constantly faces the problem of reconciling two ever-changing schedules, the timetable of office and the timetable of age. Since aging is universal, I can easily relate the politician's age timetable to the pattern of office movement which I have already measured.

In this chapter I want to establish the ages at which men typically achieve positions of prominence in American politics. I can then determine whether there is any relation between age and office careers. To determine this relationship, I will examine the ages at which the states' major political leaders begin their office careers, the offices in which they begin, and their subsequent achievements. I shall then examine the age patterns of American political leaders by states to determine the relation between age patterns and the states' opportunity structures.[5] Finally I shall consider the implications of age for ambition theory.

[4] The most important general study on age is Harvey C. Lehman, *Age and Achievement* (Princeton: Princeton University Press, 1963). W. Bell, R. J. Hill, and C. R. Wright, *Public Leadership* (San Francisco: Chandler, 1961), provide a summary of various studies on this as well as on other topics dealing with leadership. For a study of congressional candidates, see David B. Walker, "The Age Factor in the 1958 Congressional Elections," *Midwest Journal of Political Science,* IV (1960), 1–26.

[5] In my analysis of age and political advancement, I have used two different sets of data. First, I have examined the careers of men who have actually attained specific offices: Presidents, senators, representatives, governors, and legislators. When discussing such data, I have specifically referred to the office. Secondly, I have used data based on the careers of all the major party candidates for governor from 1900 through 1958 and for senator from 1914 through 1958, except that only Democratic nominees have been used for 12 southern states. Such data have been used for the analysis of age and first office, age and occupations, age at entry to politics and subsequent careers, as well as for the state-by-state analysis. When referring to such data, I have used the term "major political leaders" and have indicated its meaning in the appropriate places.

AGE AND THE ATTAINMENT OF MAJOR OFFICE

The hierarchy of office in the United States is an accurate guide to the typical age timetable of American political leaders. Examination of the 85th Congress elected in 1956 reveals that the largest single block of United States representatives, if we divide them into five-year age groups, first enter the house between the ages of 35 and 40 (Figure IX-1). Of the governors elected between 1900 and 1958, the greatest number are between 45 and 50 years of age. Of the United States senators elected for the first time between 1914 and 1958, the largest number are between the ages of 50 and 55. By far the greatest

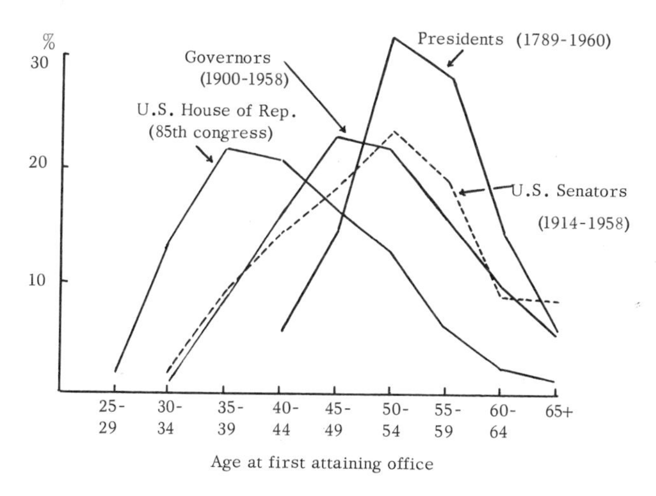

FIGURE IX-1
Age and Achievement of Major Office in the United States

proportion of the men elected President through 1960 are in their early fifties, although the age of attainment is much more sharply focused for the Presidency.

The ambitious politician, therefore, can easily detect his best periods of opportunity. Congressmen do best to arrive in the 15-year age span between 35 and 50, and better earlier than later. The period between 45 and 50 is the most likely time for a man to become governor, while the office of senator is most often achieved between the ages of 45 and 60. Well over half the Presidents of the United States have been in their fifties. Although these figures are by no means binding, they do indicate that there is a 15-year span within which the appropriate ages to attain the major offices in the United States overlap and to which the politician who hopes for advancement should pay close attention.

Age at Entry into Public Office

My findings on the ages of major achievement in American politics imply that some politicians have a more careerist relationship to public office than others. But we can get a better view of a man's relationship to public office by examining the age at which he begins his office career. The younger a man is when he enters politics the greater the range of his ambitions and the likelihood of his developing a career commitment to politics.

When I examined the careers of all the major party candidates for governor and senator, I found that most had obtained some public office by the time they were 35, half between the ages of 25 and 34. Those in the under-30 age group represent the potential career politicians. Entering politics before the age of 30, they are the most likely to consider politics their primary occupation; their interest is not likely to be due to failure in some other endeavor. At the same time, the attainment of public office at an early age represents a less costly investment than later entry to a public office career. Requiring no formal training like medicine and the law, politics is an inexpensive trial run for those whose interests are vague. Unfortunately, we do not know how many young men make their trial run and drop out. We can speculate, however, that success as this age produces firm commitments to a political career.

On the other hand, the public office career entered upon in the thirties represents a more conscious and deliberate choice than that made by the man in his twenties. It may well be an expression of failure in some other field, a dwindling law practice, an unprofitable business venture. But it is also possible for the man in his thirties to use his position outside of politics to gain entry into politics. His extrapolitical accomplishments bring him to the attention of those seeking candidates for elective office or earn him a public office appointment. But, whatever the cause, the man entering public office in his thirties, unlike the man in his twenties, arrives from some other occupation; he has been Bill Jones, insurance salesman, John Smith, lawyer, Fred Williams, shop steward. The man in his thirties is also unlike the man in his twenties in that his age does not make him conspicuous, at least in the lower office ranks. Nevertheless, all offices are open to him, even the Presidency, once he reaches the age of 35. The man who begins his public office career in his thirties, then, can also become a careerist. Of the political leaders we have been studying, three-fourths have started their public office careers by the time they are 40; of that group about one-half have started in their thirties.

The remaining one-quarter of the states' political leaders start their public office careers after the age of 40. My observations about office careers begun by men in their thirties pertain to men in their forties, except that, for these men, politics is an even more secondary occupation or subsequent career. We should, therefore, expect these men to represent more clearly established positions in society, and success more often than failure. In this age group extrapolitical accomplishment is required, more often than not, to give added luster to political candidacy.

The age at which men enter public office thus helps mark their entire relationship to politics. At one extreme, the youth brings little to politics but himself and his background. Should he be successful, he can expect to become the true careerist; but if he fails, he loses little by dropping out. At the other extreme, the man in his forties or older is likely to bring tested talents and accomplishments; but in this age group there are also the political dilettantes. The man in his thirties can bring to politics both a serious commitment and extrapolitical experience.

There is also a significant relationship between the age at which a man begins his public office career and his extrapolitical occupation. The young man in his twenties may wish to become a politician pure and simple, but the purely political career is so fraught with risk that few care to take it on. Even the young man in his twenties can, more often than not, resort to an occupational sideline. Nevertheless, the would-be politician is not free to adopt any trade or profession. Unless he enjoys independent wealth, the politician does best to follow a trade compatible with politics, an occupation to which political activities may in fact be an aid and, at least, will not be a liability. Of all occupations, the practice of law is most clearly compatible with politics, and the relation between early entry into politics and the practice of law is striking.

Among the early entrants in our group of political leaders, those starting their office careers before the age of 30, lawyers dominate almost to the exclusion of all other occupations (Table IX-1). Of those in the 25–29 age group, three out of every four are lawyers. After 29, the proportion of lawyers declines steadily. As the age of entry into public office rises, the businessman becomes increasingly prominent until, in the age groups over 40, he outnumbers the lawyer. The non-legal professions also increase in representation as the age of

TABLE IX-1

Age at First Office and Occupation (Major Political Leaders in the States)

Age at Entry	*Lawyers*	*Businessmen*	*Farmers*	*Communications*	*Non-Legal Professions*	*No Information or No Other*	*Total (N)*
Under 25	68.67%	16.27%	3.61%	6.03%	1.80%	3.62%	100% (166)
25–29	74.16	11.24	3.82	4.72	3.14	2.92	100 (445)
30–34	58.76	22.42	6.95	5.16	5.67	1.04	100 (388)
35–39	40.49	33.47	8.26	7.02	9.52	1.24	100 (242)
40–44	36.70	37.97	5.06	8.23	8.87	3.17	100 (158)
45–49	31.03	45.68	5.17	5.17	10.35	2.60	100 (116)
50+	20.71	47.74	6.30	4.55	18.01	2.69	100 (111)

entry rises, although they represent no large share of the total. Nevertheless, in the age group entering public office at full maturity, those over 50, the number of men who practice the non-legal professions approaches the number of lawyers. Farmers appear in only very small numbers in all the age groups. Journalism, written or broadcast, is only slightly better represented than farming, despite its theoretical compatibility with politics. Like farmers, journalists, editors, and publishers are no more conspicuous in one age group than in another.

The distribution of occupations by age groups supports my statement about the significance of the age of entry into politics. The overwhelming domination of the under-30 age group by lawyers confirms my suggestion that this group is made up of men casting about, testing their chances in politics while they are yet without established positions. As lawyers they have the least to lose and the most to gain from political activity. The steady decline in lawyers as the age of entry rises indicates that, even for lawyers, politics becomes less compatible, the more established they become in their profession. The very low proportion of businessmen entering politics under the age of 30 and the non-existence of other professionals in this age group demonstrates that men bent on prominence elsewhere do not make an early entry into public office. By the same token, the true career politicians enter politics before the age of 30.

The occupations of men entering public office in their thirties is more evenly distributed. Among those in their early thirties, lawyers are still dominant, although the other occupations have increased their representation. But in the late thirties, there is a sharp increase in the number of representatives from all the other occupations. In the thirties a man's professional career settles down, the marks of success or failure begin to show. After 35, then, businessmen, non-legal professionals, farmers, and members of the news media, established in their primary occupations, begin to move into positions of political leadership. After the age of 40, those for whom politics is most clearly an avocation dominate the "new" politicians.

The age at which a man enters public office is relevant not only to his non-political occupation; it is relevant also to the type of career he has in politics. The American office structure provides a variety of points of entry to a public office career; to a large extent a man's point of entry depends upon the age at which he enters office. Earlier I have pointed out that the most common points of entry to major political careers in the American states are offices, low in the office hierarchy, whose number is large and whose turnover rate is frequently high. The office of state legislator combines many openings with a

TABLE IX-2

Age at First Office Related to the First Office (Major Political Leaders in the States)

Age at First Office	*First Office Held*[a]								
	State Legislature	*Law Enforcement*	*Adminis-trative*	*Local Elective*	*Congress*	*Statewide Elective*	*No Office*	*Other*	*Total*
Under 25	20.48%	28.91%	43.98%	6.63%	—	—	—	—	100%
25–29	30.33	39.77	16.17	9.21	1.57	1.12	—	1.83	100
30–34	32.73	26.54	16.75	14.43	4.12	0.77	1.03	3.73	100
35–39	28.42	19.83	19.42	16.94	5.78	3.72	2.89	2.48	100
40–44	23.41	14.55	22.78	13.29	5.06	4.43	11.39	5.09	100
45–49	26.72	9.48	23.27	8.62	10.34	6.90	10.34	4.33	100
50+	9.00	4.50	14.41	6.30	4.50	14.41	43.24	3.64	100

[a] The figures listed in the table give the percentage of all the major political leaders who have held a first office in each category.

high rate of turnover; law enforcement office includes the many state and local, district and prosecuting attorneys; administrative office includes appointive posts at all levels of government. Of the political leaders we have been studying, the young entrants into public office are the most conspicuous users of these three major entry points.

But there are interesting variations (Table IX-2). For the youngest entrants, those under 25, administration is the major point of entry; undoubtedly most of the law enforcement men in this age group have held appointive positions as well. The earliest entrants into public office, then, are men mostly co-opted into the political system, men who started with strong enough ties in the system to gain a public office appointment. After the early twenties, use of an administrative entry point drops sharply, becoming important again only for the age group over 40. In this age group, however, the administrative entry point is undoubtedly at a higher level. In addition to administration, law enforcement office is most important as an entry point for young entrants, reaching its peak importance for those in their late twenties. The importance of law enforcement office for this group undoubtedly reflects the importance of lawyers in the group. As a point of entry, the state legislature is consistently significant until the political entrant reaches the age of 50; relatively, it is the most significant point of entry from the age of 30 on, although its absolute importance declines as the politicians grow older.

We might expect from my general statements about age and political careers that men entering public office late in life, with the advantage of prestige achieved elsewhere, will make their entry into public office at higher levels in the office hierarchy than the three common points of entry. As the age of entry into public office rises, there is indeed a sharp increase in the number of men who achieve the major positions of elective leadership without previous office experience. In the age group over 50, men without office experience are dominant. As the age level rises, there is also an increase in the number of political leaders whose first offices are the prestigious offices of congressman and statewide elective official.

What importance does a man's point of entry into public office have for his subsequent career? Since all of the men in my sample did achieve positions of leadership, they will not help us make judgments about which ages and which offices of entry are most likely to lead to advancement. To make such a judgment we need information about those who have succeeded and those who have not at every level in the office hierarchy. With our data we can, however, determine the relative influence of the mode of entry upon the subsequent achievements of the leadership group itself.

What kind of careers do the politicians who enter public office at each age level have? Does the age of entry into public office make any difference to the age at which the major position of leadership is achieved? There are two possibilities: the earlier the entry, the more rapid the rise; or, if my judgments about the men who enter politics after 30 are correct, advantages acquired outside of politics will facilitate rapid advancement in the older age groups.

TABLE IX-3

Age at Entry to Public Office and Age at Achievement of Major Nomination[a] (Major Political Leaders in the States)

Age at Starting	*Percentage to Have Achieved Major Nomination by the Following Ages:*							
	40	*45*	*50*	*55*	*60*	*65*	*Over 65*	*N*
Under 25	13.25%	28.31%	45.78%	65.06%	82.53%	89.16%	100%	166
25–29	12.36	31.24	53.49	73.27	88.33	93.50	100	445
30–34	13.89	33.17	56.05	72.50	87.15	92.81	100	388
35–39	9.09	25.21	46.28	63.64	81.82	94.63	100	242
40–44	—	16.46	39.24	66.46	81.65	97.47	100	158
45–49	—	—	21.55	51.72	75.86	89.65	100	116
50+	—	—	—	31.53	58.65	77.48	100	111

[a] Major party nominations for governor, 1900–1958, and for U.S. senator, 1914–1958.

My evidence tends to support the inference that extrapolitical accomplishment can more than compensate for an early start in public office. The earliest starters, those entering public office before the age of 25, are not the speediest runners in politics (Table IX-3). In terms of the age at which they receive their major nomination, the early starters run behind many of the older starters; a higher proportion of those entering public office in their early forties achieve their nomination before the age of 55 than those who have started their careers in their early twenties. The fastest moving group of politicians are those who start in their early thirties; of these, 56 per cent attain their position of elective leadership before the age of 50. Within the open structure of American politics, the precocious do not appear to enjoy any marked advantage over the man who comes to politics in early maturity; the early starter is perhaps even at a slight disadvantage in the race for higher office. In this sense, American politics appears to be markedly different from the other professions.

On the other hand, the evidence does support the inference that the early starter is the true career politician. Politics is not only more open than most professions, it is also more risky; the political career is often sporadic. A man's age at entry into politics and the age at which he receives his major nomination do not necessarily, therefore, give us his total office experience. An early entry into politics could well be followed by periods of no officeholding. Nevertheless, there is a positive relation between early entry into public office and the total number of years spent in office. Twenty years in public office constitutes a substantial career; of the early starters, those under 25, fully one-third have held office 20 years or more before receiving their major nominations (Table IX-4). Over half of those who start before

TABLE IX-4
Age at Entry and Number of Years in Office Before Receiving Major Nomination (Major State Political Leaders)

Age at Entry	*Percentage of Major Leaders with the Following Numbers of Years of Experience:*				
	Under 10	*10–19*	*20 and over*	*Total*[a]	*N*
Under 25	22.89%	42.77%	33.77%	99.43%	166
25–29	35.06	48.32	16.40	99.78	445
30–34	54.13	36.34	8.57	99.04	388
35–39	56.58	35.13	5.79	97.50	242
40–44	74.05	20.89	4.43	99.37	158
45–49	79.31	16.38	1.72	97.41	116
50+	90.09	9.01	0.00	99.10	111

[a] Percentages do not add to 100 per cent because of incomplete information.

they are 30 have spent at least ten years in office (not necessarily consecutively) before attaining their major nominations. After the age of 30 the total time in office drops; among those who start their office careers after 40, at least three out of four spend less than ten years in public office before receiving their nominations.

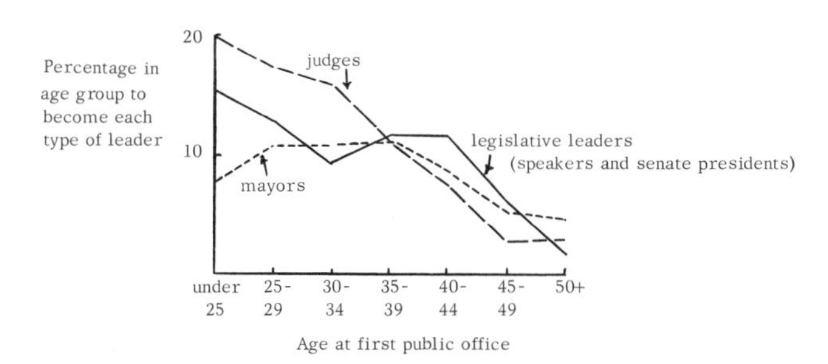

FIGURE IX-2
Age at First Office of Major Political Leaders and Attainment of a Secondary Leadership Position before the Major Nomination

The youngest entrants are also the careerists in that they have held more positions of secondary leadership before attaining their major nominations. Among those who enter public office before the age of 25, a higher proportion becomes judges and state legislative leaders (though not mayors) than those who enter office later. But it is important to note also (see Figure IX-2) that, although the earlier entrants obtain a greater number of secondary positions of leadership, the number of secondary leaders in the older age groups does not sharply decline. Despite the steady decline in the amount of office experience in the older age groups, the proportion of mayors increases in the 25–35 age group, the proportion of state legislative leaders in those entering in the 35–45 age group. The later start, then, does not handicap men in their thirties either for positions of secondary leadership or for the major nominations.

Age and Penultimate Office

My evidence indicates, however, that the achievement of some conspicuous office more often than not hastens the achievement of the major position of leadership. In general, the manifest officeholders set the typical age pattern at which the offices of governor and senator are achieved.[6] Of the manifest officeholders who become governor, most of the statewide officials are elected in their forties and early fifties, most of the state legislators in the years between 45 and 55. Of the manifest officers who become senator, most are elected in the years between 45 and 59; congressmen usually achieve the office five years earlier than governors.

Among the non-manifest officeholders who become governor, those in the more conspicuous offices arrive earlier than those in the lesser offices or without office experience (Figure IX-3). Holders of law enforcement offices are among the youngest to win gubernatorial office, typically in the years between 35 and 45. Of the few congressmen who become governor, the largest number are elected in their late forties. In contrast, local officials and administrators become governor mostly after they have reached their fifties. The same is true of men elected to the governorship without prior office experience.

On the other hand, the age pattern of the non-manifest officeholders who become senator deviates from the overall trend in which notable office experience hastens the achievement of major office (Figure IX-4). There is a marked contrast between the age distributions of the

[6] These figures are based on those who actually become governor and senator.

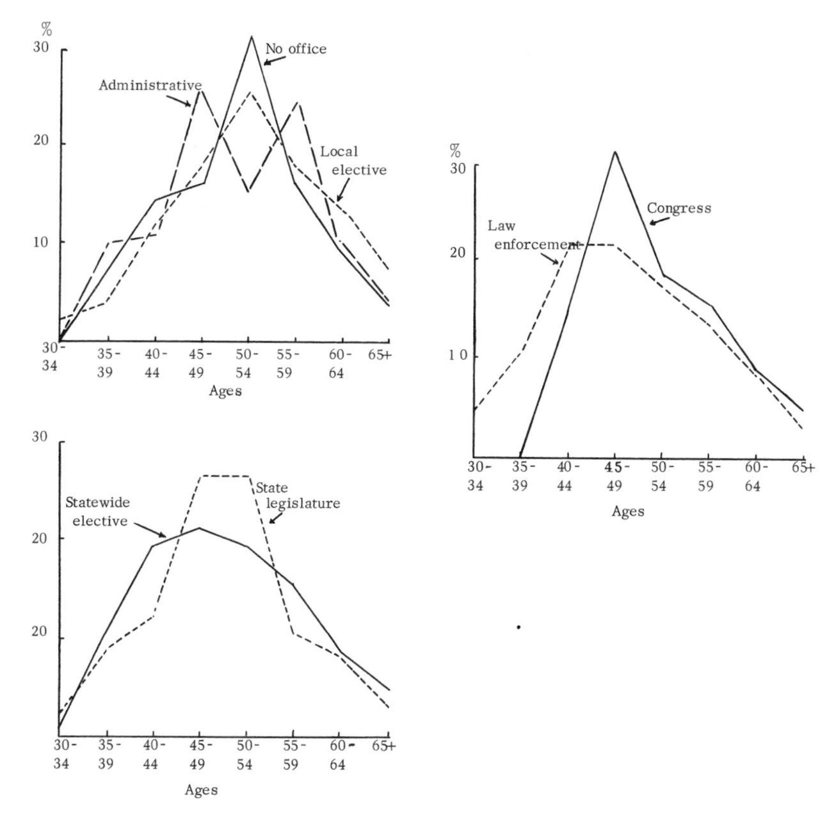

FIGURE IX-3
Penultimate Offices of Governors and Age at Becoming Governor

men who become governor without prior office experience and those who become senator. Although the number in each case is small, the proportions are about the same for each office. With respect to the governorship, these men come typically from the 50–55 group; with respect to the Senate, they are not conspicuous in any one age group and, if anything, tend to win election before they are 50. Thus, while men outside the office system usually become governor later than those from within, the reverse is true for the office of senator. Furthermore, state legislators elected to the Senate usually win election at an earlier age than those elected from the manifest offices; local officials are elected both earlier and later.

The differences in the age patterns of the two offices is probably accounted for by the differences in the positions of the offices in the states' opportunity structures. The position of the governorship is intermediate; it is conspicuously placed for later advancement. By the

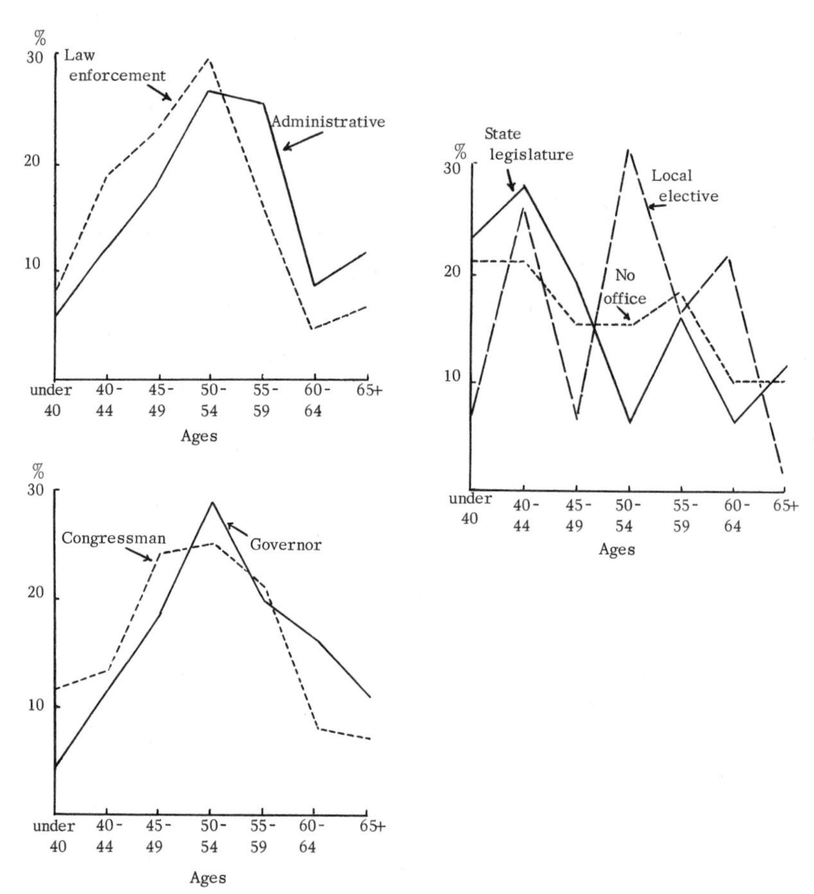

FIGURE IX-4
Penultimate Offices of Senators and Age at Becoming Senator

same token, the paths leading to the governorship are less rigidly marked; it is an office which can be assaulted successfully by a broad group of individuals. It is, therefore, an office peculiarly attractive to and assailable by men who have become conspicuous both in and out of government. A conspicuous position is more likely to be achieved later than earlier in life, but somewhat earlier in politics than in extrapolitical activity. The office of senator, on the other hand, is more the career office; the path is more rigidly defined. When the manifest office pattern breaks down, therefore, the professional requirements appear to have taken precedence. Men without office experience and lesser officials can win the office of senator and win early, not because they have become conspicuous in the public eye but because they have a close association with the party organization or other organized elements capable of helping them to office. My evidence on ages, therefore, seen in relation to my earlier evidence, suggests that the office of governor is by far the more likely outlet for those whom the French call "notables," the Senate the more likely outlet for the career politician.

AGE AND POLITICAL OFFICE: REGIONAL AND STATE VARIATIONS

The interesting differences in age patterns, however, are not confined to the differences in office careers; there are significant regional and state differences. Generally, throughout the United States the age groups which achieve major office become older and more restrictive the higher the office. Throughout the states, the age level rises progressively and the age focus narrows from the office of congressman to the office of governor, from the office of governor to Senate office. Limited evidence indicates that the range of ages is much broader among lesser

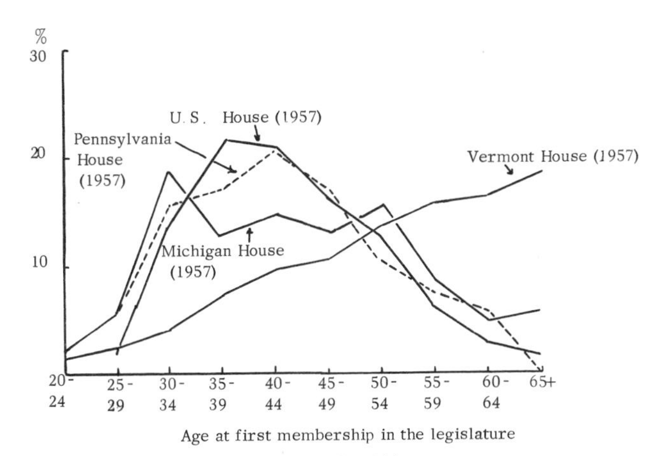

FIGURE IX-5
The Ages at Which the Members of Selected Legislatures First Attained Office in the Legislature

officials. Members of the lower house of the Michigan legislature, for example, fit a bimodal age curve; the largest number of legislators have first won election either in their early thirties or in their early fifties (Figure IX-5). In Vermont the number of new arrivals increases with each succeeding age bracket from the early twenties on, the largest number of new arrivals coming in the age group over 65. But the Vermont situation, which deviates from the normal age curve followed by other state legislatures, indicates that regional and state factors play their part, as well as the position of the office in the office hierarchy. New England, along with the border states and the south, has distinct and rigid age patterns for the three highest state offices, supporting our earlier picture of all three regions as areas where political opportunity is most rigidly ordered.

The age patterns in New England and the border states set the national norm of age progression for the three offices of congressman, governor, and senator (Figure IX-6). In both these regions congressmen are usually elected in their forties, governors in their late forties, and senators in their early fifties. The age patterns in the midwest and the middle Atlantic states are similar but not as neat. The age distributions are flatter in the midwest; the differences in the ages of governors and senators are much smaller there than elsewhere. In the middle Atlantic states, the age of election to the governorship concentrates more sharply in the later forties and senators are somewhat older than elsewhere. Men also go to the House of Representatives later, typically in their late forties.

The distinctive age pattern of the south is marked by the election of senators at an earlier age than governors, a pattern which is also characteristic of the far west, and in both regions congressmen are also conspicuously younger than elsewhere. The age pattern of both regions is clearly related to the regional treatment of the Senate as a career office. In the south, at least, the strong assurance of long tenure in office undoubtedly has its impact upon the selection process, producing younger senatorial candidates than elsewhere. In this sense, the career system helps to shift power within Congress to the southern and western states.

Distinctive state patterns emerge with respect to the age of entry into politics (Table IX-5). If we rank the 48 states according to the proportion of their major leaders who are careerists (those who have begun their public office careers before the age of thirty), the range is considerable, from a high of 61 per cent in South Carolina to a low of 11 per cent in Delaware.[7] The age rankings indicate the distinctly different approaches to officeseeking in the states.

An early start is most characteristic of southern states. In eight of the southern states one-half or more of the state's major leaders have begun their public office careers before the age of 30. The states whose leaders are predominantly late starters, i.e., more than three-fourths have entered public office after the age of 30, show little regional

[7] The analysis of state differences is based on the careers of the major party candidates for both governor and senator, with the exception of the 12 southern states where only Democratic nominees are included.

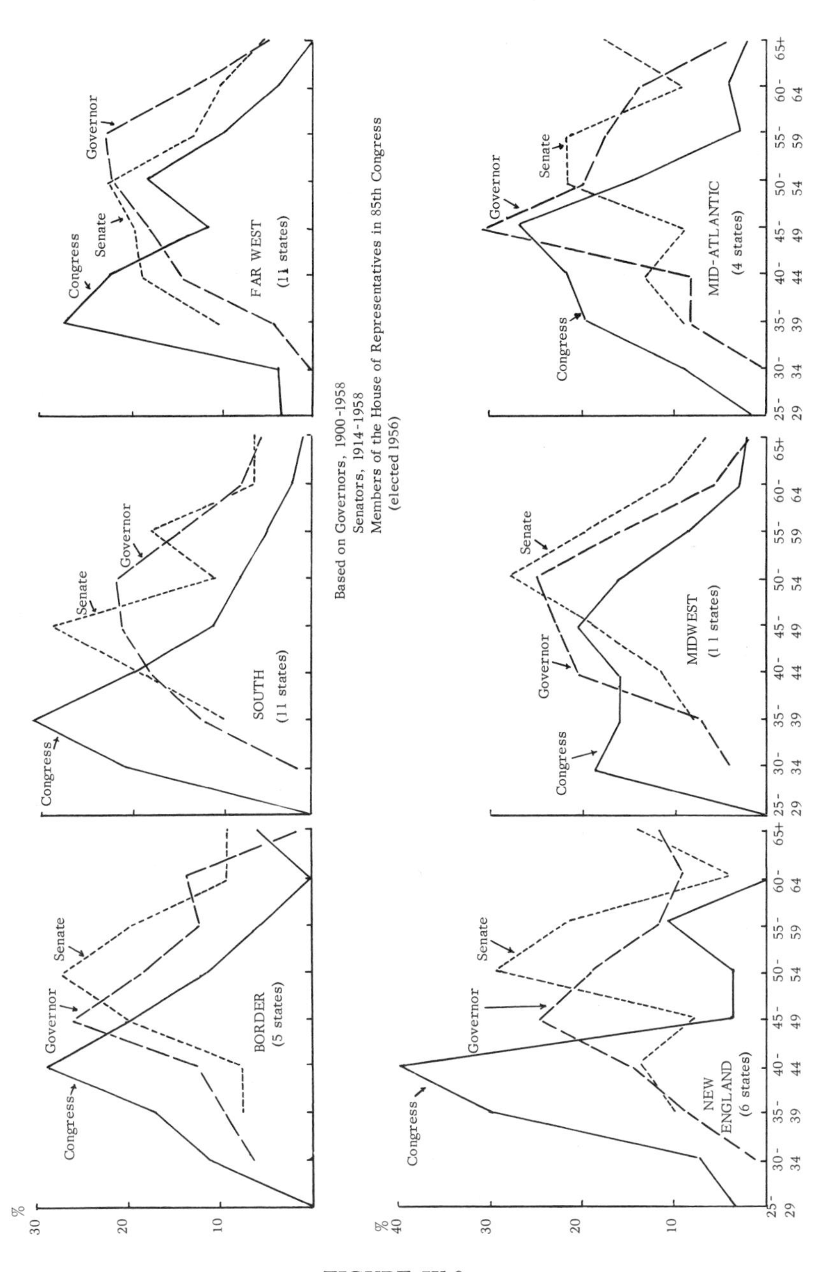

FIGURE IX-6
Age at Achievement of Major Office, by Regions

TABLE IX-5

Ages at First Public Office (Major State Leaders), by States

State	*Percentage in Each Age Group:* Under 30	30-39	40 and Over
Group I—Early Starters Dominant			
South Carolina	61%	28%	11%
North Carolina	59	26	15
Mississippi	59	41	0
Florida	56	26	18
Iowa	53	30	17
Texas	53	27	20
Alabama	52	38	10
Louisiana	52	30	18
Minnesota	51	40	9
Georgia	50	30	20
Ohio	50	37	13
Michigan	49	19	32
Maryland	47	32	21
Illinois	46	28	26
Arizona	45	27	28
California	45	33	22
Wisconsin	44	31	25
Rhode Island	43	38	19
Kentucky	42	42	16
Missouri	41	35	24
Tennessee	41	39	20
Group II—Secondary Starters Dominant			
South Dakota	18	60	22
North Dakota	22	56	22
Arkansas	36	56	8
Nevada	32	54	14
Utah	31	50	19
New Mexico	31	50	19
Maine	28	50	32
Virginia	27	50	23
Washington	38	48	14
New Hampshire	31	48	14
Massachusetts	36	47	17
Nebraska	31	47	22
Colorado	28	46	26
West Virginia	34	45	21
New Jersey	20	44	36
Kansas	21	43	36
Idaho	22	42	36
Montana	34	41	25
New York	31	40	29
Group III—Tertiary Starters Dominant			
Oklahoma	20	25	55
Delaware	11	41	48
Connecticut	35	24	41
Group IV—Relatively Even Distribution			
Wyoming	39	30	31
Oregon	35	32	33
Vermont	27	39	34
Indiana	32	37	31
Pennsylvania	31	31	39

concentration. They consist of rural states in New England and the midwest, Vermont and New Hampshire, Kansas and the Dakotas, and of urban industrial states in the east, New York, New Jersey, and Pennsylvania. A late start in public office, then, may reflect the general age distribution of the state and the exodus of the young from purely agricultural areas: I have already pointed out the peculiarly aged character of the Vermont legislature. The late start may reflect too the lack of careerism in a state's politics, the lack of patronage and control which can support young men and attract them to public service, although the lure of major office may attract them at a later date. The late start in states such as New York and New Jersey most likely reflects the competitive political situation in these states which often requires the parties to seek strong candidates outside the area of politics. Furthermore, as states whose parties are marked by strong organization, longer organizational apprenticeship may be required. In these states the stereotype of political office as the reward for party labor is more likely to be true, but the reward is likely to be delayed until a man has served a satisfactory apprenticeship in the party organization.

I should also point out that in very few states do the late starters have a serious handicap. In only three states, Mississippi, Arkansas, and Minnesota, do fewer than 10 per cent of the state's leaders enter public office after the age of 40; and only in Mississippi does no one start on a major career in public office after the age of 40. See Table IX-5.

All the evidence, then, points to a close relationship between age patterns and the states' structures of opportunity. In accordance with the American political tradition which dates from the rule of Andrew Jackson, we should expect a high rate of opportunity to be associated with lack of careerism in public office. That is indeed the case; we find an inverse relation between a state's per capita chances for major public office and the proportion of its major political leaders who begin their public office careers before the age of 30 (rank order correlation = −0.54). It would seem that the fewer the political opportunities in a state, the more likely it is that the state's political leaders will make an early start. In contrast, Delaware which provides the greatest number of opportunities for major office is the state which has the smallest number of early starters.

My discussion of age patterns implies also a relation between age and the shape of the states' structures of opportunity. There is limited support for the proposition that the more rigid the states' structures, the earlier the age of entry into public office. See Table IX-6. In all the states where more than half the political leaders have started in their twenties, there is some type of office career pattern. In contrast, ten

TABLE IX-6
Age at Start of Public Career and Degree of Structure in Office Opportunities

Type of Opportunity Structure (from Table VI-6)	*Number of States Where the Following Percentages of Leaders[a] Who Attain First Public Office before the Age of 30 Are Found:*			
	49%–61%	*36%–47%*	*31%–35%*	*11%–28%*
I Highly structured	4	3	2	2
II Semistructured	8	7	3	6
III Diffuse	0	3	7	3

[a] Major party candidates for governor, 1900–1958, for senator, 1914–1958.

of the thirteen states which I have classed as diffuse in structure are among the states whose early entrants number under 35 per cent. The less orderly structures, then, appear to advantage the late entrants into public office.

AGE AND AMBITION THEORY

In this chapter I have measured a personal dimension of the states' opportunity structures, the age timetable of political careers, and found that the age at which major office is achieved is closely related to what I have termed the size and the shape of the states' opportunity structures. The age timetable parallels the office hierarchy, showing a progressive rise in the typical age at which office is achieved. More important, the age focus is sharper the higher the office. The age focus is also sharper the fewer the number of political opportunities in a given state. Well-defined age patterns are associated too with political careerism. Since age and career data are so closely related, we expect to reach such conclusions. Nevertheless, the relation of career and age data emphasizes that the structure of opportunity provides a framework for personal ambition capable of controlling the long-range behavior of numerous politicians.

The close relation between age and career patterns can only intensify the impact of political ambitions. Both impose order upon opportunity and reduce the field of the reasonably ambitious. True, nowhere in the United States is the field so restricted by age or office requirements that any one person can be assured of advancement. But this situation merely serves to intensify ambition; certainty by definition reduces or eliminates tensions. Rather my evidence reveals that the American political system provides a probable balance or narrowing of political opportunity.

My data imply that the tensions of ambition are likely to be greater as one rises in the pyramid of office; the timetables of age and office have narrowed the field and intensified the competition. We can infer, therefore, that the impact of ambitions upon the behavior of public officials will be greater on those in high than in low office, greater upon congressmen than upon state legislators, greater upon United States senators than upon United States representatives. Such an arrangement is surely felicitous in a democracy, for it provides progressive controls over public officials as their power to do good or evil increases.

The progressive age pattern also makes for a felicitous spread of the tensions of ambition among politicians at the height of their political vigor. It allows eminence to come in politics to much older men than in other areas of activity, and it makes possible long-range career-planning in an otherwise risky business. The 35-year-old politician with progressive ambitions, although constitutionally eligible, is not likely to aim directly at the Presidency. He knows, rather, that under the proper conditions, his chances will improve over the next 15 to 20 years. The tensions of ambition, therefore, affect not only those in the age groups appropriate to a particular office, but they leave their effect upon younger men, causing them to behave so that they will create the proper conditions for subsequent advancement. If major offices could be assaulted by men of all ages with equal chances of success, the effect of ambition would be diffuse and far less useful as a political control.

The states' structures of opportunity and their age timetables work as controls because they are as obvious to the members of the political community at large as to the individual ambitious politician. They set the framework of expectations. In effect, there are both manifest ages and manifest offices. When the manifest office and manifest age coincide, the influential members of the political community, elective and appointed officeholders, party men, representatives of interest groups, reporters and columnists, begin to treat the officeholder as if he were a potential governor, senator, or President. With such expectations, the officeholder gains influence. But he also loses freedom once the goal of his ambition is clearly in focus; he becomes the creature of the newer constituency.

CHAPTER X

Conclusions

IN THIS STUDY I have brought together empirical findings about American political careers within the theoretical framework which I consider most meaningful for American politics. That the measures I have devised and their applications are crude I readily admit. But the virtue of theory is that it allows crude and tentative efforts to point the way to unexplored areas and to suggest new approaches to existing knowledge. At this point, however, it is appropriate to reconsider whether ambition theory, as elaborated by the findings of this study, leads toward a useful interpretation of the American political system.

The central assumption of ambition theory, I repeat, is that politicians respond to their office goals. The theory assumes, in other words, that politicians act in the manner which they consider appropriate to the achievement of office. But here let me again make clear why ambition theory has not led to the preoccupation with *how* politicians achieve office. If the theory has sparked my interest in data on office advancement, it has also diverted me from attempting to use that data to explain success in politics. Since, as we have seen, there are no *sure* paths to high office in the United States, a description of the frequency with which certain officeholders become governor or senator tells us little about how these offices are won. The congressman or governor who wants to become senator must still make the strategic choices concerning the conduct of his office which will determine his chances to advance. To the extent that political advancement depends upon appeals to the voters, we must look to electoral theory and to voting studies for the explanation of the strategies of advancement.

Ambition theory has diverted my attention to the source of politics, the ambitions of politicians. Thus I have used the data on office careers to build a model of the structure of political opportunities in the United States; not to discover who the men are who are likely to become governor or senator, but to help locate the men to whom it is reasonable and appropriate to assign ambitions for these offices. It is true that my concern with ambition for office rather than with its achievement has limited the inferences which I have drawn from career data. Most notably it has kept me from commenting on the behavior of specific officeholders even when I make inferences about their ambitions, because the ambitions themselves tell us nothing about the proper strategies for their fulfillment. The closest I have come to an analysis of behavior is in Chapter VIII where I deal with the problem of party convergence and policy. Nevertheless, knowledge of the structure of political opportunities does provide insights into the American political system. It helps especially to enlighten institutional relationships, which are all too easily discounted as irrelevant or, at most, of superficial importance, and political organization whose basic purpose, the capturing of office, is all too often obscured.

In this chapter I want to discuss the insights provided by ambition theory and my findings about political opportunities in the United States. In order to do so, however, it is useful to reconsider these findings, a summary of which follows:

I. The structure of political opportunities in the United States is national in scope.
   A. The principal flow of public office personnel is from the state to the nation, from state office to the Congress or the Presidency.
   B. Nevertheless, the states are the foundation of the national office structure. Two-thirds of the men who hold posts in the presidential office complex have held some kind of office within the states' control.
   C. The states, however, vary in their relation to the national structure: twelve states have no representatives among the presidential office group, while the states of Massachusetts and New York have more than twice the number of representatives warranted by their populations.

II. The arrangement of offices in the national structure reflects American institutional arrangements.
   A. Although there is considerable overlap, elective offices

provide lines of promotion distinct from appointive offices. At the national level, at least, the judiciary draws from lesser positions in the legal system.

B. There are discernible federal and state perspectives in political careers.
   1. The state career has its base in the state legislature; men advance to the governorship from the state legislature or lesser statewide elective posts; and governors advance to the Senate.
   2. The base of the federal career is the law enforcement office; while advancement to the governorship takes varied paths, the office of United States representative is the principal route to the Senate.

C. The offices which are key positions for advancement have a manifest institutional relationship with the goal office; the offices share either the same electorate or the same political arena. One-half the senators come either from the lower house of Congress or the governorship; one-half the governors come either from a lesser statewide elective post or the state legislature.

III. Although the national structure is open, in the sense that all offices can be won by men with any type of office experience or by men with no office experience, there are definite marks of hierarchy.

A. The higher the office, the more complex the typical career leading to that office. Typically, senators have held more offices than governors and there is greater difference between their first and their penultimate offices.

B. The careers of those who advance from higher offices, e.g., offices in the United States House of Representatives or the lieutenant governorship, are more complex than the careers of those who advance from lower offices, e.g., the state legislature or a law enforcement post.

C. Higher offices draw personnel from fewer, more conspicuous offices than do lower offices. The Presidency and the Vice Presidency draw more heavily on governors and senators than the office of senator draws on governors and representatives; in turn, the use of statewide elective office and the state legislature for the governorship is even less concentrated.

D. Within the individual states, patterns of promotion to the

Senate are more sharply defined than those leading to the governorship.

E. The typical age for the achievement of specific offices reflects the hierarchical status of the office.

IV. Within the national structure, offices differ markedly in their career potential.

A. The states' principal executive posts, the offices of governor, lieutenant governor, and attorney general, are highly transitory offices.

B. The career offices, those held in many states for twelve years or more, are the offices of senator and United States representative and the minor statewide elective posts such as secretary of state and state auditor.

V. The states' structures of political opportunities vary in clarity.

A. Within the state structures the base office is related to the degree of order in the structure.

1. The states whose patterns of advancement are most orderly have a high proportion of leaders with state legislative experience.

2. States whose patterns of advancement are less well defined have a high proportion of leaders with law enforcement experience or with no common base office.

B. Within the states, a well-defined structure of opportunities is closely related to the rate of turnover of personnel in office and to the age of officeholders.

1. The states whose structures of opportunity are poorly defined have either a very high or a very low turnover in public office.

2. The starting age of political leaders is higher in states with poorly defined structures of opportunity.

VI. While the two-party system helps determine political opportunities, the structure of opportunities appears to be independent of the state of competition between the parties.

A. The competitive status of the parties within a state affects the offices available to the parties and, therefore, their internal structures of opportunity.

1. In dominant parties the paths to nomination are more often well-defined than in minority parties. The use of manifest offices for nominations to the governorship and the Senate is primarily a characteristic of dominant parties.

2. Competitive parties can have well-defined paths to the Senate. Competitive parties often nominate United States representatives for the upper house.
3. Minority parties rely on varied lesser officials for nominations to high office. State legislators and local office-holders are most often the nominees of minority parties.

B. The parties internal structures of opportunities also reflect the independence of the states' opportunity structures from the party system.
1. The classification of offices as transitory or careerlike is not dependent upon party competition; the correlation between party competition and turnover in office in the states varies from office to office; the value of incumbency in gaining renomination varies with the office.
2. There is a strong similarity between the two parties in the geographical sources of their national leadership and in their patterns of advancement within the states, particularly with respect to the use of base offices.

THE STRUCTURE OF POLITICAL OPPORTUNITIES IN THE UNITED STATES, AMBITION THEORY, AND THE AMERICAN POLITICAL SYSTEM

Do the findings about political opportunities which I have just summarized justify an ambition theory of American politics? Since there does appear to be a structure of opportunities independent of the party system, we are at least justified in going beyond party theory for an explanation of the American political system. Had the opportunities for office been defined simply by party competition, there would be little point in developing new constructs.

One advantage of ambition theory is that it has allowed us to draw a plausible as well as a rational scheme of American politics. It is true that I have presented no direct evidence about the ambitions of American politicians. I have only assumed that men's ambitions are stirred by opportunities and, to the extent that experience brings order to opportunity, that opportunity will guide men's ambitions. Nevertheless, by demonstrating the existence of a hierarchy of elective offices in the United States, and one in which the key positions are the obvious positions, we bring reasonable order to the American political scene. I am well aware that I have not demonstrated either that American politicians do in fact perceive their opportunities as I have described them, or that the opportunity structure affects political aspirations.

Nevertheless, I feel that the structure of opportunity is a useful guide to the effective ambitions of American politicians and their repercussions.

The structure of political opportunities, for example, allows us to ascribe to American politicians varying ambitions and therefore varying pressures, even at the same levels of government. When we know that the local law enforcement offices, the offices of county and district attorney, are important bases from which to launch a political career and that the offices of mayor and city councillor are not, we can reasonably ascribe progressive ambitions to local public attorneys while ascribing static or discrete ambitions to local executives and legislators. We can then reasonably make the further assumption that local law enforcement officials will be most subject to electoral pressures, particularly from the constituencies of the office to which they aspire, while local executives and legislators will be more susceptible to non-electoral pressures.

The opportunity structure illuminates the relative laxness of electoral pressures at the local level in still another way. Within the American structure of opportunities, the higher the office the fewer and more sharply defined its career lines. Thus, even when ambitious men are drawn into local offices, their expectations are diffuse. Because expectations become clearer as one rises within the office hierarchy, it follows that the higher the office, the more effective electoral tensions become. In other words, the opportunity structure indicates that the higher the reaches of politics, the more things are what they seem or what they are supposed to be—parties and politicians courting popular or electoral support. Certainly this is one plausible explanation of why the hidden power structure is taken far more seriously within the local community than at the national level.[1]

At the national level, the concept of a national structure of political opportunities in which state offices, the offices of senator and governor, have a special place is most helpful to our understanding of American political institutions. I should now like to examine in some detail the implications for the federal system and the two-party system.

THE STRUCTURE OF POLITICAL OPPORTUNITIES AND THE FEDERAL SYSTEM

Within the American federal system, the Senate has been a major centripetal force. William Riker has noted that the Senate, introduced

[1] Compare, for example, the seriousness with which students of local politics have treated Floyd Hunter's *Community Power Structure* (Chapel Hill: University of North Carolina Press, 1953), with the very limited interest shown in his *Top Leadership, U.S.A.* (Chapel Hill: University of North Carolina Press, 1959).

into the Constitution as the bastion of the states, quickly became a national institution, the senators refusing to take their directions from the state legislatures which selected them.[2] As the party system emerged, state legislative elections came increasingly to revolve around the selection of a United States senator rather than around state issues. The Seventeenth Amendment, which provided for the popular election of senators, merely made constitutional what was becoming the *de facto* situation. It did, at the same time, free state legislatures from the task of choosing senators; reformers hoped that this would improve the quality of legislative work and focus the legislator's attention on state issues. By enlarging the political base of the senator, however, popular election made the office more attractive than ever to state leaders.

Because the Senate has been attractive both to governors and to congressmen, its position within the national government has been greatly strengthened. At a time when the second chambers of bicameral legislatures have increasingly lost influence, the United States Senate has become ever more important. There are, of course, many reasons why, among them the Senate's popular electoral base and the separation of presidential and congressional powers, but because congressmen can realistically aspire to the Senate, it is unlikely that the House of Representatives will ever seek to reduce the Senate's powers, as the British House of Commons reduced the power of the Lords in 1911. Similarly, as long as the states' governors see their hopes for advancement in the Senate, it is unlikely that attacks upon federal power will be directed at the Congress.

The structure of political opportunities in the United States, of course, has grown out of existing institutional arrangements. But it also affects these arrangements, modifying and reinforcing the relationships among institutions. This is best demonstrated by the long-range decline of state government and the increased importance of national institutions. There are many reasons for these developments. Most recent analyses emphasize the states' failure to resolve pressing problems as the principal cause of increased federal involvement in the traditional state areas of education, public welfare, transportation, and urban affairs. The states' failure to act in these areas is ascribed not to any inherent incapacity, but to the inflexibility produced by malapportionment and one-party politics. I would add that the states' inertia is reinforced by their intermediary position in the national structure of opportunities. Within the states the most vigorous and ambitious men are drawn in-

[2] William Riker, "The Senate and American Federalism," *American Political Science Review,* XLIX (1955), 452–69.

exorably to the national arena, either to the Senate or to some place in the presidential office complex.

The national opportunity structure helps aggrandize the nation over the states in two ways. First, as I have pointed out, it tends to deprive the states of their leaders. Secondly, and probably more important, ambition theory makes us aware that men are unlikely to demean the object of their ambitions. If the best long-range career opportunities for American politicians are at the national level, it is unlikely that promising state officials will lead the fight to reduce the nation's powers. This has been a significant influence in weakening the states; it means that the potential for leadership concerned with state problems is reduced far beyond the obvious. Because of the age patterns in American politics, which we discussed in Chapter IX, progressive ambitions are most likely to affect state legislators, county attorneys, and even public administrators at the peak of their vigor. At the same time, the superannuated state officials who have no hopes for national office are less likely to find bold new resolutions to state problems.

It is true that in Chapter VI, I discussed the state-oriented career pattern. This pattern does provide a point of resistance to the complete nationalization of American government. But the divisions between the state and the nationally-oriented career are by no means sharp. The important fact remains that the force of progressive ambitions is entirely in the national direction.

THE STRUCTURE OF POLITICAL OPPORTUNITIES AND THE PARTY SYSTEM

Since the opportunity structure consists of public offices and the purpose of the two-party system is their control, it is inevitable that one institution affects the other. Intense party competition can turn the most careerlike office into a transitory and risky post. But the place of an office in the structure of opportunities, or the treatment which voters and politicians typically afford it, can likewise affect the level of party competition. It seems plausible that the generally low level of competition for congressional seats is due as much to electoral attitudes toward the office as to the electoral composition of congressional districts. In the same way, the generally high level of competition for the governorship is as much a reflection of the attitude toward elective executives as it is of vigorous party competition. In effect, I am arguing that the two-party system which is characterized by variations in competition from office to office as well as from state to state is to a large extent the product of the way in which political opportunities are ordered. The opposition party, no matter how disorganized, can always hope to oust a President or governor. Accumulated grievances can give effect to the notion that these offices should not be held for long by anyone. But the acceptance of incumbency in legislative office tends, on the other hand, to reduce competition, to produce one-party systems in constituencies which on other grounds might be competitive.

I would argue also that the national character of the opportunity structure reinforces the two-party system. The weakness of the states' career opportunities within the federal system is compounded by the separation of powers which denies the states' leaders alternative resting-places within state government. I have pointed out earlier that state leaders ambitious for national advancement desert indigenous state parties. The movement of political leaders from state to nation may seem inevitable within a federal system. But the Canadian federal experience, without the separation of powers, shows that indigenous local parties can retain their leaders and persist where the structure of opportunities holds out the expectation of significant, long-term careers within the smaller governmental unit.

Moreover, in the United States the major opportunities for national advancement fall within the Congress, a body organized to strengthen the two-party mold. The observance of strict party seniority in the distribution of committee office is a powerful incentive for congressmen to retain their Republican or Democratic ties. While the seniority rule is not often viewed as an instrument of discipline for the national parties, it is difficult to see what else has prevented dissident and popular congressmen from running either as independents or as leaders of indigenous state parties. Surely it has not been fear of electoral defeat which has kept both Harry Byrd and Adam Clayton Powell Democrats. American electorates are conspicuously undisciplined; at this writing the maverick Strom Thurmond has shifted political affiliation three times without visible electoral costs. What makes Thurmond exceptional, however, is not his electoral success but his cavalier treatment of congressional seniority. While the federal system, then, reinforced by the separation of powers, imposes a national perspective on state party leaders, congressional traditions and procedures help keep them within the national two-party lines.

THE STRUCTURE OF OPPORTUNITIES AND PARTY ORGANIZATION

I would argue further that the structure of opportunities not only reinforces the two-party system but largely determines the nature of

American party organization. In Chapter VII I tried to demonstrate the impact of the opportunity structure as well as party competition upon party organization. Much of the apparent difficulty in understanding American parties is cleared up once we recognize the impact of both these factors. Both the party system and the opportunity structure are national and, therefore, produce national organizations concerned with the control of office. These are not textbook organizations; that is, they do not conform to the formal structure of national committees. Since the two-party system does not operate uniformly throughout all constituencies, factional organization is inevitable. Similarly, we have seen that all offices do not serve the same function within the opportunity structure; these discrepancies also provide the basis for faction. Yet the party system and the opportunity structure together create national organizations with national perspectives.

The literature of political science, on the other hand, most commonly asserts that American parties exist mostly at the local level, that the power base lies in the state parties or in city machines. The national parties are seen as ephemeral coalitions of state parties, coming together every four years with the object of nominating and electing a President. While empirical studies of roll-call voting in Congress have gone far in restoring the view that national parties count there, the dominant view remains that the Congress is primarily the gathering-place of locally organized and locally oriented men.

The local view of party organization makes much of American politics incomprehensible; Maurice Duverger, a foreign observer under the influence of the dominant American view, could write in 1951: "It is a serious matter that the greatest nation in the world, which is assuming responsibilities on a world-wide basis, should be based on a party system entirely directed towards very narrow local horizons."[3] Yet this was the time when the United States was pushing forward with the Marshall Plan, developing the NATO alliance, and carrying on the Korean police action policies, which could hardly be described as local in orientation.

On the other hand, an observer such as James Wilson, recognizing the national character of policy-making in the United States, finds that national leaders are capable of developing such policies precisely because the parties are local and not concerned with national affairs.[4] Thus the local interpretation is preserved at the cost of reading national

[3] Maurice Duverger, *Political Parties* (first published in France in 1951; New York: Wiley, 1963), p. 53.

[4] James Wilson, *The Amateur Democrat* (Chicago: University of Chicago Press, 1962), and the article by the same author in *The American Government Annual*, Vol. 1, 1962–63, ed. I. Hinderaker, et al. (New York: Holt, Rinehart, and Winston, 1963).

leaders out of the party organizations. But an explanation of American parties which asserts that men such as Mayor Richard Daley of Chicago and Robert Wagner of New York are organizational leaders while Franklin Roosevelt and John Kennedy are not hardly clarifies our understanding.

The difficulty lies, undoubtedly, with the concept of organization, a concept which has troubled the most sophisticated students of this abstraction.[5] How one defines party organization depends as much upon one's value judgments about the function of parties as upon formal definitions. Most students of American politics accept the definition of American parties as office-seeking organizations. Confusion arises only because these same students have different views of what they wish parties to be.

Duverger wants parties to be, and defines the true party as, a community organized to further its members' interests. American scholars with similar preferences abandon the officeseeking definition of American parties in favor of the search for internal goals and interests and rewards. Since most of the organized distribution of internal rewards, i.e., patronage, takes place at the local level, the local view of American party organization emerges. For Duverger, this view leads to the untenable conclusion that American parties and their policies are dominated by parochial interests. Mr. Wilson avoids this error while maintaining the local view, but only because he is satisfied that, if American parties are concerned with internal goals of patronage, they will not be concerned with public policy.

Apart from questions of policy, the local view of organization leads us astray on more important considerations. It causes us to undervalue the abundant evidence of conscious, cooperative, i.e., organized, efforts aimed at capturing the Presidency, the Congress, and indeed all offices of value. From the local view of organization, these efforts, not to mention the millions of dollars which go into the capturing of major national and state offices, must be written off as non-organization. In my opinion it is simpler to discard the local view and accept American parties as national organizations.

Party organization, I would assert, draws its strength from the visions men hold of their futures. Certainly today, and I would guess it has always been so, the local organization has only the most limited

[5] That the most intense observers of organizations have yet to agree on any properties as essential is evidenced by the explicit avoidance of any definition of the term in one major summary of the literature on organizations. See James G. March and Herbert Simon, *Organizations* (New York: Wiley, 1958), p. 1.

control over the long-run careers of political leaders in the United States. The picture of Theodore Roosevelt beholden to Thomas Platt, or Harry Truman in the control of Pendergast, accepts the Platt-Pendergast ideal of American party organization. Local organizations, however dominant they appear, are in the long run dependent on the status of the national parties among local voters. No party machine in any major city has been able to withstand for very long the loss of partisan allegiance due to a national realignment. It was not the brilliant organizational tactics of the Kelly-Nash machine which took Chicago away from the Republican machine or outstanding local organization which, some time later, permitted the Democrats to take Philadelphia away from the classic example of local Republican organization. Rather, it was the national political realignment produced by the Great Depression and the New Deal.

Surely the national parties have their factions. There are, as James McGregor Burns has argued, at least two factions within each party focused on the two national opportunity outlets, the Presidency and Congress.[6] But this is only one aspect of the total opportunity structure which provides divergent tensions of ambition. The tensions which exist between President and Congress frequently exist between governors and state legislatures and for the same reasons. Wherever the opportunity structure consistently permits divergent career expectations for offices within the same party, it sows the seeds of faction. We have seen how minor statewide officials are able to resist electoral swings against their party. Their electoral strength has often led them to resist, and sometimes to lead factions in opposition to, those dominating their state parties. Long-time Republican Secretary of State of Wisconsin Fred Zimmerman, a man who consistently led his ticket at the polls, was an outspoken critic of his state's junior senator, Joseph McCarthy, even at the height of McCarthy's local and national influence. Democratic Secretary of State James Hare of Michigan, enjoying a similar position of electoral strength, in 1960 challenged, unsuccessfully, the preferences of the dominant liberal-labor forces in his party for the gubernatorial nomination. The Democratic controller of New York, Arthur Levitt, the only member of his party to survive Republican tides, sought in 1961 to oust Mayor Robert Wagner from his post. Not subject to the same electoral fates as others, minor state officials often become a source of organizational tension within their parties. All the same, the career expectations of thousands of politicians remain the

[6] James McGregor Burns, *Deadlock of Democracy* (Englewood Cliffs, N.J.: Prentice-Hall, 1963).

motive force of American party organization, and the national structure of opportunities, which guides these expectations, gives the organization its framework.

PARTY ORGANIZATION AND CHANGES IN THE STRUCTURE OF OPPORTUNITIES

Because the structure of opportunities largely defines party organization, proposed changes in the structure should always be examined for their effect upon party organization. The local view of American parties, which suggests that there is little organization above the local level, tends to divert our attention from the consequences of proposals for change. For example, I have noted earlier that one function of congressional seniority rules is that they hamper independent state party organizations. Yet it is not unusual for students of American parties who are addicted to the local view to suggest that the elimination of the seniority rules will strengthen national party organization.

While the seniority rules undoubtedly produce incongruities in Congress, it is well to realize their relevance for the national parties, as well as for the distribution of congressional influence, before making proposals to change the rules. Release from the tensions of seniority would, barring the development of new controls, permit congressmen with strong support in their districts and states to bolt the national parties with impunity. Given the critical role of the Senate in linking state and national party organizations, it might well lead to permanent indigenous state parties on the Canadian model.

Another favorite target of reformers is the Electoral College. Were we to elect Presidents either directly or by popular vote or by some system apportioning electoral votes within states, we would be doing much more than altering the weight of this or that constituency in the choice of Presidents. The framework of the presidential party organization would be drastically changed. That may or may not be desirable, but it is irresponsible to discuss reforms of the Electoral College in abstract terms, without considering the effect of such reforms upon party organization.

In the real world of American politics purposeful changes in the structure of political opportunities are less likely to come from the major reforms mentioned above than from minor reforms whose impact is less clear. For example, Americans like to tinker with the election schedule. The federal Constitution lays out the terms of federal officials, and, after some shifting, we have reached a point where all federal officials whose terms expire in the same year run for election on the same day. Some reformers have suggested that all federal elections coincide with that of the President, giving senators eight-year terms and congressmen four years.[7] While seemingly an attractive proposal for congressmen, the proposal has not been taken very seriously, probably for the reason why the proposal was suggested in the first place: the coincidence of all federal elections would certainly bring Congress much closer to the presidential electorate.[8]

Reformers have, over the years, been more successful in changing election schedules at the state level. These changes have worked unnoticed to produce an effect opposite to that desired by the national reformers. In the past 30 years, New York, Connecticut, Ohio, Michigan, Minnesota, and Idaho have adopted a four-year term for their governors. At the same time, however, they have adopted the midterm year for election, as in Pennsylvania and California, in preference to electing the governor at the same time as the President, as in Illinois. While the four-year term takes its rationale from the desire to give governors administrative latitude and freedom from electoral pressures, the midterm election is a device to divorce state politics from national or presidential trends.

Whether one does or does not favor separating state and national politics, it is important again that the ramifications for the total political situation be understood. There is more than one possible consequence. If the separation of federal and state elections causes state officials to be less swayed by national partisan trends, they are also under less pressure to influence those trends to help themselves. Our national parties have always been under great pressure from state parties to find effective candidates and policies because they help state and local officials to get elected. Governors not up for election in a presidential year may still want the national party to put forth an effective candidate, but the terrible pressure of self-interest is greatly reduced. After 1966, for example, the governor of Michigan will have a four-year term and he will be chosen in the midst of the presidential term. No longer, then, are we likely to have the spectacle, as we did in 1964, of a Michigan governor operating under the pressure of his own electoral

[7] Burns, *Deadlock of Democracy,* and Stephen K. Bailey, *The Condition of Our National Parties* (Santa Barbara: Center for Study of Democratic Institutions, 1959). President Johnson, in his program for 1966, requested a constitutional amendment making the term for representatives four years. He did not carry the idea to its logical conclusion by asking for eight-year terms for senators.

[8] The Congressmen interviewed by Charles Clapp expressed considerable doubt that they would ever get a four-year term, and one indicated that senators would never permit such a reform if it meant that congressmen might be able to try for a Senate seat without risk to their own position. See *The Congressman* (Washington: The Brookings Institution, 1963), p. 330.

needs, fighting against a poor electoral choice for the presidential nomination. He may contest the choice because of his own presidential aspirations, as did the governors of New York and Pennsylvania, but he is just as likely to relax, as did the governor of Ohio, and permit the ideological battle to run its course. Changes in the election schedule for the office of governor, therefore, may be a critical factor in changing the presidential nominating process.

We should at least note, therefore, how in the past the opportunity structure has helped resolve one of the most critical problems facing any political party—the control of ideological commitments. How can a party, responsible for government, retain the flexibility necessary to respond effectively to complex international and domestic problems if it is controlled by men with strong ideological commitments?[9] Both American parties have enjoyed a life span greater than most of the governments in the world; their life span testifies to the parties' adaptibility. Yet we know that they do attract people with ideological commitments, and that the more involved people are in politics, the more likely they are to hold their commitments strongly.[10] The answer lies in the interdependence of politicians' fates which forces men to temper ideology with responsiveness.

There is, then, a danger in insulating state from national politics. Without eliminating the state politician from national organizational decisions, it frees him from intense self-interested concern for national victory. Normally ideological in his perceptions of national politics, he becomes free to give ideological sentiments full play.

THE STRUCTURE OF OPPORTUNITIES AND POLITICAL LEADERSHIP IN THE UNITED STATES

Much of the discussion in this study pertains to one of the most critical problems of government, that of providing leadership capable of resolving complex problems. Implicit in my argument has been the proposition that the type of leadership a man is likely to provide is affected by his ambitions. Within a nation, political ambitions are directed by the structure of political opportunities. Ambitions provide the energies and decide the policies of individual leaders. Ambitions also provide the means by which leaders can influence others. The en-

[9] Wilson, in *The Amateur Democrat,* poses the distinction between the political *professional* who uses issues as a means and the *amateur* who sees them as the end. For a discussion of the organizational consequences of different means of attracting members, see P. Clark and J. Wilson, "Incentive Systems: A Theory of Organization," *Administrative Science Quarterly,* VI (1961), 129–66.

[10] Samuel Eldersveld, *Political Parties* (Chicago: Rand McNally, 1964), Ch. 8.

tire network of political decisions is held together by the interlocking of ambitions through the structure of opportunities.

If ambition is the motive force in politics, then the leader with progressive ambitions is the hero, the man who brings others together and provides unity and cohesion. If anyone is going to search for solutions, it is the man whose career depends on finding solutions. The politician with static ambitions is far more likely to be driven by immediate pressures, whether it be the pressure of opinion, party, or special interest groups. Only the man with progressive ambitions is driven to explore current policies in the light of future consequences, for his future career is at stake. In his calculations, today's opinions can be discounted, tomorrow's put at a premium. For this reason the man with progressive ambitions is more likely to seek to lead and direct opinion, not necessarily from any idealistic sense of what is right, but from his own need to secure opinion for his future goals.

The different roles played by each of the major political institutions in the United States reflect their place in the structure of opportunities. The conservative character of the Congress is only partly understandable in terms of its consituency. As long as the typical congressional seat is held on terms which foster static ambitions, Congress will be motivated primarily by the immediate problems of reelection. It will be swayed, therefore, mostly by what it sees as contemporary opinion. Congress as a body is not, and has never been, the instrument for finding new solutions or for leading opinion. Individual congressmen have been important, but for the most part they have been men with ambitions to move on from Congress. In particular, they have been men in the Senate, a body whose term of office provides more time for a politician to seek to influence and guide opinion.

Of course, this situation is largely a matter of constitutional design. The authors of the Constitution well recognized that the lower house would reflect rather than guide opinion. But the effect of the constitutional separation of powers has also been to divide the functions of leadership in the United States. The influencing and informing function of leadership has been divorced from the responsive function. In the parliamentary system, the party leadership more clearly combines both functions. As long as the congressman's immediate desire to retain his seat is in any way at variance with the President's drives, the conflict between the president and Congress will exist.

Nevertheless, the American opportunity system does enhance the importance of one skill essential to political leadership, the ability to relate the careers of others to that of the leader. Of course, the party system helps with much of this problem, but, as I have sought to demonstrate, it can not do it all. Not all party politicians share the same electoral fate as their leader, and the controversies within parties revolve not only around which leader will help the party most, but also around individual interpretations of which leader will help individual politicians the most. The answers are not necessarily the same. This is true of the national party as well as of state and local parties. A vital ingredient in political advancement, therefore, is the ability to put together a winning coalition of politicians.

This skill might well be less important if the principal offices in the United States were limited in number, all elected simultaneously, and ordained for a similar partisan fate. All problems of leadership are more or less institutionalized in the sense that the leader does not start from scratch in the development of the machinery necessary to achieve political goals. Certainly in the United States the leader does not start from scratch in defining his team. But, and this is the essential point, the team is defined within the set of alternatives laid out by the opportunity-party system as we have described it.

Since men who have the talent for constructing coalitions rise to the top, there is a self-perpetuating quality to the politics of coalition. Successful politicians have almost always been scornful of political scientists' proposals for party reform, as well they might be, since for most of them reform would mean political death. Only political leaders who have succeeded without the need to construct coalitions, or who have developed independent strength, or who have had to battle the system to advance, ever talk seriously of changing the rules of American politics. Huey Long could have risen further only by a disruption of the party and opportunity system. Dwight Eisenhower, who commanded extraordinary personal popular support, and Franklin Roosevelt, after his election and subsequent growth as a national leader, talked of party reform and realignment. Yet even these men who had the great personal strength to effect change did nothing concrete to alter the rules. On the other hand, John Kennedy exhibited loving concern for the preservation of the political rules by which he rose to power, at the very time when the possibilities for major political change were emerging.

Kennedy's concern is worth noting, and the skill of forming and maintaining political coalitions should not be demeaned. The defense of American parties rests upon the assumption that the American political problem consists primarily of holding the country together, of producing alliances which will mute controversy. Bringing political leaders together by means of their office drives is a particularly effective way of achieving compromise among areas and interests. There is, perhaps, an even better argument in support of the ways in which American political leaders rise—the growing need for the United States to provide world leadership. Men whose national politics sharpens their skills in creating coalitions ought to be capable of forming and maintaining coalitions in international affairs. The ultimate test of any process of leadership selection is whether or not it produces men skilled in the tasks which will face them when in office. While the relationship is not a logical necessity, functionally it is essential. A political system reinforces itself through its process of leadership selection. That process must produce men capable of making the political system work and of guaranteeing its adaptability to meet the problems of the society.[11]

[11] In accord with ambition theory, international organization can best be strengthened by making international offices attractive career outlets for national politicians. Certainly the principal strength of the United Nations today is that it provides such outlets for the leaders of small states. President Johnson's appointment of Supreme Court Justice Arthur Goldberg to succeed Adlai Stevenson as delegate of the United States to the United Nations was an extraordinary example of a conscious effort to enhance the international institution. We shall have true international government when presidents and premiers, themselves, seek international office.

APPENDIX A

The Sources of Data on Political Careers

A GREAT VARIETY of sources was used in compiling the data on political careers. I found the standard sources adequate in providing information on those men who actually became governors and senators. *The Biographical Directory of the American Congress* 1744–1961 (Washington: U. S. Government Printing Office, 1961) presents as good information as any on offices held by all men who have served in Congress. Thus, it was useful not only for all senators, but also for many candidates for the offices of governor and senator as well. *The National Cyclopedia of American Biography,* 45 vols. (New York: White, 1898–), systematically covers all governors and senators, as do the multiple publications of the A. N. Marquis Company, the publishers of *Who's Who* and its various regional and historical versions.

The information on the defeated candidates of the major parties for the offices of governor and senator was more difficult to get in completely adequate form. While all of the standard sources were examined, a sizeable proportion of the candidates did not show up there. State blue books and manuals filled in some of the gaps, particularly for those who had been in state legislature. For many of the states, multi-volumed state histories have been published; most of these consist of individual biographies. I culled those that were available in the Library of Congress and they proved a most useful source. While I had expected that local newspapers published during the election campaigns would prove good sources for information of this type, they proved disappointing. I also examined *The New York Times* for each individual gap and it was frequently useful, either in providing leads to other information or in giving small bits of relevant data. The data are weaker the further back in time they go, and they are also weak for some of the more rural states. While I had originally planned to utilize data on defeated candidates for governor back to 1870, there were so many gaps in information that I started assembling those data at 1900. Of the 2000 men nominated for governor and senator, I was unable to get any relevant information on 121.

TABLE A-1
Number of Candidates for Governor and Senator, by States

	Candidates for						
	GOVERNOR, 1900–1958			*SENATOR, 1914–1958*			*Total Number of Candidates for Governor and Senator for Whom There Is Some Information (No Individual Counted Twice)*
	Number with Information on Penultimate Office		*Number with No Personal Information*	*Number with Information on Penultimate Office*		*Number with No Personal Information*	
	R	*D*		*R*	*D*		
Alabama	—	21	—	—	9	—	30
Arizona	8	11	3	4	4	5	29
Arkansas	—	26	—	—	9	—	34
California	12	9	1	12	11	0	40
Colorado	20	17	2	12	8	0	54
Connecticut	19	16	1	10	13	0	51
Delaware	11	6	4	8	10	0	32
Florida	—	17	—	—	6	—	24
Georgia	—	24	—	—	7	—	27
Idaho	15	14	2	8	11	2	43
Illinois	9	13	0	9	12	0	40
Indiana	13	11	1	7	16	0	41
Iowa	13	14	4	10	9	0	42
Kansas	18	15	2	7	9	2	43
Kentucky	14	11	0	13	13	1	45
Louisiana	—	19	—	—	9	—	28
Maine	17	18	1	7	9	3	43
Maryland	9	10	0	10	10	1	34
Massachusetts	22	21	1	9	9	0	56
Michigan	15	12	4	6	14	2	44
Minnesota	18	19	1	11	10	2	60
Mississippi	—	16	—	—	7	—	23
Missouri	15	13	0	11	12	0	48
Montana	8	8	0	14	6	0	33

TABLE A-1—Continued

	Candidates for GOVERNOR, 1900–1958: Number with Information on Penultimate Office		GOVERNOR: Number with No Personal Information	SENATOR, 1914–1958: Number with Information on Penultimate Office		SENATOR: Number with No Personal Information	Total Number of Candidates for Governor and Senator for Whom There Is Some Information (No Individual Counted Twice)
	R	*D*		*R*	*D*		
Nebraska	14	14	0	10	13	0	45
Nevada	5	6	4	8	9	1	25
New Hampshire	23	19	2	6	16	0	58
New Jersey	15	14	1	13	15	0	52
New Mexico	9	12	7	11	9	2	39
New York	17	16	0	14	10	0	55
North Carolina	—	20	—	—	11	—	29
North Dakota	13	5	14	7	11	2	33
Ohio	18	13	0	11	14	2	50
Oklahoma	—	12	—	—	6	—	20
Oregon	11	11	3	10	12	1	42
Pennsylvania	14	12	1	9	12	3	43
Rhode Island	17	17	3	11	6	3	47
South Carolina	—	22	—	—	8	—	28
South Dakota	17	15	4	9	8	0	43
Tennessee	—	13	—	—	10	—	36
Texas	—	22	—	—	8	—	30
Utah	8	10	1	8	7	0	31
Vermont	23	18	2	9	12	3	59
Virginia	—	20	—	—	5	—	27
Washington	9	7	3	10	8	1	29
West Virginia	13	12	1	8	8	0	39
Wisconsin	14	12	5	12	9	3	43
Wyoming	10	9	3	8	7	1	32

APPENDIX B

Tables on Careers within State Parties

TABLE B-1

Structure within Parties—Profile Differences between First and Penultimate Office Distributions

(1) REPUBLICAN Candidates			
For Governor		*For Senator*	
State	*Profile Difference*	*State*	*Profile Difference*
Missouri	27	Indiana	48
Delaware	38	Kentucky	49
North Dakota	38	New York	50
New Mexico	45	Montana	57
Idaho	52	New Mexico	59
West Virginia	52	Maryland	63
Utah	55	Wisconsin	65
Indiana	57	Rhode Island	67
Wisconsin	58	Missouri	69
South Dakota	59	Illinois	70
Nevada	61	New Jersey	70
New Jersey	62	Washington	80
Maine	62	Delaware	80
Pennsylvania	66	Nevada	82
Maryland	68	Michigan	90
Colorado	70	Oregon	90
New York	72	North Dakota	90
New Hampshire	73	Colorado	93
Ohio	76	Utah	95
Kansas	76	Massachusetts	96
Minnesota	76	California	96
Arizona	78	Minnesota	97
Nebraska	79	Connecticut	104
Montana	82	Idaho	109
Rhode Island	85	Pennsylvania	110
Kentucky	85	West Virginia	113
Illinois	90	Nebraska	116
Oregon	99	Iowa	120
Connecticut	104	Ohio	132
Vermont	107	South Dakota	140
Iowa	109	Maine	142
California	124	Vermont	155
Michigan	127	Arizona	157
Washington	146	Kansas	163
Massachusetts	160	New Hampshire	167
Wyoming	166	Wyoming	173

TABLE B-1—Continued

(2) DEMOCRATIC Candidates			
For Governor		*For Senator*	
State	*Profile Difference*	*State*	*Profile Difference*
Wisconsin	26	Vermont	54
New Hampshire	28	New York	54
California	28	Delaware	57
Iowa	34	Nebraska	58
New Jersey	38	Oregon	58
West Virginia	44	Missouri	59
Kansas	46	Indiana	59
Minnesota	46	Wyoming	61
Utah	46	South Dakota	62
Illinois	49	Minnesota	63
South Dakota	49	New Jersey	63
New Mexico	51	New Hampshire	64
Nevada	56	Nevada	65
New York	56	Pennsylvania	66
Maine	58	Iowa	68
Montana	60	Wisconsin	70
Massachusetts	61	North Dakota	72
Pennsylvania	64	Maine	76
Vermont	69	Massachusetts	77
Michigan	70	Kansas	79
Oregon	71	Idaho	79
Missouri	75	California	80
Ohio	76	Illinois	85
Idaho	77	Montana	87
Colorado	79	New Mexico	88
Connecticut	79	Ohio	89
Nebraska	79	West Virginia	94
Arizona	84	Washington	95
Wyoming	88	Michigan	105
Rhode Island	88	Arizona	107
Maryland	93	Connecticut	108
Delaware	93	Colorado	115
North Dakota	105	Utah	117
Indiana	111	Kentucky	118
Washington	124	Maryland	125
Kentucky	136	Rhode Island	155

TABLE B-2

Use of Manifest Offices by State Parties for Candidates for Governor and Senator (Figure is Percentage of Party's Candidates)

	Dominant Parties				Minority Parties				Competitive Parties							
State	*Party*	*Gov.*	*Sen.*	*State*	*Party*	*Gov.*	*Sen.*	*State*	*Party*	*Gov.*	*Sen.*	*State*	*Party*	*Gov.*	*Sen.*
Vt.	R	74%	77%	Nev.	R	40%	51%	Mass.	R	87%	44%	Idaho	D	42%	27%
Me.	R	65	72	R. I.	R	59	27	Idaho	R	60	65	W. Va.	D	17	50
Ky.	D	64	61	Mont.	R	51	29	Conn.	R	58	60	Ohio	D	15	50
R. I.	D	53	83	Ore.	D	55	25	Colo.	D	47	63	N. J.	R	40	23
Kan.	R	45	86	Pa.	D	41	34	Wyo.	R	30	75	Del.	D	33	30
Iowa	R	77	50	S. D.	D	47	25	Minn.	R	50	54	N. J.	D	40	23
N. H.	R	35	83	N. M.	R	44	18	Utah	D	40	57	Mich	D	0	53
Neb.	R	57	60	Neb.	D	21	47	Wyo.	D	60	29	N. Y.	D	31	20
S. D.	R	47	66	Vt.	D	61	0	Ohio	R	28	63	Ind.	D	27	25
Ariz.	D	45	50	Iowa	D	21	33	W. Va.	R	39	50	Utah	R	25	25
Calif.	R	42	50	Kan.	D	20	33	Ill.	R	33	55	Ill.	D	23	25
N. D.	R	40	43	Ariz.	R	26	25	Mich.	R	47	33	Minn.	D	32	10
Ore.	R	72	10	Calif.	D	11	36	Md.	D	30	50	Md.	R	11	30
Wis.	R	29	33	N. H.	D	26	19	Del.	R	27	50	Ind.	R	23	14
Pa.	R	14	44	Me.	D	6	33	Mass.	D	33	44	N. Y.	R	6	28
Nev.	D	17	33	N. D.	D	20	18	Colo.	R	50	25	Wash.	R	67	14
N. M.	D	8	33	Mo.	R	26	9	Conn.	D	19	53	Wash.	D	14	50
Mo.	D	29	16	Wis.	D	25	0								
Mont.	D	13	17	Ky.	R	0	23								

INDEX

PRINTED IN U.S.A.